About the authors

Erika Cudworth is senior lecturer in international politics and sociology at the University of East London. Her research interests are in political theory, broadly conceived, particularly feminisms, ecologisms and complexity theory, food consumption and production, human relations with non-human animals and educational inclusions/exclusions. She is author of *Environment and Society* (Routledge, 2003), *Developing Ecofeminist Theory: The Complexity of Difference* (Palgrave, 2005), *The Modern State: Theories and Ideologies* (with Tim Hall and John McGovern, Edinburgh University Press, 2007) and *Social Lives with Other Animals: Tales of Sex, Death and Love* (Palgrave, 2011).

Stephen Hobden is a senior lecturer in international politics at the University of East London. His main areas of interest are international relations theory, China in world politics, and North–South relations. He is the author of *International Relations and Historical Sociology: Breaking Down Boundaries* (Routledge, 1998), and editor, together with John Hobson, of *Historical Sociology of International Relations* (Cambridge University Press, 2002).

Posthuman international relations
complexity, ecologism and global politics

Erika Cudworth and Stephen Hobden

Zed Books
LONDON | NEW YORK

Posthuman international relations: complexity, ecologism and global politics was first published in 2011 by Zed Books Ltd, 7 Cynthia Street, London N1 9JF, UK and Room 400, 175 Fifth Avenue, New York, NY 10010, USA

www.zedbooks.co.uk

Set in OurType Arnhem and Futura Bold by Ewan Smith, London

Index: ed.emery@thefreeuniversity.net

Cover designed by www.alice-marwick.co.uk

Printed and bound by CPI Group (UK) Ltd, Croydon, CRO 4YY

FSC
www.fsc.org
MIX
Paper from
responsible sources
FSC® C013604

Distributed in the USA exclusively by Palgrave Macmillan, a division of St Martin's Press, LLC, 175 Fifth Avenue, New York, NY 10010, USA

A catalogue record for this book is available from the British Library
Library of Congress Cataloging in Publication Data available

ISBN 978 1 84813 514 7 hb
ISBN 978 1 84813 515 4 pb

Contents

Acknowledgements

We would like to thank Tamsine O'Riordan at Zed Books for her initial interest in our work and in this book, Ken Barlow for his help and advice in seeing it through to completion, and Sue Browning for providing excellent copy-editing services. We would also like to thank our respective partners and children for putting up with us while we struggled with the complexity of complexity!

Parts of some of these chapters are adapted from material which has already been published in journals: 'Beyond environmental security: complex systems, multiple inequalities and environmental risks', *Environmental Politics*, 20(1), 2011, pp. 42–59; 'Anarchy and anarchism: towards a theory of complex international systems', *Millennium: Journal of International Studies*, 39(2), 2010, pp. 399–416; and 'Foundations of complexity, and the complexity of foundations: beyond the foundation/anti-foundational debate', *Philosophy of Social Sciences*, 2011, forthcoming.

FOR JAKE, SAM AND FREDDIE

1 · Introducing complexity and posthumanism to international politics

Since 'we have never been modern' we have always been living through a completely different history than the one we keep telling ourselves about: until the ecological crisis began to strike hard and strong, we could go on as though 'we' humans were living through one modernisation after another, jumping from one emancipation to the next. After all, the future was one of greater and greater detachment from all sorts of contingencies and cumbersome ties until 'Free at last!'

What happens to our identities if it finally dawns on us that that very same history always had another meaning: the slow explication of all of the attachments necessary for the sustenance of our fragile spheres of existence? What happens if the very definition of the *future* has changed? If we now move from the position of taking into account a few beings to one of weaving careful attachments with an ever-greater and greater list of explicated beings, where will we be? Attached at last! (Latour 2009: 75)

This book may well annoy some of those who read it because it intends to disrupt. It follows the passion of Bruno Latour in calling for a profound rethinking – in our case, of the study of international politics, in particular with regard to its recent attempts to incorporate the 'natural world' into the scope of its study. 'Environmental problems' have emerged as issues of concern for international relations to the extent that they cross state borders and call for solutions which transcend state boundaries. Both here, and in the chapters that follow, we will suggest that this additive approach has been minimally disruptive for scholarship in international relations. We will argue that international relations remains wedded to the Enlightenment project of overcoming the hazards of nature, and is thus fully human-centred in its approach. Established theoretical approaches in international relations, such as Marxism(s) or liberal-institutionalism, have incorporated 'issues' of the environment in terms of established conceptual frameworks of regimes and questions of global governance on the one hand, or a critique of global capitalism on the other. Perhaps most influential in practical political terms have been the more mainstream links made between environmental 'issues' and conflict. The resultant environmental security perspective, which will be strongly criticized towards the end of the book, tends to reproduce a dualistic understanding of human relations to 'the environment', in which humans are either threatened by or pose a threat to 'nature'. Recent, more critical developments of the concept of 'environmental security' remain largely embedded in this dualism. The challenge we face is profound. While we are undoubtedly in a situation of risk, this is shaped by histories of social relations, economic practices and formations of political power. At the same time, 'we' have unmade many of the attachments necessary for our lives on this planet. Latour suggests that we call humans, those who have 'waged war on Gaia', 'Earthlings' (ibid.: 75). This recognizes the need for us to understand our attachments to Planet Earth, and understand ourselves as a species, among many other living inhabitants. Underpinning such terminology is the notion that 'we', the Great Apes who like to call ourselves 'human', see ourselves as 'on' and not 'of' Planet Earth. In his 'manifesto for a new millennium', drawing on ideas of ecologism and complexity alongside international politics, Edgar Morin entreats us to reinvent a politics for 'Homeland Earth' (Morin 1999). Even more critical scholars of international relations unfortunately do not undertake scholarship *for* earthlings of Homeland Earth.

Latour pushes us further in asking whom this new understanding of the world must be *for*. If the 'project' of the modernist social sciences was about emancipating humans (from exploitation or ignorance or insecurity, and so on), it needs to be profoundly rethought, reconfigured and reinvented. We need a new social science that can attend to the needs of '*Earthlings* buried in the task of explicating their newly discovered attachments' as they 'suddenly realise', in the face of ecological catastrophe, that 'all along' they have inhabited the earth (2009: 75, 84). For both Morin and Latour, their differences notwithstanding, the reinvention of politics means reflecting our condition of, and with, this planet. When Latour made this plea to an assembled throng of sociologists, many of them stood and clapped, but it may well be that they enjoyed the jokes and the charm of Latour's delivery and thought rather less of the case made. They may have smiled at some of the content – for example, the challenge of a social science that takes consideration of the needs of earthworms or one that contemplates a 'politics for the Gulf Stream'. And yet, such statements must be taken utterly seriously. The challenge of a politics that thinks beyond the narrow confines of 'the human', a politics of Homeland Earth, is, we would suggest, the most profound of the twenty-first century.

We argue that the study of international politics is transformed by the understanding that we have never been either modern or human (respectively, Latour 1993; Gane and Haraway 2006). Neither Latour nor Donna Haraway, as we will see below, approves of the term 'posthuman' as a description for this condition. Neither do they endorse the appellation 'posthumanist' for perspectives which critique human centrism. This book, however, is, in our view, articulating a posthumanist critique of international relations and suggesting a new agenda. A colleague recently described what we are doing as '*not* international relations', and some readers may well come to agree with this assessment. Within international relations, however, are a range of core assumptions and useful concepts that might be rethought and developed. Crucial to our engagements with, and recasting of, some kinds of international relations theory has been the development of complexity theory and its use in the social sciences.

Posthuman International Relations draws on reworkings of the concept of 'system' in complexity theory as multilevelled, nested, overlapping and non-saturated, while acknowledging distinctions between human and non-human systems. Compared with systems approaches in international relations, a complex systems approach has a number of significant advantages. It enables us to consider the embedded character of human relations within broader multi-species and biosphere contexts. In addition, a complexity view of systems allows the analysis of patterns of social exploitation in ways that reveal complex and dynamic configurations and intersected qualities. Yet, to date, approaches drawing on the notion of complexity have under-theorized the notion of power. To address this inadequacy, we propose incorporating an analysis of power in terms of three different types: relational power, institutional power and biopower.

The book builds upon ideas from complexity theory and political ecologism to develop a 'complex ecologism', informed by elements of feminism and (post-)Marxism/colonialism in positing that human relations to other humans, other species and natures are characterized by complex forms of social difference and domination. We call this approach 'posthuman' as it overcomes the Enlightenment anthropocentric focus of most social and political theory; and provides a post-Newtonian non-mechanistic approach. The co-evolution of human communities, non-human animals and the 'natural environment' can be understood as interpolated through institutions and practices of biopower that give rise to patterns of multiple complex inequalities. We hope to provide students of international relations with a coherent, readable discussion of complexity theory that illustrates the implications of a complexity approach, and to convince at least some of our readers of the need for posthuman international relations, where a focus on the biosphere replaces the current human-centred framing of the discipline. We will be arguing that the combined insights from complexity theory and ecological thinking provide a new focus and agenda for a progressive and critical international relations of the twenty-first century. This chapter closes with an outline of the structure of the book, but in between then and here, we want to introduce uninitiated readers to complexity theory, outline our critique of international relations theory and suggest how it might be developed, and also situate this book as a posthumanist text.

Complexity theory and the complex world

'Complexity theory' is itself a contested and problematic term because it is something of a misnomer for a range of theories and concepts. It is tempting to concur with Dillon's (2000: 4) observation that any attempt to define complexity theory 'seems bound to go wrong'. One of the tasks that we undertake in this book is to tease out some variations in the way that complexity has been applied, particularly in the social sciences. Such variations have profound consequences, we will argue, for how we think about complexity, and the implications of living in a complex universe.

The usual understanding of complexity by complexity scientists is 'the occurrence of complex information in which order is emergent' (Hayles 1991: 176), while also being dynamic and imperfect (Hayles 1990: 292). At this point it is perhaps useful to distinguish between complicated, complexity and chaos. Complexity theory had its origins in the study of apparently chaotic processes (for good introductions to the development of complexity theory, see Capra 1996; Gleick 1988; Waldrop 1994) observed in the non-animate world. The underlying order in the rate of drips from a tap is often cited as an example (Gleick 1988: 262–6), or grains of sand dropping on a sand pile, causing apparently random collapses (Waldrop 1994: 304–5). The chemist Ilya Prigogine and philosopher Isabelle Stengers (1984) suggest that even in the most apparently chaotic situations we can see the emergence of coherence, structure, order and pattern. The concept of complexity became synonymous with this study of underlying order which appeared in many processes. Complexity theories and concepts emerged in the natural sciences, in physics, biology, chemistry, mathematics and in computing sciences. The scientific study of complexity has

4

been neatly summarized as 'the *study of the phenomena which emerge from a number of interacting objects*' (Johnson 2009: 3–4, emphasis in original). In other words, complexity implies something more than just the study of complicated things. A car engine might be described as complicated (by a non-mechanic, anyway!). It has many parts which perform different functions, but which, when combined, make a car go (until one part wears out). How a car engine works can be understood by breaking down the separate parts and thinking about how they work together. Ultimately, a car engine is nothing more than the sum of its parts. Complexity occurs where there are emergent features – a complex system is more than the sum of its parts. Interactions between elements lead to the appearance of new phenomena. There are features at the level of system that are not apparent by looking at the constituent parts, the key point being that these new phenomena cannot be deduced from the study of the parts. Complex phenomena need to be studied holistically.

A comparison can be drawn here between Newtonian and post-Newtonian physics. Newton's study of gravity and force paved the way for many of the features of the contemporary world, such as industrialization. However, even Newton was aware that his theories did not explain everything, and through the nineteenth and early twentieth centuries shortcomings in the Newtonian world-view became apparent, especially with the advent of quantum mechanics. It isn't so much that Newton was wrong – it is more that his laws described only a limited subset of physical reality (Wallerstein 2000: 30–31). The problem is that much of the social sciences is based on a mechanical and Newtonian view. In particular, the world is seen as ordered, systems are seen as closed, and the same rules apply regardless of time or space. Post-Newtonian perspectives would dispute all of these ideas. The world may be ordered at times, but it is also subject to disorder, systems are open and subject to 'time's arrow', what has occurred in the past will affect the present and future, and locality can matter.

Some are greatly concerned at the modification and application of concepts and theories in the natural sciences by social scientists, yet historically, both the social and natural sciences have borrowed and borrowed back from one another (López and Scott 2000: 10). For example, at perhaps one of the leading centres of the 'non-linear' science of 'complex adaptive systems', the Santa Fe Institute in New Mexico (Waldrop 1994: 11–12), there have been concerted attempts to theorize beyond the natural sciences. Complexity scientists have themselves sought to apply their ideas to various aspects of human behaviour – from the actions of traders in financial markets, commuters in cities and voting panels in the Eurovision Song Contest, to the behaviour of states and militaries in warfare contexts and the strategies of 'terrorists' and counter-insurgency organizations (Johnson et al. 2003; Johnson 2002; Fenn et al. 2008; Johnson et al. n.d.). While some of these applications are more credible and significant than others, it is notable that scientists have been using complexity to make sense of social phenomena for some time, with limited engagements by the social sciences until very recently. Early chapters of this book develop the arguments that complexity sciences are a rich source in the attempt to transcend unhelpful but powerful dichotomies between the 'social' and 'natural' worlds and the disciplines of their study. In addition, we will be arguing that complexity concepts allow us to better understand the complex features of world politics.

Complexity theory provides us with a range of concepts and ideas that are usefully developed in the study of international politics. In complexity science, natural systems are understood to exist in a web of connections with other systems and to be internally differentiated. The term 'emergent properties' is used to describe those specific qualities that emerge at a certain level of systemic complexity, but which are not apparent at lower levels (Capra 1996: 34–5). This is a non-reductionist position in which phenomena cannot be reduced to the sum of their parts but gain their character from interaction. In international relations, this enables us to consider multiple kinds and levels of institutions, processes and relations and to avoid the pitfalls of reductionism.

Secondly, complexity science has transformed the understanding of the concept of a 'system'. Systems in complexity theory are multi-levelled and layered, and complexity scientists often speak of systems as 'nested', with larger-scale systems enclosing myriad smaller-scale systemic processes (Holling et al. 2002b: 68–9). Complexity also sees systems as existing in the context of other systems and as interacting with them and often developing cross-system dependencies (Maturana and Varela 1980: 109). Systems have 'autopoiesis' and are self-making, self-reproducing, self-defining or regulating. One of the main criticisms of the use of the concept of 'system' in the social sciences was that it was associated with stasis and the maintenance of equilibrium. However, complex systems avoid the problem of stasis by using notions of positive (reinforcing) feedback and 'co-evolution' (in which systems are internally changed by their interactions with other systems external to them).

Such concepts for understanding systemic patterning have seemed

6

increasingly attractive to social scientists. Much of the theoretical legacy of the social sciences has, until recently, been concerned with large-scale conceptualization and modelling, usually invoking some kind of conception of a system or structure. In the path of Marx, for example, the capitalist system of relations has been seen as operating globally (Wallerstein 1979). The critique of systems theory in the social sciences has focused on an inability to account for the shifting nature of social life and its multiple differences, a rigid understanding of the relationship between parts and wholes and a preoccupation with notions of balancing in the maintenance of equilibrium, or social order, as apparent in the functionalism of Talcott Parsons (1951, 1960). Complexity thinking avoids such rigidity and stasis, understanding systems as simultaneously ordered yet disordered, stable yet unstable (Prigogine 1980). Instabilities lead to new forms of order and disorder, and these are often (but not necessarily) of increasing complexity. Change and development depend on the systems' history and various external conditions and cannot be predicted (Prigogine and Stengers 1984: 140). So, these kinds of understandings of complexity provoke a rethinking of notions of order, pattern, system and change.

However, social scientists have made a very different use of complexity insights, and in Chapter 2 we identify four distinctive approaches. Some consider that complexity theory can be used metaphorically. Here, complexity provides a series of models that can be used as a means of describing social events. At the other end of the spectrum, 'social physicists' perceive complexity as being an inherent quality of all matter. In this view, the social world is subject to the same forces as all other material entities. A further two approaches consider the presence of complex phenomena in both the human and non-human worlds, but acknowledge distinctive features of the human world. Within these, there are those who see complexity as a network, or rather as a range of interlinking networks capable of understanding processes from localized minutiae to global events. Our favoured approach, which we call 'differentiated complexity', allows for analytical separation between social and natural systems and can account for the distinctive features of the social, while also allowing for inscribed complexity in both human and non-human systems. It also enables the possibility of overlapping, interrelating and co-constituting qualities of social and natural systems. Complexity allows us to consider 'human' social relations as being both embedded in and constituted with non-human systems. In addition, it allows us to consider human social relations with 'the environment' as systemic and exploitative.

So far, then, we are not necessarily at odds with Latour's entreaty at the opening of this chapter. However, a major departure from Latour (and his actants, networks and worlds of attachments) is that we remain concerned with the politics of inequalities and the persistent and dynamic features of systems of human relations. This is not clinging to the wreckage of a politics of modernity. Many critiques of the politics of modernity conflate 'modernity' with the notion of 'progress' (Walby 2009: 24–8). Further, they set up a false distinction between the emancipatory politics that Latour scorns as that of 'detachment' and a reflexive, postmodern ambivalence (Bauman 1991). While the landscape of inequalities has been revealed to be complex, this does not make the production of better-nuanced and more sophisticated theories of this landscape an outdated or epistemologically redundant task. Rather, multiple complex inequalities are apparent in political relations, institutions and processes from micro to macro levels. Relations of multiple inequalities have recently been addressed by the development of concepts and theories around 'social intersectionality'. This has mainly been associated with feminist work on the complicating effects of 'race' for gender relations (Crenshaw 1991; McCall 2005; Phoenix and Pattynama 2006). Complexity is also useful in developing our understanding of human relations as socially intersectionalized, in terms of the co-constituted qualities of systems of social relations, such as those based on class, gender and ethnic hierarchy.

In Chapter 5, we will be drawing on political ecologism in considering the interplay between human domination of nature and our systemic domination of each other. For many, environmental exploitation is the direct result of 'intra-human domination', and the exploitation of humans by other humans has been crucial to explaining the human exploitation of the natural environment (Bookchin 1990). Systemic analyses of capitalism have been deployed in suggesting that the nexus of environmental exploitation is the social organization of labour power in capitalist societies around the production of goods for the market (Dickens 1996). For others, contemporary developments in capitalist relations mean that 'nature' becomes increasingly internal to the dynamics of capital accumulation (Castree 2001; Harvey 1996). Environmental difficulties have also been understood in terms of their embedding in the social relations of (post-)colonial capital and gender (Anderson 2001; Cudworth 2005; Demeritt 2001). In developing our 'complex ecologism', we will argue that there is a social system of human domination, but we also consider that this takes historically and geographically specific formations. Such domination is linked to multiplicitous intra-human formations of domination. It is here that complexity theory can help us to consider intermeshing multiple systems. We conceive these systems as both analytically distinct and mutually constitutive. The domination of non-human nature is a system of exploitative relations that overlaps and interlinks with other systems of power and domination based on gender, capital, ethnic hierarchy, and so on. The contribution of a complex ecology approach is the potential to analyse intersectionality and multiple power relations beyond the human. We will consider how this kind of theorizing might be situated as 'posthumanist' in a short while, but first we turn to the challenge it poses for the discipline of international relations.

The problem of 'IR'

In international relations, the study of politics at a systemic level has a long history. International relations is preoccupied with large questions, often global in scale, and the understanding of 'relations', so key to complexity, is the endemic feature of the discipline. We consider, however, that there are some serious shortcomings with international relations theory as it is currently constituted. From the perspective of complex ecologism, two of the main difficulties – human centrism and linearity (in particular as associated with methodological positivism) – might be addressed and overcome by a complexity approach.

What are the difficulties with the contemporary study of international relations? First, it is a small and narrow discipline, which, despite the presence of academic organizations, publications and communities of scholars in Japan, Britain and elsewhere in Europe, is overwhelmingly associated with North American scholars and scholarship and the theories and concepts these have generated (see Wæver 1998: 697–700). The US-centrism and small size of the discipline facilitated, Ole Wæver charges, the so-called 'Great Debates' of the discipline among different strands of American theory. What the Great Debates have not moved us far from in Wæver's account, however, is methodological individualism (from behaviourism to games theory) and the theoretical domination of realism in its various forms. Steve Smith concurs, arguing that these debates serve to suggest that there has been far more openness and pluralism than has in fact been the case and that there has been "progress" as the discipline gets nearer and nearer the "truth" about international relations' (Smith 2000: 377; see also Smith 1996). Rather, these debates have been iterations of a 'foundational myth' – the replacement of idealism with realism – that has served to centre the discipline on various forms of realist explanations of international politics (Schmidt

9

1998). While British international relations, the main national competitor to US hegemony in the disciplinary field (Holsti 1985), might be less positivist and more epistemologically and methodologically open than that in the USA, the US academic community still overwhelmingly dominates the discipline (Smith 2000).

Smith suggests that realism, state-centrism and positivism underpin the discipline of international relations as a whole, more strongly than international relations *theory* (ibid.: 379). Nevertheless, this unfortunate triumvirate dominates much of what is considered serious or legitimate scholarship in international relations theory. This is characterized by what Wæver (1996) terms the 'neo-neo synthesis' between neo-realism and neoliberalism. This mainstream is characterized by considerable agreement on the subject matter of international politics and the most suitable approach to its study. The 'neo-neo' approach is state-centric and it assumes that state actors are unitary and that state interests drive behaviour internationally. As Smith remarks, 'this results in a very limited view of what international politics is and can be' (2000: 382). Smith characterizes the international relations neo-neo mainstream as rationalist – positivist and empiricist. What is perhaps remarkable about such approaches is their incredible rate of failure. For all the searching for 'law-like regularities', none of the major events of the past twenty-five years has been foreseen: the end of the Cold War; the collapse of the Soviet Union; the rise of China (in the early 1990s the 'hot money' was on Japan as the next challenger to US hegemony – for example, Rosecrance and Taw 1990); the 9/11 attacks and subsequent 'war on terror'; the global turmoil associated with the 2008 banking crisis. Surprise seems to be a typical feature of international relations, at least in the current era.

Smith counterpoints the rationalist perspectives with 'constitutive theory' (also referred to as reflectivism, post-positivism or, more generally, Critical Theory in the international relations literature), which encompasses the diversity of positions outside and opposed to the mainstream: (Frankfurt School) Critical Theory, feminism, postmodernism, post-colonialism, normative theory and anthropological and sociological approaches (2000: 380). A posthuman approach to international relations draws on elements of critical theories, while also critiquing these positions for their anthropocentrism. Using complexity in understanding international politics provides a clear alternative to positivism as a basis for making claims about the 'international system'. This is international system(s) but not as we know it.

How, then, might complexity be able to reinvent the ways in which we understand international systems? We do first need to note that in the study of international politics, complexity concepts have most often been used in two ways, and these are both very different from our application in this book. There have been some attempts in international relations to move beyond the notion of system to that of complex systems. However, the majority of these attempts have adopted the use of computational simulation models in order to test the emergence of certain kinds of system behaviour (Axelrod 1997). Such agent-based models profile the characteristics and capabilities of various kinds of 'agents' (both states and non-state 'actors') in order to predict behaviour and outcomes. Others have focused on individuals as actors, for example in theorizing the participation of individuals in collective ethnically based violence (such as the Rwandan genocide – Bhavnani 2006). Secondly, complexity has been used by scholars situating themselves as 'new institutionalists' and using complex systems theory to argue that political networks are characterized by non-linearity and to describe political processes as 'path dependent'. Some have applied non-linear models to subjects such as alliance formation, outbreaks of war, federal political formations and environmental policy-making (see Richards 2000; and in the case of the latter, Hoffman 2006). Others have used a complexity-informed notion of 'emergence' to theorize the processes of the formation and collapse of nation-states (Cederman 1997; Clemens 2001). Paul Pierson (2000), for example, has suggested that the investigation of political developments using the economic notion of 'increasing returns' can provide a more rigorous framework for developing some of the key claims of recent scholarship in historical institutionalism: patterns of timing, a range of possible outcomes and large consequences resulting from relatively small or contingent events. Additionally, new institutionalist analysis of international political developments has suggested that particular courses of action are difficult to halt or change once they are introduced, and thus political development is punctuated by critical moments (tipping points, in complexity parlance). Such insights, he suggests, stretch the temporal horizons of political analysis and can lead to greater appreciation of the centrality of historical processes in generating variation in political life and in helping us to understand sources of stability and change.

While agent-based modelling and institutionalism are the main current engagements with concepts from complexity theory, perhaps the first sustained engagement by an international relations theorist is that of James Rosenau (1990). In particular, his *Turbulence in World Politics* focused on the notion of turbulence, a term taken from organization theory, but which might be equated to non-linearity, or chaotic behaviour. Rosenau argued that with the end of the Cold War, international politics was entering a new 'postinternational' phase, which would be characterized by increased uncertainty and rapid unpredictable change, and in particular a decreased role for the state. While Rosenau's book is interesting and has been influential, it suffers from several major flaws. First, it has not stood the test of time as well as it might. It was written and published in the short period between the end of the Cold War and the collapse of the Soviet Union. Since then there have been major developments in international politics (a unipolar world, rapid growth in economic integration, the rise of China, the war on terror, and in particular, of course, concern about environmental issues). While much of this could be equated to Rosenau's conception of turbulence, a post-international world has yet to emerge and, if anything, with the combined economic and political crises that have emerged since 2000, the state has reasserted itself as the key actor, while international organizations have proved ineffective at restraining states or alleviating crises. Furthermore, there have been many developments in complexity approaches, and applications of complexity to the social sciences, which Rosenau's account could not incorporate at the time of writing. A second weakness is that the approach to complexity theory derived is a rather limited one. While the non-linear aspects of complexity theory contribute to the idea of turbulence, ideas related to recent thinking about systems, such as autopoiesis and emergence, are not developed. A third weakness is the focus on human-centred interactions and systems. What we will be developing in this book is a wider and more nuanced discussion of complexity concepts which foregrounds the analysis of the relations between human and non-human systems, leading to a *posthuman international relations*, rather than a *post-international politics*.

Given Rosenau's early intervention here, it is rather ironic that he has emerged as a critic of complexity applications in international relations. He is now among those who contend that there are serious theoretical and methodological difficulties with the application of complexity concepts from the sciences to social and political life. This is because 'social systems have structures of authority that may be inconsistent with the theory of complex adaptive systems' (Earnest and Rosenau 2006: 144). In following the simulation methods adopted by complex systems scientists, international relations scholars make assumptions about who the significant actors are and where political authority resides. However, Earnest and Rosenau (ibid.) seriously underestimate both the incredible diversity of complexity theory in the study of the social world (something we attend to in Chapter 2) and, at the same time, the bifurcation of these approaches into two broad schools of thought. One school, following the chemist Prigogine, emphasizes the unknowability of the world and is often called 'chaos' theory, with a reflexive approach to knowledge as a social construct which alters its object of inquiry. The other, associated with the Santa Fe institute, emphasizes the search for, and realization of, patterning and order in apparently chaotic systems (see Walby 2003: 16). When Earnest and Rosenau (2006: 145) 'take complex systems theory at its word and assume that it is indeed "theory"', they make a fundamental error. The breadth and disciplinary range of applications mean that, in effect, there is no such 'thing' as 'complexity theory'.

Earnest and Rosenau further claim, on the basis of a very few applications in international politics (primarily Axelrod 1997; also Cederman 1997), that 'complex systems theory' demands a positivist epistemology. They then argue that complex systems theory only makes 'theory-like claims' when linked to its 'principal method' of actor-based modelling. The problems here lie with a limited reading of complexity applications in the social sciences. Earnest and Rosenau (2006: 144) consider that complexity can be a powerful paradigm (by which they seem to mean 'metaphor') for international politics but not a theory (with explicatory power). Yet this is precisely what complexity is – a paradigm – a framework within which various concepts might be developed and utilized for theory building (Harrison 2006c: 193; also Cudworth 2007). It is not 'a theory', and nor does it have, and certainly not in the social sciences, a single or a preferred method. The false assumption Earnest and Rosenau make is that 'complexity' is a single theory claiming to provide a transhistorical and generally applicable theory with which everything in world politics might be explained. Rather, it is a framework, with a range of useful concepts, adaptable by social scientists, within which to build theories explaining specific processes and phenomena. The case for many complexity theories and various kinds of social application will be made in the following chapter, but suffice to say here that our use of complexity could not be more different to that of Axelrod, although it does owe something to the historically embedded work of Pierson.

A final, although very small, set of applications involves those who have drawn on the work of Niklas Luhmann, and in particular his account of systems theory and world society. Mathias Albert and Lena

Hilkermeier (2004) provide a comprehensive discussion of Luhmann's systems theory, and examine the ways in which it could be used to illuminate some core concerns of international relations theorists, such as sovereignty, governance and war. Luhmann's work represents the first thorough attempt to bring complexity concepts into the study of the social world. However, the core of Luhmann's account of systems is that world society is constituted through communications. While accepting the importance of communication in constituting human systems, we view this as just one feature – social systems are constituted by a mixture of ideas and material features. As well as being lingua-centric, Luhmannian systems theory is human-centric. Luhmann himself, in his well-known disagreement with Ulrick Beck on sociological understandings of 'risk' (see Luhmann 1993; Beck 1999), considered the 'environment' to be outside the scope of social scientific study. *Posthuman International Relations* argues that as human social systems are dependent on, and are co-constituted by, natural systems, this position is untenable. We would dispute the all-encompassing character of world society as depicted by Albert and Hilkermeier – such a view seems heavily influenced by globalization theory, about which we are sceptical. There are human and non-human systems operating outside of the world society envisaged by Luhmann.

Our approach, as we will see in Chapter 3, develops the concept of system in international relations and the notion that there is something to be gained from an analysis of international politics at the inter-state level as opposed to analysing international politics at the level of the actions of political figures or the study of the foreign policy of different states. Using complexity means for us, however, that we do not use systems as a descriptive device. Rather, epistemologically, complex realism (Walby 2009: 17) allows us to consider systems as having distinct properties, powers and causal effects (emergent properties, in the language of complexity theory). In terms of thinking about international systems in contemporary international relations theory, distinctions can be drawn between realist, constructivist and Marxist/ International Political Economy discussions. Realist and constructivist views of system have tended to regard the state as the key actor, while Marxist and International Political Economy approaches have regarded a capitalist system to be the focus of analysis. While our project is largely critical of existing systems work, this does not mean that there are not elements of overlap and complementarity. As we will see in Chapter 3, for example, from Waltz (1979), we would draw upon the idea of specific forces operating at a systems level, while Wendt (1999) and English School theorists have pointed to the role of ideas norms and law in the regulation of international affairs. We would see these as forms of self-organization within international relations.

Barry Buzan and Richard Little (2000) have undoubtedly made a major contribution to work on systems thinking in international relations. They argue for a pluralist approach, which attempts to allow for a variety of different aspects to international relations. To encompass this they advocate a historical and multi-causal approach. This comprises a theorization of different levels of analysis, different sectors of analysis, plus three central sources of explanation: interaction capacity, process and structure. Perhaps the most important contribution of Buzan and Little's approach is the inclusion of different sectors of analysis. These include an economic system and a military system, but also include a political sector concerning relations between states, and an environmental sector relating to relations within the earth's biosphere. An important point is that within each sector the units and system might be different, and some international systems might exclude certain sectors. For example, it is possible to imagine an international system where the units were militarily competitive but did not have economic relations (or vice versa). We share some of Buzan and Little's concerns; in particular, the focus on multiple systems and the historical approach taken. Their analysis of interlinked systems provides a starting point for our discussions of intersectionality and nested systems. However, Buzan and Little do not sufficiently rework the understanding of system, and complex systems theory enables us to develop it in innovative ways, in particular in terms of non-linearity, emergence and intersectionality. While they would like to see boundaries around 'international relations', we would see these relations as embedded within a whole range of other systemic features. A complexity approach would see differences from conventional views of system in terms of the boundaries, constitution, power and dynamics of international systems. Buzan and Little's inclusion of the consideration of the biosphere is a major advance for an international relations analysis. However, their theory considers relations with the biosphere as an 'add-on' and, like the overwhelming majority of other theorists of international system, they remain wedded to an anthropocentric view.

In Chapter 3, we demonstrate how complexity understandings of systems undermine the realist focus on states in constituting the international system, while avoiding the marginalization of the state apparent in other systemic accounts, such as varieties of Marxism. In addition, complexity sees systems as multilevelled and intersected, allowing the analysis of multiple influences. It is here that relations of complex inequalities and forms of social domination might be brought into the analysis. The international system may be affected by the global economic system and systems of patriarchy and ethnicity. However, the ways in which these intersections occur are historically and geographically specific rather than simple combinations of influences. Intersectionality points to the ways in which complex systems can affect each other, rather than providing a comprehensive account of all forms of power interaction. Chapter 4 will exemplify our application by considering the emergent features of the international system. This is a system within which the traces of the emergent properties and interactive effects of various types of system can be seen. The majority of social science approaches, including both dominant and more marginal approaches in international relations, assume a direct link between cause and effect, and one that can be mapped mathematically (representing the influence of Newtonian physics). By contrast, complexity approaches assume that the relationships between events may be hard to trace, that small effects can create large outcomes, and that at times of instability future events will be difficult to predict.

Finally, our approach to international politics draws in elements of various kinds of what Smith calls 'constitutive theory' in a complexity frame. Smith refers to the work of Cynthia Enloe as a powerful and important challenge to the ontological and epistemological assumptions of rationalist mainstream international relations. Asking feminist questions of the constituting features and processes of international politics encourages us to see a whole range of different kinds of relations of systemic power. Asking questions informed by the politics of complex ecologism pushes Enloe's considerable intervention farther – it asks questions of international politics in terms not only of gender but of 'race', locality, class, age and other human differences and inequalities. It also asks questions about politics that involve wolves, bears, mosquitoes, eucalyptus trees, soya beans, cattle, chickens and bananas. In posthuman international relations, then, the banana itself would be an important element of Enloe's story of the gendered and colonialist international politics of the Chiquita banana! (See Enloe 1990.)

Two moves are then required in order that international relations can produce an understanding of environmental questions which is not state-centric and 'humanocentric' (Bekoff 2002). First, we need a shift away from a dualist approach which fails to see the embedded situation of the human species in networks and scapes populated with non-humans. Secondly, we need an approach that can account for different levels of governance and different kinds of power relations. We will argue that elements of complexity theory can assist both moves and take us far from the positivist and conservative mainstream of the predominantly American social science that calls itself 'international relations'.

The posthuman future of international relations?

Our social world and our understandings of it have been defined and understood as human-centred or 'anthropocentric' and as 'exclusively human' (Naess 1973; Midgely 1996: 105). The recently popularized term 'posthumanism' has been used as a descriptor for critical perspectives on our human-centrism, and, as is clear from our choice of title, we see this book as part of this posthumanist project. However, the term posthuman is highly flexible and ambiguous, and also contested. In closing this chapter, then, we locate our approach within this conflicted and uncertain terrain.

'Posthumanism' has operated as a somewhat inaccurate collective descriptor for a range of discourses and philosophical claims about the constitution and construction of minds and bodies (both human and non-human) and of nature and artifice (see Miah 2007). First, we should make clear that we do not consider 'transhumanism' to be a posthumanist position. Transhumanism is an ideology that emphasizes the possible good of a future in which humans are able to acquire 'posthuman capacities' and extend their life and health spans, their capacities for happiness and their intellectual capabilities (Bostrom 2003). While such positions use the term 'posthuman' and 'posthumanist', we do not consider that these challenge human-centrism. Rather, they represent an apotheosis of the human through physical extension and disembodiment.

Alternatively, there are a range of biophysical, philosophical and political posthumanisms that centre on the relationships between human beings, other species and the whole other worlds of 'nature'. Some forms of ecologism and earth systems science have been read as suggesting an anti-humanist form of posthumanism. The particularly apocalyptic recent pronouncements from earth systems scientist James Lovelock (2009) about the irreversible harm we humans have now effected on our planet and the extensive and (certainly for humans and other mammals) catastrophic changes which are currently emerging would be a good example. Lovelock's Malthusian statements on overpopulation and management strategies in the face of climate change have met strong criticism. Others, however, have linked earth systems science to left, green and anti-colonialist political projects. Fritjof Capra (1996, 2002), for example, has linked deep ecologism to ideas emerging from complexity approaches in the sciences. In this analysis, we become part of a multitude of various levels of natural and social systems, in which we humans exploit non-human natures as resources. Simon Dalby argues that human-induced changes mean that 'the environment' is increasingly artificial – we have remade the environmental context of our own existence (Dalby 2009: 11–12). Dalby's account is influenced by certain kinds of political ecologism, and he considers our current predicament to be constituted through collective human activity that has been structured by carboniferous consumer capitalism, and relations between rich and poor regions and peoples. It is from this position that, as we will see in Chapter 5, Dalby has made a sustained and important intervention in the literature on 'environmental security'. For Dalby, our ecologically embedded and increasingly perilous situation demands a rethinking – an 'ecological security'.

This understanding of 'humanity' as a fundamentally socially and culturally constituted category, and of humans as existent in webs of relations with other species, has been foregrounded in the range of work within animal studies across the humanities and, more recently, some of the social sciences. From philosophy, literature, art history and cultural studies, to sociology and politics, disciplines are delimited by human exclusivity. For Cary Wolfe (2010: 1), we need to develop modes of social and cultural inquiry that reject the classic humanist divisions of self and other, mind and body, society and nature, human and animal, organic and technological. This philosophical posthumanism enables different kinds of readings of the cultural, the technological and the biological, and also a rethinking of established social forms of difference and exclusion. What Wolfe and others emphasize is that it is not so much 'the human' which is a difficulty, but the human-centric understanding of the human as the unique individual striving in the world, and not embodied and embedded in complex biotic lifeworlds.

Less politically committed than these posthumanisms coming from ecologism and animal studies, but more engaged in some ways with established notions of 'politics', are a range of positions within science and technology studies and cultural studies. These approaches want to move beyond an outdated understanding of the human in our current social, cultural and material context of technoscience. Here we may find Latour, who considers that there is a fundamental deceit at the centre of 'modernity'. We modern 'humans' consider that the real world of nature and the discursively constituted social world of ideas and beliefs are 'pure', exclusive. We are, however, pretending to be modern; in the real natural/cultural world all kinds of hybrids of natures and cultures are produced. In this sense, we have never been modern, but rather we are 'a-modern'; the separation of nature and culture never was. More reticent in her assessment is Katherine Hayles (1999), for whom the notion of the 'posthuman' simply indicates the extent to which narrow definitions of what it means to be human have lost credibility.

Focused on explicitly political questions is Chris Hables Gray, whose *Cyborg Citizen* (2001) has become a cult 'manifesto' for those drawn to postmodern cultural studies. Hables Gray considers we are entering a new postmodern era in which we are becoming cyborg. Much of the book constitutes a liberal prescription for a politics that acknowledges the influence of technology on the bodies of citizens. Thus a 'cyborg citizen' has a bill of rights that includes rights to bodily modification through genomic intervention, or a right to secure their own death. Abounding with examples of advertising, televisual motifs and celebrities which exemplify cyborg citizens, this kind of posthumanism is concerned with the technological mediation of everyday culture, rather than matters of political power more traditionally defined. However, there is, lurking among the commentaries on the various images of popular culture, an analysis of political crisis, the solution to which is a redefinition of political community as 'the earth as a whole'.

There is, then, a wide range of perspectives associated with the notion of the 'posthuman'. Common to them is a critique of humanism as a guiding normative framework for understanding the social/natural world, and all are preoccupied with the consequences of developments in technology, albeit that they are often ambiguous about the desirability of biological interventions. Critical cultural posthumanists, such as Hayles, Haraway and Wolfe, and political ecologists such as Capra and Dalby, emphasize the extent to which the liberal humanist subject is undone by a consideration of both the embodied condition of the human animal, and of life beyond the human. As Wolfe (2008) suggests, posthuman work undertakes two related tasks. First, it challenges the ontological and ethical divide between humans and non-humans that has been the philosophical linchpin of modernity. Secondly, it engages with the challenge of sharing this planet we inhabit with 'non-human subjects', and of the co-constituted conditions of multiple species and biosphere. This book, we hope, is a posthumanist work on both these counts.

Posthuman International Relations has questions of political power (broadly conceived) and environment–society relations at its core.

We understand political systems as dependent on natural systems involving multiple species, and as affecting and affected by them. If international relations is to become posthuman, it must reflect such an understanding. But why, sceptical readers might ask, might theories of international politics feel compelled to take a posthuman turn?

We would argue that international relations theory is biased in its humanocentric ontology and provides a poor and partial representation of international political structures and processes. The theoretical bedrock of all kinds of international political theory has been humanistic in its core assumptions of dualism (the human/nature dichotomy), the elevation of reason as a master category (and as constitutive of the political subject) and its understanding of political agency in rationalist and human-referential terms (see Plumwood 1993, 2002). The underpinning of Western secular and humanist political theory has been distinction from and dominance over 'nature'. We have been understood fundamentally, as Latour (2009) reminded us at the start of the chapter, as a 'detached' species. Our detachment makes us 'modern' and 'human'. Yet such detachment is increasingly unravelled. The varied contributions of environmental sociology, political ecologism and science studies and the insights of transdisciplinary complexity theory illuminate the folly of explanations of the world embedded in Newtonian and humanocentric assumptions.

Complexity science undoes the notion that 'matter' can be subjected to abstraction and prediction. Rather, it suggests that the operation of natural systems is incredibly difficult to predict with any accuracy. The currently compelling evidence of ecological crisis, and the role of human social organization in contributing to it, suggests that our technologies may no longer enable an apparent 'mastery' of the non-human world. While Latour may be right in arguing that we have never been properly modern – that this ideal has never been actualized – various more critical political ecologisms have suggested the narrow and unrepresentative nature of humanocentric modern political theory and the unsustainability of our systems of human relations (such as the capitalist free-market economy, for example; see Hutchinson et al. 2002). Given this, then, the question posed for international relations theory specifically (and for international political theory more broadly) is the extent to which it wishes to represent the constitution of the political world.

The structure of the book

As we come to the close of this chapter, readers will have some familiarity with the idea of complexity approaches, and the possibilities for the development of theories of complex systems in international relations. The next two chapters will detail the applications of complexity approaches in the social sciences more widely, and assess the uses of complexity approaches in international relations specifically. We have also considered the various usages of the term 'posthuman' in the social sciences and situated our usage in this book as an approach to international relations that moves beyond the current human-centred paradigm of the discipline. We have argued here that complexity approaches provide a means of analysing multiple and overlapping systems. This provides a more effective means of analysing global processes, but additionally emphasizes the embeddedness of human systems within a range of non-human systems.

'Complexity theory' has had an impact across the social sciences, and in Chapter 2 we look in some depth at the questions complexity raises for the study of social and political life. The ways in which complexity has been interpreted have been diverse. Is its prime contribution as a metaphor that can be used as a way of explaining social phenomena, or are complexity phenomena related to physical concrete patterns in human relations? Is it that events in the social world are 'as if' complexity phenomena are at work, or is it 'physics all [or most] of the way down'? The answers to such questions are significant in terms of ontology, methodology and epistemology in the social sciences. This chapter assesses a diversity of ways in which complexity has been appropriated in the social sciences, before arguing that social systems do manifest complex phenomena. Complexity is apparent in the social world in different types or kinds of systems – relational and institutional. In addition, and as critics have pointed out, a particular feature of social systems as opposed to non-human systems is that human actors have cognizance of their situation; complexity approaches need to allow for this in their analyses. This chapter establishes a typology of social science approaches to using complexity theory. The chapter ends with a consideration of the types of approach that have been most prevalent in complexity applications within the discipline of international relations, such as 'actor-based modelling'; and sets out the limits of this approach.

Chapter 3 provides an alternative complexity application to 'actor-based modelling', one of complex systems theory. The significance of complexity theory for international relations is that it offers us different ways of thinking about connections and linkages. It offers a toolkit with which to examine interlinked and multilevel relations, between different scales of activity and processes, and it challenges the way the notion of 'system' has most often been deployed. The chapter discusses conventional approaches to systems thinking in international relations before arguing that concepts derived from complexity approaches can be applied to thinking about international systems. It considers how 'complex' international systems might be distinguished from the views developed to date by theorists of international relations. A number of features of complex systems are relevant to the study of international systems, in particular the interconnected notions of self-organization, emergence and non-linearity.

Following this theoretical discussion of systems, Chapter 4 provides an empirical discussion of examples of emergent features in international systems. A key feature of a complexity approach is that systems are self-organizing, and have emergent features – in other words, features that are apparent only at a systemic level of analysis. The chapter applies these theoretical concepts to examine such international features as international organization (the League of Nations and the United Nations), the balance of power (the Cold War), and periodic systems breakdown (the post-Cold War world). The chapter contains a case study which considers how complexity theory can help us make sense of a key contemporary question in international relations – human insecurity, particularly in relation to food. We will look at key changes in animal food production and the development of an international market in animal food and animal feed and the impact of very recent developments in animal food production on local, regional and global environments. Animal-based food has come to be seen as a solution to food poverty, yet the promotion of Western eating habits and intensive production methods is likely to increase social inequalities and make food availability more precarious. Using complexity in explaining these developments, it will be argued that the linked insecurities around food availability and climate change are produced by a combination of continuities and changes in patterns of persistent social inequality and political power. The chapter argues that a complexity approach is more effective at explaining international phenomena than alternative approaches to international systems.

Chapter 5 focuses more comprehensively on the issues of human relations with non-human natures and the ways in which the 'environment' has been theorized in international relations. International relations has historically been preoccupied with questions of security, considered in terms of nation-states and military capabilities. This notion of security has been extended to consider, for example, 'human security' and, most recently, 'environmental security'. The development of environmental security as an academic project has been seen as an important contribution in theorizing the politics of global environmental change, yet critics suggest that ecological matters are not usefully understood in terms of 'security'. This chapter argues that theories of environmental security tend to reproduce a dualistic understanding of human relations to 'the environment'. Alternative approaches to understanding 'environmental issues' in international relations have focused on governance. The chapter will argue that, although on a seemingly separate trajectory from security, the environmental governance and policy literature is also framed by securitization. Drawing on understandings of complex systems as co-constituted and co-evolving, we suggest there is a need to account both for changes in the biosphere resulting from human endeavours, and the ways in which multiple and complex inequalities shape the environmental impact of different populations and raise region-specific issues of insecurity for humans, other species and scapes. The chapter also argues that in order to theorize the environment as implicated in human systems and fundamentally altered by them, we need to draw on various strands of thinking in 'green' political theory, or political ecologism. We develop elements of eco-socialism, ecofeminism and liberation ecologism in arguing that human relations to environments are characterized by social intersectionality and complex inequalities resulting from complex systems of social relations such as colonialism, capitalism and patriarchy. Complexity approaches can help capture the patterns of these relations. So, the chapter draws on complexity in order to understand, first, the co-constitution of human communities and the 'natural environment' and, secondly, that human relations with non-human species are shaped by persistent relations of power around gender, class, ethnicity, locality, and so on.

The closing chapters develop arguments which call for a 'posthuman international relations' and a concerted move away from anthropocentric international relations. Chapter 6 argues that theorizations of international relations should be critically posthuman in quality, by which we mean they should both understand our human condition as embedded in relations and practices with other species, for example, and acknowledge forms of power and domination over them. The category 'human' is a human invention, a social construct linked to formations of power. The power relations and dominant social, economic and political institutions of Western modernity have been constituted by and through constructions of social inequality, of class, race and gender. However, these social categories of difference and domination have also been cross-cut by prevailing ideas about 'nature' and the separation of the human from it. In addition to understanding relational power as posthuman, we also suggest that political power is embodied and this also involves us thinking beyond the human. To this end, a Foucauldian notion of biopower is added to the discussion of complex systems to examine the ways social relations are inscribed on to and embedded in human and other bodies. Both humans and non-human species may be subjected to certain forms of biological control or manipulation with political implications. This understanding of power as embodied has important implications for the study of established preoccupations in international relations, such as warfare, territorialization and human rights. Posthuman international relations, then, does not *only* mean thinking about non-human species and scapes and the interlinking of human and non-human complex systems. Posthuman international relations *also* means thinking differently about the human and about the political.

In conclusion, we examine the wider implications of a posthuman approach to the study of international politics – including practical politics as well as matters of theory. We argue that such an approach would have radical implications for the discipline in terms of the subject of study and the approach to knowledge. In particular, we will pose the question of what constitutes the 'international', and how the posthuman approach advocated by the book differs from conventional accounts in international relations. From a posthuman perspective, the international is composed of multiple and overlapping human and non-human systems that interact in a complex set of relationships. Only a complexity-based approach provides the tools which enable an understanding of such interactions, but also includes an awareness of the limits of our knowledge. Such an approach would supply the discipline of international relations with the tools to theorize key issues of the twenty-first century and suggest new agendas for future research priorities.

2 · Complexity theory in the study of the social world

In this chapter we examine the ways in which complexity ideas have been adopted across a range of social sciences and humanities. We do this for two reasons. First, to establish that complexity approaches have found a wide range of applications. This does not, of course, mean that it is necessarily the case that a complexity approach is appropriate in the study of international relations. However, it does suggest, given that complexity thinking has established a foothold across a range of studies of the social world, that its potential is worthy of consideration.

Secondly, we wish to draw attention to the variety of different ways in which complexity ideas have been appropriated. In short, there is not one complexity theory, but a variety of approaches, all of which draw upon a shared cluster of ideas. While virtually all of the approaches that have been developed using complexity ideas share some similarities, this is often fairly limited. There are various conceptions of what constitutes complexity, how we might analyse it, and what the implications are for our understanding of the human and non-human realms. A particular distinction can be drawn between those approaches that view complexity as a feature of models or metaphors that we might use to analyse the social world (a majority view) and those that see complexity as ontologically real. In the second half of the chapter we draw up a typology of approaches which could be described as complexity, and attempt to distinguish between them and their implications. We advocate an approach that we describe as 'differentiated complexity', which we see as radical, thick (Strand 2007) and general (Morin 2007).

Complexity and the social sciences

For some parts of the social sciences, the impact of complexity thinking is a very recent affair. Certainly, in international relations, work drawing on complexity ideas is very new. While Emilian Kavalski (2007) suggests that contributions from complexity thinking to international relations constitute a 'fifth debate', we would consider that the impact on the discipline to date has been fairly limited. We have discussed some appropriations of complexity thinking in Chapter 1. There may be good reasons for this limited engagement, and it is possible that complexity thinking does not provide a suitable framework for thinking about international relations. It may also be the case that the implications of complexity are ones that the discipline does not wish to engage with, because, at least in our analysis of complexity, they would require a fundamental reorienting of the discipline. Either way, international relations is somewhat at odds with developments elsewhere in academia. Complexity-inspired approaches have made a considerable impact across a wide range of disciplines. It is not our intention to produce a comprehensive account of all these contributions, which would be far beyond the scope of this book, but to give an indication of the kind of work being done. Here we will consider the contributions of complexity to economics, history and sociology.

Much of the material referenced below is 'new', but it should be acknowledged that there are historical precedents. In sociology, for example, the use of the concept of 'system' to describe and explain social interconnections and the emergence of social phenomena, social change and stasis has a long history. The sociological use of 'system' also engages perspectives across the discipline (Durkheim 1952, 1966; Parsons 1951, 1960; Weber 1968; Marx 1954), and such work can be read as containing some isolated elements of complexity thinking; for example, see Urry (2003) on the legacy of Marx, and Luhmann (1995) on that of Parsons. In politics, there is a similar legacy in the use of the concept of system. On the one hand, we have the Parsonian use of the concept of self-regulating political system (Easton 1981), and comparative approaches to different kinds of political systems (Almond and Bingham-Powell 1966). Alternatively, those working in the Marxist tradition have drawn on systemic understandings in explaining changes in global capitalism and its relationship with other processes such as economic development and democratization (Cortes et al. 1974; Przeworski 1985, 2000). We consider any such use of system 'proto-complexity' thinking, however. This distinction is perhaps more difficult to sustain with the discipline with which we begin – economics.

Economics Economics is perhaps the discipline where complexity thinking made both an early and a significant contribution. In some ways, perhaps, this is not surprising. A key feature of contemporary capitalism is its tendency to exhibit periods of rapid expansion and contraction. The fluctuations in the financial and equity markets appear to be completely chaotic and irrational, and complexity-inspired work has sought to analyse these apparent periods of instability. However, at the core of the discipline (at least in its classical and neoclassical formulations) has been the contention that markets move towards equilibrium. Where this has not happened (in effect everywhere), economists have blamed 'exogenous shocks' or market-distorting activities, either by firms (monopoly or cartel activities), or governments (subsidizing uncompetitive activities). Remove the market distortions, and markets will move into equilibrium, ensuring maximum efficiency, and hence wealth creation. Complexity economics approaches are rather more dubious about the claims regarding automatic balancing tendencies in markets. The claim to automatic balancing tendencies is based on a classical model of physics. Hence for Ricardo (cited in Mainzer 2007: 316), conclusions drawn from economics could be 'as certain as the principles of gravitation'. Complex economics, by contrast, views economic processes as 'too complex, too nonlinear, too dynamic, and too sensitive to the twists and turns of chance to be amenable to prediction over anything but the shortest of terms' (Beinhocker 2006: 17, 323).

Klaus Mainzer (2007: 345–6) points to four assumptions shared by classical economists that are undermined by complexity approaches. The first assumption is that economic actors are rational. When presented with economic information they will choose the most rational option and as a result boost wealth. However, outside of economic models human beings do not act like calculating machines and do not always act to maximize their self-interests. A second assumption is that all economic actors are alike. Confronted with the same set of economic conditions, all actors will act in the same way. In practice, there are many different types of economic actors – as an example Mainzer distinguishes between 'fundamentalists', who trust that all stock values are related to underlying value and will revert to that value at some point, and 'chartists', who believe that trends in stock market values are more important. The interactions between these two types of investor can lead to stock market crashes and booms. Thirdly, classical economics sees price changes as continuous, allowing the application of relatively straightforward equations to track and analyse economic formations. However, stock prices, like quantum states in physics, do jump, and 'reality is actually discontinuous' (ibid.: 346). Finally, there has been an assumption, akin to the concept of Brownian motion in physics, that price changes are statistically independent (in other words, unrelated to previous changes), statistically stationary (always caused by the same processes) and that price change distributions would conform to a normal, bell-curve distribution. In practice, price movements conform to none of these features.

Equity markets are frequently referred to in order to illustrate the complex features of economic activities. Conventional economics would anticipate that equity markets would move towards equilibrium, where the value of market shares would reflect the underlying value of the relevant company. If shares become overvalued then we would expect shareholders to sell them, resulting in a loss of value, while under-valued shares would be expected to be purchased, thus pushing their value up. Share values should be consistently moving towards their equilibrium value. However, in practice, share prices tend to be much more volatile, indeed chaotic, with shares being irrationally overvalued at one moment, and ridiculously undervalued the next – the classic stock market boom and bust. A traditional model finds it difficult to account for such fluctuations because it assumes linearity and nega-tive feedback (in this instance price signals) (Rihani 2002: 22; Bein-hocker 2006: 27–8; Mandelbrot and Hudson 2004: 54–7). Conventional approaches assume that there is one model of the way the economy works, and that all actors share this model. Complexity approaches suggest both that there is no one model, that it changes continually and that actors (in this case, investors) are not only constantly re-vising their models, but also reacting to how other investors react. In a famous illustration of this, the 'El Farol Bar Problem', Brian Arthur (1994) drew parallels between the operation of the stock market and the attendance at a local bar. In the Bar Problem model sixty potential clients would base their decision on whether to attend the bar on their expectation of how busy the bar would be – hence they not only had a model of bar attendance, but also were considering how others might be acting. Any one individual who wishes to frequent the bar (but only when it is not too busy) will base their model on what they expect others to do. However, other bar users will be modelling their expectations on their predictions of the behaviour of other bar users, and so on in a constant loop. Any common pattern of expectations will soon be broken up – if all expect few attendees, then everyone will turn up, quashing the model. While this might be expected to be a recipe for complete chaos, when Arthur ran a computer simulation of the model he found that an emergent structure appeared – while models of bar attendance were being constantly re-evaluated, and bar attendance fluctuated, a pattern in the number of visitors to the bar appeared. This, Arthur claimed, could be equated to the actions of investors in a stock market. Here again, investors were constantly reassessing their models in the light of stock market developments. A computer simulation based on these factors produced in a similar fashion the volatile fluctuations that are seen in the stock market – periods of stability intercut with boom and bust.

In one of his last works, Benoit Mandelbrot (Mandelbrot and Hudson 2004), the inventor of fractal geometry, summarized his long-term interest in economics and in particular the analysis of financial markets. Financial markets have a tendency to fluctuate to a far greater extent than classical models suggest, and are 'dynamic, unpredictable, and sometimes dangerous' (ibid.: 121). In this volatility they share a characteristic of turbulence with a great number of natural phenomena, and Mandelbrot argues that in comparing wind and market turbulence 'you can see the same bump, bump, bump; the same abrupt lurches between wild motion and quiet activity; the same discontinuities; the same intermittency; the same concentration of major events in time' (ibid.: 114). While the source of this turbulence is uncertain, Mandelbrot claimed that his mathematical models, based on fractal geometry, can come close to replicating the fluctuations in the market.

Issues of development and inequality have also been a concern within complex economics. Samir Rihani (2002) argued that models of development were based on a linear account of how development occurred. This was the basis of the modernization approach adopted following the Second World War, which assumed that all countries followed a similar path towards development, each passing through a number of phases until the point of economic 'take-off' was reached (Rostow 1959). It was simply a question of assisting poorer countries to get on to the appropriate pathway, and then almost automatically economic development would occur. The history of post-war development attempts suggests that this has been a far from effective way to promote development. Two basic assumptions underwrote these development programmes: linearity (the same inputs would result in the same outputs), and mechanicalism, the idea that the social world can be treated like a machine that can be reproduced at will. Rihani's argument is that development programmes have failed to consider that economic development does not occur in a vacuum; there is a need to give priority to human development, in particular the ability to interact. 'Repressed, diseased, illiterate and malnourished people are neither free nor capable of interacting locally to energize the Complex Adaptive System we recognise as "nation", and they are certainly not in a position to bring the invisible hand [as in Adam Smith] into action' (Rihani 2002: 141). Rihani's argument is that developing nations need the active participation of their citizens. Development is not something that can be given, it has to emerge from the interactions within a complex adaptive system. 'Haphazard interactions without appropriate rules that command support produce chaos and little else' (ibid.: 164). There are two elements to the human development that Rihani advocates – the promotion of freedom (for example, democracy and human rights) and capabilities (such as health or education).

Rihani applies complexity concepts to a crucial global issue, and his critique of traditional development programmes for adopting linear and mechanical assumptions is effective. However, his approach shows some potential weaknesses in complexity applications. Discussing these, we hope, will enable us to indicate more clearly how our approach differs from some other complexity approaches. There is little account of power. While he does discuss fitness landscapes (a concept that we will develop more fully in the next chapter), there is no analysis of how more powerful actors may be able to transform the fitness landscape to their own interests. A related point is that there is no discussion of colonialism, and the results of colonialism that persist. In other words, while a focus on a failure in terms of human development as undermining economic development is a valuable insight, what is missing from this analysis is an international context – indeed, Rihani appears to fall into the same mechanistic/ linearity trap of conventional development thinking – that given the same ingredients (in this instance human development), then a similar outcome will result. There are wider systems in operation than Rihani accounts for.

As well as failing to take into account a broader range of historical and global systems, Rihani's account of development processes is markedly anthropocentric. Development is presented as a purely human process that has little connection to other species or the environment more generally, nor does it have an impact upon them.

History While economics, with its abundance of numerical data, and a tradition in classical economics of assuming that efficiently running economies move towards equilibrium, has proved a fertile ground for complexity approaches, history might not seem as obvious an area for complexity perspectives. In this section we examine the contribution that has been made by applying complexity thinking to history. What is particularly interesting is that complexity has been used across the historical scales, from 'big history' at the largest scale possible, to much more specific accounts of particular events. We focus on both here, and as in the last section, consider the relevance for thinking about posthuman international relations.

Fred Spier places human development within the largest scale possible – the history of the cosmos since the 'big bang'. He defines 'big history' as 'the rise and demise of complexity at all scales' (Spier 2010: 21). In other words, his work is an examination of the unfolding of various types of complexity over the past 13.7 billion earth years. Since that point, history has been an account of ever-increasing complexity, but also, on occasions, of the demise or breaking down of complexity. At the time of the big bang there was no complexity, in the sense that there was no differentiation between matter and energy. As the universe started to expand and rapidly cool down, a pattern of increasing differentiation (or increased organization) of matter began to occur. This encompassed the emergence of matter, and then within the furnace of stars the appearance of the range of elements that make up the periodic table. Matter also became organized into the galaxies and solar systems which comprise the universe. Underlying this process was a series of propitious historical accidents. Spier (ibid.: 36–40) uses the term 'Goldilocks principle' to describe these fortunate occurrences. In essence, this refers to the conditions being 'just right' for certain forms of complexity to emerge. So, for example, the complex forms of life that have emerged on earth could only have done so if its orbit was just right – not too close to the sun, which would have boiled all the water off, and not too far away, which would have locked all the water up as ice. The size of the planet had to be just right – big enough to have the gravity sufficient to retain an atmosphere, but not so big that the gravity force was such as to crush everything on its surface. A similar instance was the conditions that existed only in the first four minutes after the big bang for the basic characteristics of the universe (the strong nuclear force, electromagnetism and gravity) plus all of the elementary particles to emerge (ibid.: 45–6).

With the exception of the first four minutes after the big bang, cosmological history proceeds at a relatively slow pace. By contrast, life on earth has developed at a much faster pace. Biological complexity increases at a faster rate than non-animate forms because of the capability to adapt and learn from the environment – in Darwinian terms, certain organisms are more able to adapt to their environment and thrive within it. Of these biological organisms, humans, according to Spier, have developed as the 'greatest known complexity'. What has changed significantly over the past 2 million years is the human capability to exploit and affect the environment, and this would appear to be related to an increase in brain size. There is mounting evidence that this increase in brain size is linked to tool use (ibid.: 121). By approximately 10,000 years ago all the ingredients were present which permitted human beings to achieve their current accomplishments.

A significant part of Spier's observations is that complexity is not a one-way street. Systems can become more complex, but they can also become less complex: stars burn out; biological development on earth has also been punctuated by periods of mass extinction; ultimately the universe will consume all the energy made available at the time of the big bang, and complex atoms will decompose into low levels of energy. Whether human beings can maintain their position as the greatest known complexity depends on their capacity to maintain the passage of energy through human systems. Humans have possibly developed a tendency to amass more energy than is needed for survival – in which case the continued existence of the species will depend on finding social ways of mediating this propensity.

Perhaps such a decline in complexity is what Roger Beaumont (2000) had in mind in his analysis of the collapse of the Nazi regime. This work marks a distinct contrast from the vast historical scale of the 'big history' described by Spier. Beaumont explores the possibility of applying a complexity lens to the study of a more restricted period of history. Of particular interest to Beaumont is the study of the way that complex systems can be affected by sensitivity to initial conditions. With particular reference to Germany of the 1920s, 1930s and 1940s, this raises interesting questions – how could such a brutal and irrational regime appear in perhaps one of the most developed countries in Europe? And how was it possible for the regime to collapse in such a dramatic fashion? Beaumont (ibid.: 34) argues that 'from the standpoint of chaos-complexity theory, various points along the path of National Socialism's rise and fall suggest "sensitivity to initial conditions"'. As a result very minor changes or decisions may have resulted in a very different set of outcomes, either for better or worse. An example, perhaps, could have been the decision to switch the Luftwaffe attacks from air bases to cities during the Battle of Britain in 1941. In itself a comparatively minor choice, though potentially one that resulted in the postponement of the invasion of Britain, and conceivably major ramifications for the final outcome of the Second World War. Such matters, Beaumont argues, 'reinforce historians' and philosophers' concerns about the elusiveness of certainty in their tracing of causality' (ibid.: 178).

While we would have criticisms of both these historical accounts, they do show the possibilities of complexity-inspired history. A particular strength of Spier's account is to show the appearance of humanity within the context of vast cosmological processes, and within material and biological processes on earth. While there is a hint of teleology and anthropocentrism in this account, Spier (2010: 121–6, 193) acknowledges co-evolution with animate and non-animate systems, and the ephemeral character of human existence. These would support the post-humanist argument that we advocate of seeing humanity as embedded within a range of other systems from which it cannot be differentiated to a large degree. Beaumont's work, while perhaps being open to a critique of human-centredness, raises important epistemological issues related to what it is possible to assert in analysing complex adaptive systems, which are sensitive to initial conditions.

Sociology Much recent work in sociology has been concerned with issues that have overlapped with international relations, in particular the study of globalization. As with history and economics, complexity thinking has also had an impact on sociology, encroaching across the discipline as a whole from health studies to urban development. Sociologists have discussed complexity both from a philosophical (for example, Morin 2008) and an applied perspective. In a wide-ranging review of what they describe as '*the complexity turn* in sociology', Brian Castellani and Frederic Hafferty (2009: viii–x) point to five areas of research: 'computational sociology, the British-based School of Complexity, complex social network analysis, sociocybernetics and the Luhmann School of Complexity'. We do not attempt to provide a survey of this entire field, but focus on a subject that sociologists have been interested in which has a particular relevance to the study of international relations.

Sociologists influenced by complexity thinking have made a number of contributions to the study of globalization. Where the study of globalization and complexity seem to have developed particular overlaps is in terms of increasing interconnections on a planetary scale. Some sociologists have analysed this in terms of social networks (Castells 1996, 1997, 1998), while others have argued that 'global complexity' (Urry 2003) is emerging as a result of these interconnections. We will discuss John Urry's conception of complexity as a *metaphor* for understanding the social world in the next section. Here we are concerned with the main points of his analysis.

Urry's central claim is that the processes collectively grouped together under the label of globalization imply a major rethinking of the central categories that have been the core of sociology, in particular the notion of 'bounded or "organized" capitalist societies' (ibid.: 3). Complexity theory might provide the basis for such a rethinking because it depicts systems as emergent and frequently far from equilibrium. In such systems there can be huge disjunctures between cause and effect. Urry's work draws heavily on Castell's network analysis, but attempts to move this forward through making the global character of network relations more explicit. The core of this argument is that in terms of social relations within an emergent global system there is both order and disorder, or 'moorings *and* mobilities' (ibid.: 138, emphasis in original). The dynamism comes from the combination of mooring and mobility. Either would constitute non-dynamic and non-complex systems, yet the possibilities for new mooring or stabilities permit the appearance of greater mobility – in other words, the globalizing world comprises an interrelationship between elements of order and disorder – a feature which is well suited to a complexity-based analysis.

Urry's contributions to the development of complexity thinking have been influential across a range of disciplines, and his work has overlapped in particular with that of geographers. Gatrell (2005), for example, points to the significance of Urry's work in his survey of complexity-influenced studies of the geography of health. However, while, as Nigel Thrift (1999: 32) suggests, complexity thinking is 'preternaturally spatial', geographers have been comparatively reluctant to engage with complexity concepts. Thrift (ibid.: 32) suggests that this might be due to an early engagement with more mathematically inspired approaches to complexity. Complexity thinking has been used by a number of geographers to examine the dynamics of urban development. A particularly significant contribution to this literature is from Batty (2005), who used a battery of quantitative methods to examine the dynamics involved in the development of cities. From a somewhat different perspective, Byrne (1998: ch. 5) uses complexity concepts such as varying scales, perturbations and bifurcation points to develop an analysis of 'complex spaces', in particular Teesside in north-east England. Thrift (2005) has drawn on less quantitative understandings of complexity theory in his analysis of the development of global capitalism – work that shares much of the focus on globalization of Urry.

The subject of globalization is also taken up by the sociologist Sylvia Walby (2009). Her approach is perhaps the closest application of complexity to the 'differentiated complexity' that we will discuss later in this chapter. We draw considerable inspiration from Walby's analysis of systems, and in particular of intersectionality. Central to Walby's discussion is the question of how to analyse multiple forms of social inequality. Rather than focus on one form of social inequality (the classic example would be class relations), Walby seeks to understand how different forms of social inequality interact, or intersect with each other. These intersections occur within the broader context of globalization. As she notes, 'there is a need both to capture the distinctions, differentiations and nuances of complex inequalities that have been part of what has been driving the postmodern turn, and to keep the global horizon in sight' (ibid.: 2–3). In complexity theory she finds the toolbox to analyse these multiple systems. Hence, a key point of her work is to point out how developments in complexity theory permit a rethinking of the concept of system. In particular, she argues that systems, when reconceptualized from a complexity perspective, do not have an inherent tendency to move towards equilibrium. While feedback can be negative, drawing a system towards equilibrium, it can also be positive, reinforcing and amplifying forces for change. Systems, while having boundaries, also intersect with other systems, allowing the possibility of thinking about their mutual influence. However, these intersections are always far from straightforward (linear), and forms of inequality interact in ways that can only be understood from a complexity-based analysis.

Urry's and Walby's works provide significantly different takes on the analysis of globalization, and through a comparison we can draw out some distinctions in the ways in which varieties of complexity theory have been applied. First, there are epistemological differences between these approaches. Urry, as will be developed below, sees complexity theory as a metaphor for processes in the social world. Walby (ibid.: 74), by contrast, draws on critical realism to provide an ontological depth analysis of levels within systems. Secondly, they differ in their means of analysing power. While Urry employs systems terminology, his analysis is of networks. Interactions across a network bring forth emergent behaviour. This has the effect of 'flattening' the analysis, and while there is a chapter entitled 'Social ordering and power', the discussion is on forms of state power over the individual through the mediation of scandal. By flattening out the analysis to series of networks carrying information, Urry lacks the tools for an analysis of power relations between the actors. By contrast, Walby's analysis develops ideas about systems and their forms of interaction. This permits the analysis of unequal power relations between different systems. Central to this analysis is the concept of fitness landscape (a concept we will draw upon in the next chapter), which provides a way of understanding power differentials. Additionally, it allows the analysis of the context in which actors operate, including the ability to manipulate the fitness landscape to the more powerful actors' advantage.

A typology of complexity approaches

Despite this increasing influence, it is only recently that some of the deeper philosophical issues related to the application of complexity theory have begun to be examined (see, for example, Rescher 1998; Cilliers 2007; Gershenson et al. 2007), and there are few attempts to grapple more deeply with the issues involved in developing a complexity approach. In particular, there are two main problems. First, there are diverse complexity approaches, and complexity has been applied in different ways by different authors. Secondly, there are profound implications for what it is possible to know and not know about the social world when a complexity approach is utilized.

The key factor that differentiates different approaches is the extent to which complexity has a material base. In other words, the extent to which complexity is manifested as a physical quality. While all the authors we examine argue that a complexity approach provides us with a means of interpreting the social world, they differ on what constitutes the relationship between theory and the social world. In short, is complexity theory a model or metaphor (in other words, do some features of the social world operate 'as if' they had complex characteristics), or is there an underlying physics at work which impinges on the social world – a characteristic that has been described as consilience (Wilson 1999), or as 'social physics' or quantum social science.

Consilience and metaphor comprise the end points of a spectrum of thinking about complexity in the social world. We advance an intermediate position. We argue that regarding complexity theory as a metaphor for understanding social phenomena is a weak position, and one that reflects a human-centred approach, ignoring the embodied character of human systems and existence. We argue that complex phenomena in the social world are underpinned by physics, and social systems overlap and intersect with biological and physical systems. However, it is not physics 'all the way down'.

The biologist Stuart Kauffman (2008) has recently argued that scientists of complexity need to theorize 'upwards' in avoiding traditional reductionist models of the natural sciences. The understanding of more complex animals, particularly species with higher levels of complexity in group behaviour, communication and sociality (such as humans and other Great Apes, other primates, all kinds of felines, canines and cetaceans), requires scientists to move beyond their science. While social systems share characteristics with non-human systems, they are also distinguished by human cognizance. In other words, complexity approaches to the study of the social world need to account for the human capability to study and construct their social world, and this, for Kauffman or the physicist Murray Gell-Mann (1994), constitutes an area in which complexity scientists must engage beyond their disciplines. Not all are so open to the permeability of disciplinary boundaries around subjects and groups. Among social scientists, Niklas Luhmann (1995) has undertaken the most thorough working through of complexity concepts in sociology. Luhmann understands the reproduction of language, meaning and families as social systems constituted by and through self-reflexive human agents. However, for Luhmann, non-human species are not social and non-human systems are discrete, bounded and cannot be considered by social scientists.

We identify four approaches to the application of complexity insights by social scientists. We begin by examining those authors who consider complexity theory as a metaphor. We then turn to the other end of the spectrum, and look at the work of 'social physicists' who perceive complexity as being an inherent quality of all matter. Finally, we examine two approaches that consider the presence of complex phenomena in both the human and non-human world, but acknowledge distinctive features of the human world. Herein, there are those who see complexity as a network, or rather as a range of interlinking networks capable of understanding processes from localized minutiae to global events. Finally, we consider our favoured approach, which we call 'differentiated complexity'.

These approaches can be differentiated epistemologically. Paul Cilliers (2007: 4) argues that we can draw a distinction between 'hard' and 'metaphorical' complexity: 'in this understanding, the first category would imply true scientific activity whereas the second refers to the softer, more interpretative strategies of the social sciences'. He argues that the distinction between 'hard' and 'soft' complexity equates to the distinction drawn by Edgar Morin (2007) between 'restricted' and 'generalized' complexity. Morin's argument was that a 'restricted' complexity failed to understand the deeper epistemological implications of complexity for the study of both human and non-human worlds. A similar argument is made by Roger Strand (2007), who differentiates between 'thick' and 'thin' complexity.

These four positions can be considered against two axes, one indicating an epistemological standpoint, and one indicating an ontological

TABLE 2.1 Complexity and social science

| | Model | EPISTEMOLOGY | |
| | | How do we know about the social world? | |
	Model	*Hermeneutic*	*Naturalist*
	Complex realism	Metaphor	Network
		Differentiated	Consilient
ONTOLOGY			
Where is the complexity?			

viewpoint. The first axis asks: how do we gain knowledge about the social world; specifically, is the social world different? The second one asks: where is the complexity – is it a real-world phenomenon that we are examining, or is the complexity in our models? Putting the two axes together gives us four ways of thinking about complexity. Meta-phoric and differentiated approaches are similar in that they consider the social world to be 'different', though they differ in where they consider complexity to be. For metaphoric approaches, the complexity is in the metaphor, whereas differentiated approaches consider the complexity to be a real embedded phenomenon, although, owing to human cognizance, it requires a particular form of analysis. Network and consilient approaches are similar in seeing the human and non-human worlds as a continuous tapestry with the same methods being appropriate for all analysis. Where they differ is in the view that, for network approaches, the complexity is in the model, whereas consilient approaches, as with differentiated perspectives, see complexity as real.

Complexity as a metaphor 'Soft' approaches to complexity tend to use complexity concepts as descriptors for social processes. Complexity here provides a terminology, a conceptual repertoire for talking about the social. Urry's approach to the global, as discussed in the previous section, provides a clear example of such approaches.

Urry considers that the global is not a single system, but 'a series of dynamic complex systems' (Urry 2003: x). He applies elements of complexity theory in order to understand the non-linear, non-unified quality of globalization, where 'regions' (clusters of bounded societies based on the notion of a nation-state) persist, despite being (re)shaped and affected by and implicated in 'networks' of international relation-ships often involving an array of new technologies, and 'fluids', flows of people, money, environmental hazards, commodities and other objects (ibid.: 40–5, 53–74). These regions, networks and fluids are themselves non-linear, complex and self-organizing systems, and collectively they constitute the 'global', which, itself a system and distinct from those systems nested within it, has its own emergent properties (ibid.: 76).

Yet, in Urry's account, complexity is a 'concept' (ibid.: x), albeit one that can contribute significantly to understanding social events. He also argues that complexity acts as a metaphor and that notions from com-plexity thinking can be 'interrogated in order to assess their fruitfulness in representing those processes implicated in ... global ordering' (ibid.: 16). While drawing on ideas from complexity theorists such as Fritjof Capra and Ilya Prigogine, Urry (2004: 58) explores whether complexity theory can generate 'productive metaphors' that could illuminate global-ized social and political events, such as those in New York on 11 Sep-tember 2001. 'The science of complex systems', he argues, 'provides a way of thinking about social order' (2003: 105). In other words, for Urry, complexity would appear to provide a set of concepts for describing the social world, rather than deploying a scientific understanding of complexity as an inherent quality of material reality.

A traditional way of thinking about metaphors is to consider them as a word or phrase that stands in for something to which it is not exactly applicable – 'raining cats and dogs', for example. For Urry (2000: 21) the term 'metaphor' refers to 'the wide variety of modes of substitution of one figure for another; such a process suffuses language and meaning'. He argues that 'being and thinking sociologically cannot be undertaken outside of metaphor' (ibid.: 23). This stress on seeing complexity as a metaphor for studying the social world suggests that he wants to downplay the significance of complexity in social activities. Urry's use implies that he views complexity concepts as something less than a theory, or model of the social world. That is to say that complexity functions as a description of how things are rather than an understanding and explanation of the social, in Morin's terms, as 'irreducibly linked at all levels to physical phenomenality' (2008: 105). All theories about the world, whether social or physical, are ultimately ideas, representations of what are almost inevitably more complicated sets of interactions (a central claim for theorists of complexity), rather than entities that have a direct physical relationship with that which is being studied. Yet Urry's use of the term implies that he wishes to distance concepts drawn from complexity from the social events that he is trying to study.

There may be epistemological reasons for this defensive position. Global ordering is 'epistemologically and ontologically unknowable' (Urry 2003: 16). In other words, the sheer intricacy involved in studying the social world is so great that our knowledge will always be slight, and our models and theories insufficient. As Cilliers (1998: 58) argues, 'models of complex systems will have to be as complex as the systems themselves'. This fits well with a reading of 'complexity theory' as closely allied to an understanding of the world as postmodern. For Cilliers (2000: 9), 'there is no accurate (or, rather, perfect) representation of the system that is simpler than the system itself. In building representa-tions of open systems we are forced to leave things out, and since the effects of these omissions are nonlinear, we cannot predict their magni-tude.' Clearly, in terms of thinking about globalization, or international relations, or any complicated social activity, this is unobtainable. Our knowledge of a complex world will always be impartial and incomplete.

Yet in this situation of partial knowledge, Cilliers nevertheless appears to be making an assumption that the social world operates 'as if' complexity were at work. There may be very good reasons for taking such a position. Complexity theory emerged from the study of the physical world rather than the social, where patterns in apparently chaotic behaviour were observed. While these patterns could be modelled, no physical explanation of the phenomena has been discovered, so that, as Kauffman (2008) suggests, physics does not actually explain biological 'life'. Given this limitation in complexity theory with regard to the physical world, it is perhaps not unreasonable to be guarded with reference to its application to the social world. However, there seems to be little difference for Urry between a metaphor and a model or theory with explanatory power. He argues that different metaphors can be evaluated and assessed using empirical means (Urry 2000: 22). Here he appears to be trying to navigate a path between an unreconstructed positivism and complete relativism.

Urry's position ultimately appears to be rather defensive. It suggests that complex phenomena in the social world do not have a material basis, and may be purely coincidental, and hence are not an enduring characteristic. While this may be the case, it seems more likely that, if phenomena can be characterized as complex, the explanation for that complexity has the same basis as the explanation of complexity in the non-social world. Our view is that if the social world operates 'as if' it were subject to the same chaotic phenomena, and there is no reason to argue that this is just coincidence, then a stronger position would be to argue that there is a material basis for this that is open to study, rather than considering it to be a metaphor.

Both Urry and Cilliers suggest that there is a distinction between the study of the human world and that of the non-human world – hard, foundationalist, intrinsic complexity would be appropriate for the non-human world, while 'soft', interpretive, metaphoric complexity would be more appropriate for the study of the social world. However, our opinion is that this view draws a dichotomy between the human and non-human worlds, and reifies a distinction which does not exist. Human systems are embodied in non-human systems, and in order to gain some understanding of the human world we have to analyse it as embedded within a range of other systems. This would suggest a need to engage with the literature on consilience, which attempts to produce a unified theory of the human and non-human worlds.

Complexity as a unified science A very different kind of approach to complexity is one that seeks to utilize its insights as a means of providing a unified approach to science. The goal of developing a unified science has been one that has attracted theorists across the social and physical sciences. E. O. Wilson's discussion of consilience is perhaps one of the clearest calls for such an approach, though it should be noted that, with regard to complexity theory, Edward Wilson (1999: 96) located himself somewhere between a 'fervent advocate' and a sceptic. Unified approaches can be divided into discussions more influenced by mathematics, and those with a more social science/systems approach. With regard to the latter, we discuss here the work of Capra, a physicist who has turned his attention more to social sciences and ecological issues, and Morin, whose interests have spanned political science, psychology and sociology.

Capra's most recent work (2002) builds on his previous explorations of ecology and complexity physics (Capra 1975) and a broad range of complexity science approaches (Capra 1983, 1996) in specifically analysing 'upwards' to the social world. Capra argues that 'it makes sense to ground the understanding of social phenomena in a unified conception of the evolution of life and consciousness' (Capra 2002: 3). In other words, Capra's view is that it is possible to develop means of thinking about the social world which link it with the wider non-human world. Capra (ibid.: 70) makes the 'assumption that there is a fundamental unity to life, that different living systems exhibit similar patterns of organization'. If we can gain an understanding of these patterns then this can allow us insights into the workings of human societies.

All life on the planet shares similar patterns of development, Capra argues. These can be understood as 'self-generating networks' (ibid.: 28), which have led to the development of, and from, the earliest life forms through to the most intricate of animal and plant species, and, crucially, social systems. From this perspective, cognition and consciousness emerged as part of a process of lived experience. 'From the beginning of life, [living organisms'] interactions with one another and with the nonliving environment were cognitive interactions. As their structures increased in complexity, so did their cognitive processes, eventually bringing forth conscious awareness, language and conceptual thought' (ibid.: 58). In other words, process is a significant element in the development of networks and more complex organisms. Consciousness and thought emerged and developed from the interactions between living organisms and with their environment.

The same tools and patterns can be seen in the social realm. Capra argues that we need to combine an analysis of four interrelated factors: form, or 'pattern of organization', which refers to the 'configuration of relationships among the system's components that determines the system's essential characteristics'; matter, the material environment in which a system exists; process, the ongoing interaction between form and matter; and meaning, the inner world of concepts and images which give significance to our environment. Understanding the social world, Capra (ibid.: 64) argues, 'must involve the integration of four perspectives – form, matter, process and meaning'.

The cornerstone of Capra's analysis is the concept of system. Capra argues that all forms of both social and natural 'life' are bounded, interrelated, living (i.e. self-making) systems which possess cognition (i.e. the ability to learn from the process of being in the world; see ibid.: 30–3). In any social system there will be sets of rules and norms that influence and constrain activities – this, in Capra's terminology, would be the form of the system. Any system would also be founded on a material base, the matter, comprising the individual members/ elements of the system, tools of communication, and so on. The system would develop over time through a series of processes, and for human systems would have meaning for its individual members. The internet would be a prime example of such a social system, as it has rules and norms of activity, a material base in the computer hardware and connections that it has developed over time through repeated use, and it has and provides meaning for its users.

In contrast to metaphorical accounts of forms of human organization, Capra (ibid.: 88) argues that they 'can literally be understood as living systems'. What he means by this is that through acts of communication, social systems are self-organizing (autopoietic). 'Each communication creates thoughts and meanings, which give rise to further communications, and thus the entire network generates itself – it is autopoietic' (ibid.: 72). Luhmann (1995) has applied these ideas to the social world in a similar way, but has been careful to separate an analysis of social communications as autopoietic from the process of autopoiesis in the biosciences. For consilience approaches, any such distinction is sociologically reductionist. Ultimately, there are self-organizing processes at work from the simplest cellular creatures through to the most complex of social systems.

Likewise for Morin, complexity is a feature of existence as well as a transdisciplinary epistemology (Morin 1999: 131). 'Complexity is in fact the fabric of events, actions, interactions, retroactions, determinations, and chance that constitute our phenomenal world' (Morin 2008: 5).

Compared to Capra's more biological approach to understanding systems, Morin's is perhaps best described as cosmological. Morin locates the 'phenomenal world' between a micro- and a macro-physics. Quantum theory had the impact of making the realm of micro-physics one of uncertainty, though Morin argues that this was seen as a 'borderline case', and the implications for this uncertainty were forgotten when it came to larger physical entities, including our bodies and brains (ibid.: 19). Macro-physics likewise introduced notions of complexity and the collapse of the distinction between time and space. In between, Morin argues, Newtonian science provides an account of the regularities of the experienced world. 'Between the two, in the physical, biological and human domains, science reduced phenomenal complexity to simple order and elementary units' (ibid.: 20). While Western science has made extraordinary leaps, it relies on a 'hyper-simplification', or 'modern pathology of mind ... that makes us blind to the complexity of reality' (ibid.: 6). All reality is characterized by complexity, and Morin sees similar processes operating across natural, social and technological 'life', all physical forms within which can be regarded as a 'machine' (Morin 1999: 68). Morin understands various 'crises' as co-constitutively social and natural, and as 'polycrisical sets of overlapping and interwoven crises' (ibid.: 73).

Morin has a surer grip than does Capra on the specifically social realm as characterized by complexity. He considers the actual complex characteristics of the local/global human social condition (ibid.: 16–18), and, in making the case that we are 'citizens of the earth', he argues for a reduction in the power of nation-states, strengthening of external associations and creation of 'planetary public opinion' in order to allow for the development of a genuine cosmopolitanism (ibid.: 93–7). He makes insightful points about the differentiated politics of time in terms of scope and place (planetary, rural), history (industrial, archaic) and distance (immediate/present, intermediate, etc.) and how this influences human organizations and decision-making and impacts on non-human systems (ibid.: 118–19). Such a radical politics is developed on the basis of an understanding of complexity across social and natural systems, for a complex understanding of the earth as a system (as in Gaia theory) leads to an understanding of the polity as 'Homeland Earth' for which we have 'planetary responsibility' (ibid.: 143, 113). Morin's political project here shares much in common with that of Latour, with which we opened Chapter 1.

Morin does admit that there are different kinds of system constraints in social and natural systems, but considers that what appear to be insurmountable constraints in economic and social systems can 'eventually be overcome' and physico-chemical systems may 'appear absolutely constraining' but 'harbour their own breach' (ibid.: 103). Thus both Morin and Capra see complexity as far more than providing a metaphor for understanding the social world, Morin (2008: 20) argues that complexity is 'inscribed in phenomena'. In other words, it is part of the make-up of the material and ideational world. Both these writers point to the need for an understanding of phenomena that breaks down a distinction between the natural and social sciences – complexity in this sense provides a unifying feature that dissolves distinctions between phenomena that are described as natural and those that we see as social. This overplays, however, the extent to which natural and social systems, while mutually constitutive, also have their own systemic boundaries, and the ways in which the constitution of those boundaries is played out in terms of a system's attempt to distinguish and differentiate itself. One of the benefits of Luhmann's concepts of complexity is that he stresses both the ways systems differentiate and are co-constitutive at the same time. There are distinct, hyper-complex features of social systems that are underplayed in the position of consilience. As we will consider in the final section, the kinds of large-scale systemic power relations that are evidenced in human relational systems have distinctive features.

Complexity as a network So far we have examined approaches to the study of the social world that have regarded complexity as a useful metaphor for understanding social phenomena, and others that have attempted to produce a unified account of the social and natural world. A variation of this unified approach is found in the work of physicists and mathematicians who have developed a network approach to understanding social phenomena. The key implication of such an approach is that it opens up the social world to mathematical and computational modelling. Potentially, through the use of such an approach, 'it may be possible to discover mathematical laws and meaningful patterns in the human world' (Buchanan 2003: 2). Researchers drawing on this perspective go farther and argue that the ubiquity of networks in the human and non-human worlds implies 'that many of the inherent complexities of human society actually have little to do with the complex psychology of humans; indeed, similar patterns turn up in many other settings where conscious beings play no role at all' (ibid.: 2). Here, rather than 'physics all the way down', it would appear that to understand the world it is 'mathematics all the way down'. Such an approach has profound implications for the study of the social world.

The 'small world' approach originated from an experiment carried out by Stanley Milgram in the 1960s. Milgram chose a random selection of people in Kansas and Nebraska and asked them to forward a package to a friend of his in Boston – except he did not supply an address for that friend. He simply asked the original recipients of the package to forward it to anyone they knew who might be 'more likely' to know his friend. Many of the packages made it to their destination in Boston. What was surprising was how few hands each package passed through – typically six (see Barabási 2002: 27–30). This led to the popular notion of 'six degrees of separation' – the notion that no person is separated by more than six others from any other human being on the planet. Milgram's research, apart from its entry into popular culture, was mainly ignored until picked up by physicists and mathematicians seeking to understand how certain cells in the body (that is, those that control the pumping of the heart), or insects such as fireflies and crickets, are able to synchronize their activities. Network analysis provided the link between these disparate phenomena, but also led to the suggestion that network analysis can be used to explain an enormous diversity of social and non-human phenomena (Watts 2004). Networks, according to Albert-László Barabási (2002: 7), 'are present everywhere'.

Network-influenced analyses have been used to examine a variety of areas such as wealth creation (Beinhocker 2006), food webs (Solé and Montoya 2002) and irrigation systems in Bali (Lansing 2006). These approaches to the study of complexity are significantly different to those that we have examined so far. In particular, on a methodological level, they suggest that mathematical and computational methods can be applied, while epistemologically they take the view that complexity theory can be predictive. John Miller and Scott Page (2007: 4), for example, 'hope that there is a complex systems equivalent of Newton's Laws of Motion'. They advocate the use of computational methods to analyse complex systems: 'such tools are naturally suited to these problems, as they easily embrace systems characterized by dynamics, heterogeneity, and interacting components' (ibid.: 27). Given the rapid developments in the 'speed and ease of use of computation', they argue that 'computation will become a predominant means by which to explore the world, and ultimately it will become a hallmark for twenty-first-century science' (ibid.: 27).

While we would accept that computational methods and network analysis have provided insights into certain areas of the social world, we doubt that their utility would extend to the analysis of systems across the scales required to analyse matters, for example, of international politics or environmental issues. We would critique this form of analysis on epistemological, ontological and methodological grounds.

Epistemologically, we regard the small worlds/social physics/ networks analysis as a retrogressive step, in that it is underpinned by the view that there are laws to social life that can be uncovered. In Strand's terms this is a 'thin complexity' – the traditional methods of science can be utilized with some revisions to the 'methodological prescriptions for science' (2007: 201). Likewise, Morin drew a distinction between restricted complexity and generalized complexity. The former 'remains within the epistemology of classical science'. The implication is that such an approach 'still attaches complexity as a kind of wagon behind the truth locomotive, that which produces laws'. By contrast, generalized complexity 'requires … an epistemological rethinking … bearing on the organization of knowledge itself' (Morin 2007: 10). In other words, the network approaches appear to revert to an unreconstructed positivism that would overlook what we consider to be a central contribution of complexity to the study of the social world – its unpredictability. We exist in an 'inherently unpredictable situation: a situation unpredictable in itself, not just by virtue of the limits of the observer' (Turner 1997: xiv), or, as Shelton Gunaratne (2003) has neatly summarized it: 'thank you Newton, welcome Prigogine'.

We would also argue that there are ontological problems with the 'social physics' approaches. In particular, for computational purposes, actors become reduced to data points, with interconnections becoming the focus of analysis, rather than relationships. As Axel Leijonhufvud has rather acidly commented, 'if all one is doing is playing with the equations that specify the interactions among pixels, the result, obviously, is just another Nintendo game' (quoted in Perona 2007: 51). While acknowledging the heterogeneity of actors, computational approaches tend to level out the actors, meaning that differences between them are reduced. Computers are not yet able to model the social structures in which action occurs (Byrne 2005: 103). This is particularly important when considering power relations between different actors. Crucially for studies of the social world, the actors' interpretation of their situation cannot be incorporated. While there may be similarities in terms of patterns between the social world and situations where no consciousness is at work, as Buchanan argues, in our view there are also situations that require an analysis of cognition, particularly at times of system bifurcation.

Methodologically, this equates to a distinction between quantitative and qualitative methods. We would argue that both can provide insights into particular social situations, but that neither can tell us everything about the social world. In particular the search for law-like regularities in the social world is probably a futile exercise, given that the study of complexity 'elevates variation, change, surprise and unpredictability to the center of the knowledge process' (Baker 1993: 123).

Differentiated complexity As we have seen, the difficulties with models of complexity as metaphors are that they are too weak, and use complexity as a descriptive rather than an analytic device. They also do not take the social sciences beyond the social and cannot consider the co-constituted qualities, as well as the differences, between social and natural systems. The consilience approaches are divergent, but in some cases there is an inability to account for the distinct features of social systems. Approaches which understand complexity in terms of networks give insufficient attention to the multilevelling of complex systems, while also containing a determinism that is at odds with the notion of dynamic and unpredictably emerging and creative systems. We favour an approach that allows for analytical separation between social and natural systems and can account for the distinctive features of the social, while also allowing for inscribed complexity in both human and non-human systems and the possibility of overlapping, interrelating and co-constituting qualities of social and natural systems.

There are impacting and co-constituting systems that result from the interrelation between human social systems and those involving non-human natures. Lance Gunderson and Buzz Holling (2002) use the notion of 'panarchy' to describe such systemic configurations that are themselves living systems, with internally dynamic and historically non-static structures which develop mutually reinforcing relationships that are co-constitutive and adaptive. There are multiple connections established by feedback mechanisms between both different kinds of system, and different levels of a system. It is not only panarchies involving human systems which demonstrate decision-making properties; rather a huge variety of non-human animals make collective decisions and engage in individual decision-making behaviour with a cumulated system effect (Holling et al. 2002b: 85–7). Living systems of humans, non-human animals and plants develop self-organized interactions with physical processes. These self-organized interactions do not result in stability. Rather, systems may be vulnerable – ecosystems may collapse or be undermined by human endeavours, political systems may be vulner-

[handwritten margin notes: "Systems are adaptive / complex / Always Change"; "Loosely shaped by norms no such thing as true anarchy / Always a Changing System"]

able owing to the collapse of natural systems on which populations depend for resources, or social shifts (such as economic exploitation, increased literacy rates and so on). Importantly also, these conflagrations of systems in interaction are themselves complex systems with their own emergent properties (Holling et al. 2002c: 411).

This does not collapse the social into the natural (as do network and consilience models) or the natural into the social (as metaphorical approaches tend to do). Rather, there are some qualitative and quantitative differences between 'natural' and 'social' systems, in particular because the self-organizing properties of intra-human systems outstrip those of natural systems (Westley et al. 2002: 104–5). Ecosystems and human social systems are all complex systems in their own right (Scheffer et al. 2002: 210). While social and natural systems may be shaped and structured by similar processes, 'signification allows human systems to divorce themselves to some degree from space and time, the critical organizing dimensions of ecosystems', and the reproduction of social systems means that they are more mutable (Westley et al. 2002: 110). In addition, while natural systems have the capacity for 'remembrance' (for example, biotic legacies), humans and intra-human systems have properties of consciousness and reflexivity.

This, however, does not mean that change operates towards self-regulation in terms of the maintenance of equilibrium. Rather, human systems may become more easily locked into paths of development that may have serious consequences for certain human and non-human species populations. And of course, human systems reproduce and develop formations of relational social power, which, like capitalism, patriarchy and so on, are usefully understood as complex adaptive systems. It is perhaps this which gives us an added challenge in using complexity in social relations. Thus in a differentiated complexity account, there is much to be accounted for. In any specific cases a social scientist might examine, there are likely to be various systems of social power relations at work. These will operate across and through different kinds of institutional systems in the social world that implicate multiple species, and ecosystems in which various kinds of human collectivities are embedded.

While human and non-human systems have distinct features, ultimately they are co-constitutive, overlapping and intersected. Rather than seeing a separation between the human and the non-human, differentiated complexity sees the human world as embedded within the natural world, with the variety of human social systems intersecting with those of other natural systems. Varieties of social systems overlap and intersect, with resulting implications for a range of other natural systems (species, scapes and the wider biosphere). The notion of panarchy provides an effective depiction of the sets of interrelating systems.

Differentiated complexity allows us to consider systems as distinct, interactive and co-constitutive. It allows for both the embedding of social systems in a range of non-human systems and for specific properties of human social systems, such as the operation of systems of social exclusion and inclusion and multiple power relations. A variety of different sets of power relations have been analysed by social scientists. These represent the operation of different sets of systems, such as patriarchal, capitalist, ethnocentrist, which can have an impact on each other, and have implications for non-human systems. We would argue that, while these can be considered as distinct systems, the development path of each has implications for other systems. This allows for the development of multiple levels and scales of analysis from the smallest of scales to the biospheric. Ultimately, envisioning human systems embedded within a wider range of systems overcomes the duality inherent in the majority of approaches in the social sciences in which the non-human lifeworld is 'out there', rather than constitutive of, and reactive to, human systems.

Conclusion

This chapter has attempted to demonstrate the considerable inroads made by complexity-inspired approaches to a variety of social science and humanities disciplines. In the brief survey of the impacts of complexity thinking, we found that there were a number of diverse approaches to what actually constitutes complexity, and the second part of the chapter provided a framework for thinking about these. We have mapped the differences in the use of complexity theory in the social sciences and developed a typology of four kinds of approaches. While these four approaches claim to be inspired by complexity thinking, they have rather different notions about what complexity is. They have very different epistemological and ontological commitments. We argue that the key factor that distinguishes these different approaches is the extent to which complexity has a material base. While all those who deploy complexity theory and complexity-informed concepts would concur that complexity provides us with a means of interpreting the social world, they differ on the precise nature of the relationship between theory and the social world. Consilience and metaphor comprise the end points of a spectrum of complexity applications to the social.

Network approaches sit both somewhere in between and in some ways outside the spectrum – having a quantitative application and a determinism that in some ways sits ill with the thoroughly dynamic notion of a complex system apparent in many understandings of complexity. Complexity provides us with a way of grasping the dynamic, multilevelled patterning of social life, and its embedding in non-social systems of multiple species. However, when social scientists introduce complexity 'theory' into their analysis, they should first decide on what complexity it is that best suits.

We have argued for a 'differentiated complexity'. We consider that complexity theory provides us with more than a metaphor for understanding social phenomena. Metaphorical complexity in the social sciences is a weak position, and one that is anthropocentric, ignoring the embodied character of human systems and existence. Like theorists of consilience, we see complex phenomena in the social world as underpinned by physics. However, differentiated complexity allows us to consider the particular and unique features of different kinds of social systems, inflected as they are by the operation of power in social relations and institutions. It also assumes that social systems have both distinct features and co-constituted qualities – social systems overlap and intersect with biological and physical systems.

The approach that we advocate perceives complexity as a concrete phenomenon of a range of human and non-human systems, and because of the way in which it manifests itself we support a qualitative approach, describing complex adaptive systems, rather than a quantitative, networks or modelling approach. Over the next three chapters we start to think about these ideas in terms of international relations.

3 · Complex international systems

The idea of 'system', and the view that there is utility in using systemic approaches, is one that is common to both the discipline of international relations and complexity approaches. While, as we saw in the previous chapter, there is not 'one' complexity approach, complexity-inspired approaches have made significant contributions to a wide range of the social sciences. Although ideas derived from complexity thinking have been applied in a large variety of ways, not all approaches incorporate systems thinking. For example, network approaches draw less upon systemic concepts. We introduced an approach to thinking about complexity that we called 'differentiated complexity', which does draw heavily on ideas of systems developed by complexity thinkers. At the core of differentiated complexity is the complex adaptive system (to be elaborated in greater detail below), which in our view is appropriate for analysing the human and non-human worlds. Human systems are embedded within natural systems, and are subject to complex phenomena. However, because of the human capacity to interpret, react and shape systems, these require specific forms of analysis.

This chapter extends that analysis to the study of international relations. Our purpose is, first, to expand our discussion of complexity by discussing how complex systems are distinct from systems thinking in international relations, and, second, to build a toolbox of complexity-inspired concepts in order to provide the means for discussing international relations. This will lay the foundations for establishing our core arguments – that the development of thinking about international relations has been hampered by its 'Newtonian' approaches and anthropocentric focus.

Systems thinking in international relations

That international politics can be studied at a systemic level is a view that has a long history in international relations. While to say that systems theorizing has 'fallen on hard times' (Albert and Cederman 2010: 3) perhaps overstates the case, such approaches have been undermined by a scepticism with regard to 'grand narratives' within the discipline. Systems theorists support the view that there is something to be gained from an analysis of international politics above the interstate level. Rather than analysing international politics at the level of the actions of political figures or the study of foreign policy of different states, a systemic approach suggests that there are features that can be captured only at a holistic level of analysis.

One broad distinction that can be made in systems theory is between those who regard systems in descriptive terms, and those who argue that systems have distinct causal effects (emergent properties, in the language of complexity theory). These approaches can be equated to the distinction made in Chapter 1 between things that are complicated, and things that are complex. An example of the former would be Morton Kaplan's work. Kaplan (1957: xi) argued that international politics could be analysed 'systematically and theoretically'. There were six possible types of international system, and each type had different rules of behaviour. In this analysis, systems were descriptive rather than emergent.

Our interest in this chapter is with the second approach to systems theory. Rather than being simply a descriptive device, international systems have their own distinct properties, which need to be examined at a systems level. A failure to analyse at this level would mean that we have an incomplete view of international politics. However, what characterizes a system, its constitution and the features of the interrelations between the component, or units, of a system have varied widely.

In terms of thinking about international systems, distinctions can be drawn between realist, constructivist, and Marxist/International Political Economy discussions. Realist and constructivist (at least in the Wendtian account to be discussed here) views of system regard the state as the key actor, while Marxist and International Political Economy approaches regard a capitalist system to be the focus of analysis. In this section we examine the Waltzian (realist), Wendtian (constructivist), and Wallerstein (neo-Marxist) views of system, before concluding with Barry Buzan and Richard Little's pluralist approach, which develops a multi-causal, multi-actor approach. Something can be drawn from all of these in developing a differentiated complexity approach. However, from a complexity perspective these viewpoints share common problems in their Newtonian and anthropocentric positions.

Realist accounts of systems The central feature of realist views of international system is the focus on the state as an actor. While not specifically a systems theorist, Hans Morgenthau did, through his analysis of a balance of power, see, at least partially, systemic forces.

For Morgenthau (1960: 167), the balance of power 'is only a particular manifestation of a general social principle to which all societies composed of a number of autonomous units owe the autonomy of their component parts ... The balance of power and policies aiming at its preservation *are not only inevitable but are an essential stabilising factor* in a society of sovereign nations.' Hence for Morgenthau, systemic and stabilizing factors occurred through the actions of states. Morgenthau's approach could be described as a subsystem-dominant approach in that his focus was on the interaction of states, though the 'inevitable' emergence of a balance of power suggests that he saw forces at work at a systemic level (for a detailed discussion of Morgenthau's notion of balance of power, see Little 2007: ch. 4).

The extreme contrast to such a subsystem-dominant view is Kenneth Waltz's neorealism (or structural realism). Waltz's (1959) *Man, the State, and War* made the argument that most explanations of war could be focused at one of two levels (or 'images'): the level of 'man' – which argued that war occurred owing to human nature (i.e. the classical realist account); or at the level of the state – certain types of state were more prone to conflict than others (for Marxists, capitalist states, and for liberals, non-democracies). While these theories could provide explanations for particular wars, they could not provide a general explanation for war. To do this a third image analysis would be required. This level was the international system, which provided a 'permissive' cause of war – wars happened because there was nothing in an anarchic system to prevent them (ibid.: 233).

Man, the State, and War made the argument that an analysis of the international system was needed. It did not, however, proceed very far in defining what an international system actually was. Such an analysis was pursued in *Theory of International Politics*, which provided an analysis of what constituted the international system, and what impacts such a system had on the behaviour of states. Contrary to much of the criticism of Waltz's work, he did not claim that an explanation of all state international behaviour could be found at the systemic level, only that systemic structures theory 'could tell us a small number of big and important things' (Waltz, 1986: 329). These 'big and important things' were primarily the pressure towards balance in international politics, and the different character of the system related to its polarity, in particular the stability of bipolar systems.

In order to analyse the international system, Waltz argued that it had to be defined in terms that did not include a description of the units – to do so would be, in Waltz's terminology, *reductionist* (Waltz

1979: 60–7). Including an analysis of the units would mean that it would not be possible to differentiate between what were unit-level effects and what were system-level effects. All previous systemic theories had been reductionist, Waltz claimed, and therefore not truly systemic for this reason. In order to escape the reductionist trap, great care would be needed in defining the elements that composed the international system.

Waltz argued that all systems comprised three elements: an ordering principle; the characteristics of the units; and the distribution of capabilities. The ordering principle described the relationship between the units; either hierarchic, or anarchic. Domestic political systems are hierarchic because the units are ranked by levels of greater or lesser power, with those units in higher positions in the hierarchy able to command those lower down. By contrast, international systems are anarchic: although some states are more powerful than others, there is no overarching government able to impose its will on states.

Although a discussion of the character of the units might appear to contravene Waltz's position on reductionism, Waltz argues that in anarchic systems all the units have to fulfil the same functions – they are 'like units' (ibid.: 93–7). This contrasts with hierarchic systems, where the units specialize in different activities. In international systems all the units are sovereign, and have to be self-supporting – there are no other units to which they can turn for support if attacked. As all the units have to fulfil the same functions, this level 'drops out' of the analysis and the reductionist trap is avoided.

The third element of the constitution of systems, the 'distribution of capabilities', might seem to open up the risk of reductionism, as this would appear to require an analysis at the unit level. However, Waltz claims that it is not the power level of individual units which is important, but instead the way that power is dispersed across the system. It is a system-wide rather than unit-level characteristic. In other words, it is the relative distribution across the system which counts, rather than the specific power of individual units.

The distribution of capabilities is, perhaps, the most significant part of Waltz's account of systems, as it is the only element liable to change. In anarchic systems, according to Waltz, the units will always be undifferentiated, and their primary feature will be the requirement of self-help. A change of the ordering principle from anarchy to hierarchy would be a change *of* the system, rather than a change *in* the system. The only way this would occur is through the initiation of a world government, an event that Waltz finds unlikely. More likely is a change *in* the system, as a result of variations in the distribution of capabilities. This leads to what is perhaps Waltz's major contribution – the analysis of polarity, and in particular which type of system is most stable. Much of *Theory of International Politics* is devoted to arguing that a bipolar system is more stable, and preferable to a multi-polar system. The apparent durability of the Cold War bipolar system would have seemed to confirm this view when the book was published in 1979. Unipolar systems are not considered specifically, though Waltz's (2000) more recent works have addressed this issue, and he has argued that unipolarity is unlikely to persist.

Waltz's central contribution was his attempt to isolate what constitute system-level forces, in a sense to analyse what the term 'international' means. However, this focus also opened his work up to a major criticism: without an analysis of the unit level how was it possible to understand change? Neorealism was unable to predict the end of the Cold War (a change in the system), or to provide an account of how it happened (see, for example, Kratochwil 1993; Wohlforth 1995: 92). Furthermore, a change of system, which for Waltz would mean the development of a world government, was not conceivable.

From a complexity perspective, Waltz's work is significant because it points to systemic-level features, which cannot be derived from an examination of the units. A holistic level of analysis, as opposed to a reductionist approach, is required in order to perceive these attributes. Waltz's work is also interesting because of what it is *not*. In particular, there is no element of change. Everything stays the same – the units are all alike, and have always performed basically the same functions. The system has always been anarchic, and is unlikely to change. The system is closed in that no interaction is seen between the international system and other systems – for example, the global economy or biosphere. And it is an entirely mechanical system– like the planets circling the earth in an astrolabe, the activities of states will be directly correlated to the system's polarity.

Wendtian constructivism Despite many years of sustained criticism, Waltz's neorealism remains a major source of inspiration to a number of realist writers, and his ideas have been developed in a number of new directions (see, for example, Mearsheimer 2001). This resilience could perhaps be accounted for by the insight regarding systemic-level forces, which remains relevant however much the rest of the model is criticized. It is also noteworthy that for most alternative accounts, to attack Waltz is effectively a rite of passage (Hobden 1998: 55–68).

In this section we examine a major challenger to Waltz's neorealism, namely constructivism, in particular the systemic constructivist work of Alexander Wendt. We single out Wendt as his work has focused particularly on the notion of an international system. His work should not, however, be taken to represent constructivism as a school of thought – many 'constructivists' are critical of his approach (see, for example, the essays in Guzzini and Leander 2006). It should also be noted that Wendt's more recent work has moved away from the position described here, and, potentially, towards a posthuman perspective. He uses the term 'pansychism' (see Wendt 2006, 2010).

That Alexander Wendt owes a considerable debt to Waltz is apparent from the title of his major work on systems theory – *Theory of International Politics* becomes *Social Theory of International Politics*. Wendt accepts two major aspects of Waltz's approach: states are the major actors in international politics; and they operate in a condition of anarchy. However, whereas for Waltz it was the distribution of capabilities which was the prime determinant of state behaviour in the international system, with 'self-help' being the sole response to the condition of anarchy, for Wendt ideas matter. 'Self-help' is an idea, or institution, and only one of a number of responses to anarchy. There is no predetermined response, and 'anarchy is what states make of it' (Wendt 1992).

Ideas and identities emerge through the interactions between states. These generate sets of norms and rules which provide structures that constrain states' actions. Thus state identities and the international system are co-constitutive – ideas about the international system are important in the creation of the sets of rules and norms that constitute the international system, which in turn provides a constraining factor on state activities. Furthermore, identities can change, resulting in changes to the sets of rules and norms that constitute international relations. Wendt argues that there have been three main 'cultures' of international relations. First, a Hobbesian culture, which dominated relations between political entities through to the seventeenth century. This is the realist world-view: all other states are probable enemies who will use violence without restraint to pursue their aims. Following the Treaty of Westphalia, a Lockean culture started to emerge, where, although some rules restraining activity existed, states accepted that ultimately there might be a resort to violence in the pursuit of national interests. In the twentieth century, a Kantian culture started to develop, between democracies, where the norm was for disputes to be resolved through negotiation, and cooperation became a standard reaction to security threats (Wendt 1999: ch. 6). Each of these transformations in culture was dependent on changes in the underlying identities of states, which led to transformations in the international system.

Critics have argued that there is little to separate Wendt from Waltz (e.g. Behnke 2006), and Wendt (2006: 181) accepted that the focus on states and anarchy 'looks admittedly a bit old-fashioned'. However, compared to Waltz's work, his 'social' theory of international politics did make several innovations.

First, Wendt stressed the important role of ideas. States operate in a social world where social structures are at least as important as the material structures of anarchy and the distribution of capabilities. Secondly, for Wendt, the units and system are co-constitutive, and the analysis of one is incomplete without the inclusion of the other. This provides a notable distinction from Waltz's approach, where his definition of the system excluded a consideration of the units. Assuming that units and system are co-constitutive suggests a major advance over the Waltzian approach. Thirdly, the analysis of agency, and the co-constitution of units and structure, opened the way for analysis of change – a possibility, as we have noted, considered absent by many in Waltz's neorealism.

Neo-Marxist accounts of system As already noted, in ontological terms Waltz and Wendt are similar – states are the major actors in international relations. Where they differ is in terms of their views of the constitution of the international system. For Waltz it is primarily a materialist conception, while for Wendt its constitution is primarily idealist.

The major alternative to a state-oriented view of the international system has come from neo-Marxists, in particular Immanuel Wallerstein's World-System Theory. Wallerstein's work has been influential throughout the social sciences (especially sociology and anthropology), though, perhaps surprisingly, less so on international relations.

At the centre of Wallerstein's approach is the notion of a world-system. Through human history there have been a succession of world-systems, alternating between world-empires, where political control is centralized, and world-economies, where political control is dissipated among a number of competing centres. Historically, Wallerstein argues, world-empires have tended to be more stable. However, this changed in the sixteenth century, when a modern world-system started to emerge in Europe. The modern world-system is an example of a world-economy, though additionally a capitalist system (Wallerstein 1979: 66).

World-systems have both geographic and historical features. In spatial terms, Wallerstein drew on the notion developed by dependency theorists of a core and periphery, but also added an intermediate zone, the semi-periphery. While the main purpose of the periphery is to provide raw materials, and to be a site of very low-cost production, the semi-periphery plays important economic and political roles. It acts as a site for manufacturing that is no longer profitable in the core. It also acts as a reserve pool of labour which can be used to undermine wage militancy in the core. It also acts to 'deflect the political pressures which groups primarily located in the peripheral areas might otherwise direct against the core areas' (Wallerstein 1974: 349–50).

In the core are found those activities involving the highest levels of skills and the greatest concentration of capital. The three geographic regions of the world-system are linked by a process of 'unequal exchange', whereby wealth is systematically extracted from the periphery and semi-periphery to the profit of the core. This process entrenches the divisions in the world-system, making the transition from one geographic sector to another (e.g. periphery to semi-periphery) difficult, though not impossible – as evidenced by a number of East Asian states.

As well as highlighting the geographic features of the world-system, Wallerstein also argued that all world-systems have a history, in that all will have a beginning, a middle and an end. All systems contain cyclical rhythms, secular trends and contradictions, all of which ultimately result in a condition of crisis. A period of crisis represents the final phase of a world-system, indicating its ultimate demise and replacement by another world-system. Wallerstein's more recent writings have focused on his claim that the modern world-system has now entered a period of crisis which will ultimately result in its collapse (see, for example, Wallerstein 2003).

A number of features of Wallerstein's approach to systems thinking differentiate it from the work of Waltz or Wendt. The focus is much more on the systems level, with very little discussion of what comprises the units. In this sense, Wallerstein's work out-systemizes even Waltz's neorealism. As Wendt (1987) argues, Wallerstein's epistemology and ontology are both systemic, whereas he views Waltz's ontology as statist. The modern world-system is a capitalist, economic system, not an interstate system. Wallerstein does acknowledge that an interstate system exists, but both this, and states themselves, are epiphenomena to the world-system. 'The development of the capitalist world-economy has involved the creation of all the major institutions of the modern world: classes, ethnic/national groups, households – and the "states". All of these structures postdate, not antedate capitalism; all are consequence, not cause' (Wallerstein 1984: 29).

Wallerstein's world-system is highly deterministic. 'Within a functioning historical system there is no genuine free will. The structures constrain choice and even create choice' (Wallerstein 1991: 235). These constraints are reduced only at a time when the world-system is approaching collapse (as now). It is worth pointing out that in his more recent work, Wallerstein (2004: 104) has sought to graft on a complexity analysis, arguing that in the period of crisis a world-system is much more susceptible to unstable phenomena.

World-systems allow for a hierarchic distinction between different sectors of the world. The notions of core, periphery and semi-periphery provide a much greater analytical potential than Waltz's distribution of capabilities. Through his analysis of the forces that lead to the end of a particular world-system, Wallerstein provides an analysis of change, both in the system, and of the system.

This is, then, perhaps the most systemic of the ways of thinking about international relations that is available. However, this highly systemic approach has its own price – it is highly deterministic, and we lose sight of the units of international politics.

A pluralist approach to international systems In a major contribution to work on systems thinking in international relations, Buzan and Little (2000: 43) make the point that systems theorists such as Waltz and Wendt 'operate from a position of methodological and theoretical monism'. Waltz's focus is on the distribution of capabilities, a material concern, while Wendt is concerned with inter-subjective reactions to anarchy, an idealist approach. We might add that Wallerstein is similarly monistic in focusing on the economic features of international politics.

In a criticism of existing systems theory they argue that there has been a tendency to: presentism – a failure to engage with the history of international relations; ahistoricism – a search for general laws of interactions between international actors rather than acknowledging that these may be historically contingent; Eurocentrism – viewing the experience of European states (especially since the Treaty of Westphalia) as being the model for international relations; anarchophilia – an unquestioning assumption that anarchy is the defining environment in which states act; state-centricism – the view that states are the only significant actors in international relations (ibid.: 18–22).

Buzan and Little argue for a pluralist analysis, which enables a study of a variety of different aspects of international relations. To encompass this they suggest taking a historical and multi-causal approach. This comprises an analysis of different levels of analysis, different sectors of analysis, plus three central sources of explanation: interaction capacity, process, and structure.

Whereas Waltz argued that to include an analysis at the unit level was reductionist, Buzan and Little (ibid.: 68) argue that 'each level generates its own distinctive outcomes and sources of explanation'. They identify five separate potential levels of analysis: international systems, or the highest level of analysis; subsystems, clusters of units within a greater international system (e.g. the European states within the contemporary international system); units, for Waltz and Wendt states, but perhaps also including other international actors, such as international organizations, transnational corporations, criminal organizations; subunits, conglomerations of individuals such as bureaucracies, lobby groups and companies that attempt to influence the international actions of the unit; and finally individuals.

Perhaps the most important contribution of Buzan and Little's approach is the inclusion of different sectors of analysis. Waltz's analysis focused on the distribution of power, Wendt's on the role of inter-subjective rules and norms, and Wallerstein on the global economy. Buzan and Little (ibid.: 73-4) include these as separate sectors of analysis, but also include a political sector concerning relations between states, and an environmental sector relating to relations within the earth's biosphere. An important point is that within each sector the units and system might be different – and some international systems might exclude certain sectors. For example, it is possible to imagine an international system where the units were militarily competitive, but did not have economic relations (or vice versa).

Buzan and Little therefore envisage the international system as comprising a multiplicity of levels and actors ranging across a variety of different sectors. Additionally, they incorporate three main sources of explanation. First, process refers to the character of relations between the units. Both war and trade might provide examples of different types of process. Secondly, interaction capacity refers to the intensity of different processes within an international system. Interaction capacity is central to analysing international systems, as it is interaction between the units which indicates the presence of some form of international system. The more profound that interaction the greater the system effects: 'If interaction capacity is low, then structure will have little or no effect. Higher levels of interaction capacity allow structural forces powerfully into play' (ibid.: 81). This leads to the third source of explanation, structure – in other words, the limits to which the units are constrained by structural forces. Again these may vary across the different sectors of an international system.

Systems analysis in international relations Buzan and Little's account provides the most sophisticated attempt to broaden the analysis of international systems in international relations. We would concur with their criticisms of previous systemic theorizing, and welcome their attempts to broaden the analysis by considering other sectors, actors and interactions. While this constitutes a considerable advance on previous analyses, we would argue that it still is very much the product of a Newtonian/linear analysis.

That their analysis is partially based on a mechanical view of the world is directly acknowledged (ibid.: 106–7), and their analysis of inter-action capacity suggests a direct link between the level of activity and the character of the system (ibid.: 96). We would also suggest that the range of sectors should be increased by including patriarchy and (post-) colonialism, which we would argue are fundamental characteristics of international relations. Furthermore, we would also argue that an analysis of intersectionality (discussed below) is needed in terms of examining the relations between sectors. Although Buzan and Little (ibid.: 75) acknowledge that these sectors are not autonomous, in terms of analysis they are seen as primarily independent and separate. By contrast, we would regard the intersection of these sectors (or systems) as significant points of analysis. While they have considered structuration between the system and the units, we would suggest the analysis of co-evolution between systems more generally. Finally, while acknowledging the significance of the environment as a sector, this largely drops out of the analysis (ibid.: 84). We would argue that this is a mistake given the impact of environmental factors in influencing the development of relations globally, with respect to topography and climate (Braudel 1995), to the significance of supply chains of raw materials in the development of North–South relations (Dalby 2002b), and to the increasing role environmental issues play in contemporary international relations. It is a central theme of the argument of this book that there is an urgent need to analyse international relations as occurring within and co-evolutionary with environmental and non-human systems. It is a core element of the posthuman project to decentre human activity and to perceive it within the development of a range of non-human systems. The possibility of using some tools from complexity thinking is central to this project, and the next section begins an analysis of what the key elements of such an approach would be. The final section of this chapter assesses how a systems analysis from a complexity perspective would diverge from the approaches discussed so far.

Key elements of complex theorizing

The significance of complexity theory for international relations is that it offers us different ways of thinking about connections and linkages. It offers a toolkit with which to examine interlinked and multilevelled relations between different scales of activity and processes, and challenges the way the notion of 'system' has most often been deployed. The remainder of this chapter examines the contribution that concepts derived from complexity approaches can contribute to thinking about international systems.

Complex adaptive systems At the centre of complexity theorizing, at least in the approach that we advocate, is the concept of the 'complex adaptive system'. All other elements of complexity approaches are related to and build on this central concept. Examples of complex adaptive systems would include the human body, the capitalist system, flocking birds, through to matter itself. Complex adaptive systems are precisely what the terminology suggests – systems that are 'complex' and 'adaptive'.

As we have seen, systems theorizing in the social sciences and in international relations has a long history, and complexity theorizing builds on this. Complexity approaches regard systems as distinct units of analysis. In other words, systems encompass features around which it is possible to distinguish particular boundaries. It is possible to distinguish systems from their immediate environment. However, it is a key insight of complexity approaches that the boundaries of complex adaptive systems are permeable – they will be influenced and directly impacted by their environment, composed of other complex adaptive systems. So, for example, we can describe the human body as a discrete system that can be analysed in isolation from other systems. It will, however, also be directly impacted by its environment. Viruses (in themselves complex adaptive systems) can breach the boundaries of the body – with potentially lethal effects for the system. Likewise, in terms of the social world, racism can be analysed as a distinct system, with its own boundaries. However, it will be influenced and impacted by other systems, such as capitalism and patriarchy. Central to this analysis is the idea of intersectionality, which will be discussed below. Systems in this perspective are constituted by the interactions at a unit level. These result in what complexity theorists describe as emergent features – characteristics that are apparent only at a level above the units. Kevin Mihata (1997: 31) describes emergence as 'the process by which patterns or global-level structures arise from local-level processes'. They are not reducible to the interactions of the unit level but develop from those interactions. Hence, the capitalist system has emergent features (such as a propensity to crisis) which result from the interactions of innumerable individual actors, but which can't be traced back to those actors. Nor are they controlled by those actors, and they are potentially inimical to their interests.

One way in which complexity theorists have discussed the interrelations between complex adaptive systems is to regard them as 'nested' (see, for example, Holling et al. 2002c: 402). The idea of nested systems provides a way of thinking about systems that are closely interacting but still maintain some boundaries which allow them to be analysed separately. For example, all human social systems can be envisaged as nested within a global environmental system. Nested systems can also be analysed in terms of hierarchy. One way of doing this is through the concept of fitness landscape, considered below.

Hence a system from this perspective constitutes a specific frame of study, which can be considered discrete from its environment, while not free from developments within that environment. This interdependence with the environment points to the significance of adaptation. Complex adaptive systems are in a constant state of flux as they adjust to the external stimuli and energy flows through their interactions with other systems. Perhaps the ultimate example of adaptation might be the processes of evolution – with species showing the capacity (or, in the case of extinction, an inability) to adjust to local environments.

We consider social systems as sharing many of the features of complex adaptive systems. Yet they also have particular characteristics – for example, the increased passage of information, the goal-directedness of human beings. These can have an impact on the adaptation capability of human social systems and mean that changes can occur very rapidly (Franco Parellada 2007: 159–61).

In Chapter 1 we drew a distinction between what is complicated and what is complex. While systems can be complex without being complicated (a flock of birds), and can be complicated without being complex (a mobile phone), in the social world complex adaptive systems tend to be both complicated (having many interconnections, actors and variables) and to exhibit features that we might consider complex. A central feature of such systems is non-linearity.

Non-linearity Non-linearity is a defining attribute of complexity which distinguishes environments that are complex from those that are not, and marks a break between what has been described as Newtonian and non-Newtonian theorizing (see Ulanowicz 2007; Wallerstein 2000; Gunaratne 2003). Linear systems are those where there are consistent, predictable and constant relations between actors or parts of a system. Linear relations imply that there are mathematically consistent relations between two elements. For example, in a linear relation there would be a direct correlation between the force applied and the distance a ball could be thrown; applying twice the force might mean that a ball might go twice as far. A linear relationship is assumed in statements that anticipate a specific decrease in consumer spending when interest rates are increased by a certain amount. Waltz's *Theory of International Politics* provides a clear example of a linear account of international relations – a bipolar world will be very stable, a multipolar one less so. In other words, there is a direct relationship between the number of great powers and international outcomes, between cause and effect. In the Newtonian world-view there is an expectation of consistent and predictable relations between forces. However, this view has broken down in the physical sciences, particularly physics, but not entirely following the development of quantum mechanics (Wendt 2010: 283–4). Although this has had an enormous impact in disciplines such as physics, the impact on the social sciences has been comparatively and surprisingly slight (see Homer-Dixon 2009: 10). Theories of world politics, John Ruggie has noted, are 'reposed in deep Newtonian slumber' (cited in Harrison 2006b: 6).

By contrast, in non-linear relations there is no direct or constant relationship between agents. According to Roger Beaumont (2000: 9), in non-linear systems 'inputs may vary widely and unpredictably from output'. In complex systems no direct mathematically calculable relationship would be expected between two elements; even repeating exactly the same action may not result in the same outcome, and may theoretically have a completely different effect. As we saw in the last chapter, the implications of this are disputed by complexity theorists, with some arguing that with the use of powerful computers and network analysis, simulations can be created that can model the paths of complex systems. Others argue that complex systems are inherently unpredictable.

An implication of non-linearity for complex systems is that very small changes can result in very large and unpredictable results. This is often described as sensitivity to initial conditions. This means that very small changes in the early conditions of a system can result in the development path of a system changing enormously. The most dramatic and frequently cited example of this is Edward Lorenz's (1993 [1972]) question regarding whether a butterfly flapping its wings in Brazil can result in such large changes to the meteorological system that a tornado hits Texas. Sensitivity to initial conditions indicates the possibility that small events can have large impacts. It is also important to remember that, in a non-linear system, the contrary is also true – large events can have minimal impacts. Non-linearity implies that, at a minimum, events in a complex adaptive system are unpredictable. However, there are other factors at work which suggest that complex adaptive systems also develop elements of order.

Self-organization Non-linearity indicates the inherent unpredictability of complex adaptive systems, but does not imply that within a complex adaptive system all is chaos. Perhaps one of the most fundamental features of complexity is that there appears to be an inherent tendency towards higher levels of organization and order. It is important to stress that this is not a teleological stance, nor is the increase in order necessarily progressive or sustained. Ordered systems can suddenly 'flip' or bifurcate into other, possibly disordered, states. That said, there is a general propensity towards greater order, or what some call, rather awkwardly, 'complexification' (Casti 1994).

Self-organization is closely linked to emergence. As we have seen, emergence refers to those features that are evident at the level of the system, but that cannot be deduced from an analysis of the units. Self-organization is the source of those emergent features in the sense that the self-organization of units within a complex adaptive system results in emergent features. Examples of self-organization can be found across the material and social world, most apparent in the appearance of order in apparently chaotic circumstances (for example, the dripping of a tap, or a flock of birds, where there is no apparent leader, but where there is the appearance of order in terms of the flight patterns). In the social world, self-organization can be seen to develop in the ever-increasing complexity of social institutions. Without self-organization there would be no emergent features, and no complex adaptive systems. In this sense self-organization is the basis of complex adaptive systems. However, this does not mean that order is inevitable, or will persist. Human history is replete with instances of the collapse of complex social systems (see Diamond 2005; Tainter 1988).

Fitness landscape Thus far we have looked in general terms at the ways in which complex adaptive systems can be analysed. These are systems around which boundaries can be drawn, and in which their development, while resulting from self-organization, also occurs as the result of interaction with other systems. A significant way in which the interactions of complex adaptive systems can be analysed is through using the concept of fitness landscape.

Most accounts of fitness landscapes trace the origins of the idea to the work of the biologist Sewall Wright (1932). Evolutionary biologists have used the term as a means of understanding the ways in which particular species have been particularly successful related to their competitors. The fitness landscape can be envisioned as all the potential mutations that an organism can make. Some may be more effective for the organism (a peak), while some may mean that an organism is less effective (a valley). Organisms for which evolutionary changes lead to a better 'fit' with their environment have ascended in the fitness landscape and proliferated in numbers. In other words, the more successful mutations in a species are those that have been able to produce more offspring. The notion has been developed most directly by Stuart Kauffman (1993, 1995, 2000, 2008), a biologist whose work has combined complexity thinking with evolution. Kauffman brought together a number of insights in thinking about fitness landscapes to ideas about evolution. First, whereas fitness landscapes had been thought of as related to specific organisms, Kauffman extended the idea to think about particular genotypes within an organism. This was significant because the features of different genotypes do not interact in a regular way – mutations in specific genotypes might combine in a way that leads to an organism ascending a fitness landscape, or possibly descending the landscape – there are 'constraints within the organism' (Kauffman 1993: 242). Hence we need, in terms of understanding developments in species, to think about how lower-level characteristics within the organism develop and interact. So, as a simple example, a plant that through mutation develops a gene which means its taste is less attractive to animals might improve its chances of survival through avoiding being eaten. However, this gene mutation might interact in a negative way with the plant's capacity to photosynthesize.

This leads to Kauffman's second insight, which was to think about the development of organisms in relation to others. It wasn't just a question of thinking about the evolution of one species – species do not develop independently, but at the same time as others: 'in coevolutionary processes, the fitness of one organism or species depends upon the characteristics of the other organism or species with which it interacts, while all simultaneously adapt and change' (ibid.: 33). For example, a mutation in the gene of a rabbit which leads to faster-running rabbits means that rabbits move up the fitness landscape – this has implications for foxes, whose fitness landscape is degraded as a result of rabbits being more able to evade pursuit. A mutation among foxes which leads to improved eyesight might counterbalance this and lead foxes to a higher position in their fitness landscape. Hence developments in one species can have an impact on the fitness landscape of a different species. The landscape is constantly dynamic as species either degrade or improve the landscape for others.

Kauffman's third point was to argue that there is an underlying order to the way in which evolution has proceeded. Darwin and most evolutionary biologists have pointed to natural selection as the key factor in explaining how species have developed. Mutations have developed in species which allow certain members of the species to prosper, or to perform less well. Those that prosper produce more young and their mutant genes are hence 'selected'. Kauffman's argument is that this is not sufficient to explain the evolutionary process. Selection is certainly important but it occurs within an underlying process of order. The 'order of the biological world', he (1995: vii) argues, 'is not merely tinkered, but arises naturally and spontaneously because of these principles of self-organization'. This self-organization, however, is '*inherently* beyond prediction' (Kauffman 2008: 5; emphasis in original).

Kauffman's model of a fitness landscape originated as a way of analysing the ways in which species moved in their environments, either becoming more capable of prospering (ascending to a new fitness level) or less successful (descending). Important points that surface in his account are that mutations that occur within organisms interact with other features of that organism; that species co-evolve, and that developments within one species impact on others (potentially degrading their fitness landscapes); finally that while there is an underlying order in terms of self-organization and emergence, these developments are intrinsically unpredictable.

While Kauffman (2000: ch. 9, 2008: ch. 11) has extended his analysis to human systems, there have been a number of other examples where the notion of a fitness landscape has been adopted. For example, Lee Fleming and Olav Sorenson (2001) have drawn upon patent data to examine the ways in which technology develops. In a similar way to Kauffman's use of interdependent genotypes within an organism, they analysed the interrelationships between the component parts of inventions. As with genotypes, modifications (or mutations) can have contradictory impacts. For example, Fleming and Sorenson cite the development of bicycle gearing. Cyclists prefer a greater number of gears because this increases the variety of terrain over which they can ride. However, increasing the number of cogs and gear wheels also has an impact on the gear shifting. Inventors have overcome this problem by decreasing the width of the chain, enabling a larger number of gears to be traversed without seriously undermining the capacity to shift gears. What this example demonstrates is the close interlink between components, which has the possibility of both undermining and improving the position of a particular piece of technology in the fitness landscape.

This example shows the potential for using the concept of fitness landscape to analyse social circumstances, and the idea has been used to analyse a whole range of other disciplines, such as management and organization form (Stacey 1996; Lewin and Volberda 1999), anthropology (Lansing 2003), ethnography (Agar 2004), information systems (Gill 2008), and sociology (Walby 2009). What this variety of applications suggests is that the concept of fitness landscape has explanatory power beyond its initial deployment in biological systems. It permits ways of thinking about the interaction between complex adaptive systems and how the situation in a fitness landscape of complex adaptive systems can alter as a result of modifications internal to the system, but also as a result of co-evolution with other systems or actors. Hence the notion of a fitness landscape, when combined with the complexity approach to system analysis, enables the possibility of 'opening' the box, to consider developments within actors/systems. Crucially, central to such an approach is the significance of other actors/systems. All actors within a fitness landscape interact and co-evolve with other actors, and, crucially, the actions of one system can impact on the fitness landscape of others. This introduces the possibility of incorporating an analysis of power into complex co-evolving systems, as the possibility of degrading the fitness landscape for others while improving it for oneself increases the possibilities for one actor in terms of its relations with another.

Intersectionality Intersectionality is a term with a long history in sociology and particularly in feminist approaches. It has been used in international relations, though primarily by feminist and post-colonial theorists (see, for example, Brah and Phoenix 2004; McClintock 1995). We argue that, given the developments in thinking about systems, when combined with complexity it can yield a great deal in terms of the analysis of different areas within international relations. It has been used to describe the ways that multiple forms of inequality can be analysed – for example, in feminist studies the combinations of class and ethnicity. For Avtar Brah and Ann Phoenix (2004: 76) it refers to 'the complex, irreducible, varied, and variable effects which ensue when multiple axes of differentiation – economic, political, cultural, psychic, subjective and experiential – intersect in historically specific contexts. The concept emphasizes that different dimensions of social life cannot be separated out into discrete and pure strands.' A variety of different ways have been attempted to overcome the problems of analysing multiple forms of social life, from prioritizing one aspect (for example, class), through to the rejection of all categorizations. The issue is that it is not simply a case of 'adding' one set of social relations to another. In their interactions (say, between class and ethnicity) changes will occur. These will, of course, be affected by the specific historical context. Sylvia Walby (2007, 2009) argues that advances in systems theorizing from the application of complexity thinking permit much more effective means of thinking about cross-cutting and multiple inequalities. Complex adaptive systems are seen as open, overlapping and nested – allowing the interactions between systems to be considered along with ways that different systems can affect the processes of others. These avoid problems of reductionism to a single key form of inequality while maintaining distinct areas of analysis. In her analysis of inter-species relations, Erika Cudworth (2011) points to the intersections in relations between human and non-human species which structure the interactions between the two.

This section has made a start in defining the main parts of the toolbox that will be used in the rest of the book to analyse complex social systems. In the next section, we begin to analyse what differentiates a complex approach to international systems from conventional approaches, and in what ways they overlap.

Complex international systems

In this section we argue that a number of features of complex systems are relevant to the study of international systems. We will outline the commonalities between the approaches to analysing international systems as described in the first section, and discuss the areas where complex approaches can make a specific contribution. While our project is largely critical of existing systems work, this does not mean that there are not elements of overlap and complementarity. From Waltz we would draw upon the idea of specific forces operating at a systems level, while Wendt and English School theorists have pointed to the role of ideas norms and law in the regulation of international affairs. We would see these as forms of self-organization within international relations. Buzan and Little have made a considerable contribution in terms of their analysis of sectors and the broad historical scope of their analysis. Their analysis of interlinked systems provides a starting point for our discussions of intersectionality and nested systems. While they would like to see boundaries around 'international relations', we would see these relations as embedded within a whole range of other systemic features. A complexity approach would see differences from conventional views of system in terms of the boundaries, constitution, power and dynamics of international systems.

The boundaries of systems For complexity theorists, systems are self-organizing to the extent that the features of a system can be modelled without reference to factors outside the system. This does not mean that a system is closed and that it has no relationship with other systems – for complexity theorists, particularly within the social sciences, a key feature of systems analysis is such interaction. However, complexity theorists suggest that a particular system can be analysed by considering the interaction of its parts independently from other systems. Waltz saw the international system as a closed system which, at least in analytical terms, could be sealed off from other levels. Where Waltz and complexity approaches concur is that there are systemic features that emerge from interaction which cannot be investigated solely at the unit level. Robert Jervis described these as 'system effects', though his (complexity-influenced) approach to the study of systems focused on interactions rather than emergent properties (Jervis 1997: 17).

Analyses of international relations have typically seen the international system as one comprised of states as units, with little to distinguish them apart from their relative power. Hedley Bull drew a distinction between an international system, where state actions were interconnected because states needed to take the actions of other states into account, and an international society, where states had developed certain rules and norms to help promote smooth interactions between them. In both system and society, though, it was states which were seen as the key actor – though Bull (1977: 279) also had a notion of a 'world society' made up of a much wider range of international actors. The core distinction from a complexity perspective is to see systems as open. While it is possible to draw a boundary around what comprises an international system, the boundary with other systems is permeable, and there are influences and effects from other systems. Likewise the influence of the international system intersects with other systems. A complexity perspective suggests that for a given system all other systems comprise its environment, and any system will comprise part of the environment for all other systems.

This has two important implications. First, complexity understandings of systems undermine the realist conception of states as solid 'billiard balls', relatively unchanged by the process of interacting with each other and with the international system. Neither states nor the international system have a hard shell providing insulation from their environment. Secondly, systems are seen as intersected, allowing the analysis of multiple influences. Hence the international system may in turn be affected by the global economic system and systems of patriarchy and ethnicity. However, the ways in which these intersections occur are historically and geographically specific rather than simple combinations of influences. Intersectionality points to the way in which complex systems can affect each other, rather than providing a comprehensive account of all forms of power interaction. Hence while complexity approaches see boundaries around a particular system, the form of these boundaries differs distinctly from previous systems thinking, having implications for the influence on and from international relations.

The composition of the international system Realist accounts of international systems have seen them as constituted by states. Waltz's neorealism is perhaps the paradigmatic instance of this, seeing international relations effectively only constituted by the interactions between states – though Wendt (1999) shares a similar ontology. An alternative viewpoint in world-systems approaches has been to largely marginalize states and to conceive of capitalism as a world-system in which states are nodes of secondary importance. Considering international actors as complex adaptive systems which interact with each other opens a route for analysing relations between them, whether they are, for example, states, governmental or non-governmental international organizations, or transnational corporations. For Buzan and Little (2000) the overarching system of (exploitative) economic relations (global capitalism) provides one level of analysis, relations between polities and environments are another, and an international system is seen to result from the interaction between the units (states, but also non-state actors) of the system, and to operate at different intensities. At each level of the international system, we have what might be seen as 'emergent properties'. However, Buzan and Little underplay the extent to which the properties of each kind of unit in their model are shaped, constrained and remade by their interactions – in other words, the extent to which they are co-evolving. In addition, there are only certain processes at work for Buzan and Little. Gender relations, for example, are not seen as constituting a significant component of power at any level. Likewise, ethnicity is not included as a feature of international relations.

Envisaging the international system as itself made up of interacting subsystem elements opens up the possibility of considering the system as comprising multiple forms of actor, rather than being restricted to just one (and in the case of neorealism, undifferentiated) actor. From a complexity viewpoint, international relations systems comprise a variety of different actors, and the same actors themselves will not be undifferentiated, but distinct systems constituted by their own subsystems.

System dynamics Where complexity approaches differ most distinctly from previous theorizing with regard to systems is in relation to their dynamics. Arguing that human social and political networks are characterized by non-linearity, some have applied non-linear models to subjects such as alliance formation, outbreaks of war, federal political formations and environmental policy-making (see Richards 2000, and, in the case of the latter, Hoffman 2006). Others have used a complexity-informed notion of 'emergence' to theorize the processes of the formation and collapse of nation-states (Cederman 1997; Clemens 2001). An international system would appear to be a paradigmatic example of a self-organizing system, in that under anarchy there is no overall direction to the system. What patterns and regularities there are materialize from the actions of the units.

In other words, these are features which cannot be evaluated purely from an examination of the interactions of the parts. When units interact in a complex system, properties can be seen to be present which are not manifest at the unit level. This is, of course, a feature of much systems analysis, and formed the centre point of Waltz's approach to the study of systems. However, complexity theorists are much more ready to collapse the levels of analysis than Waltz's approach, and see the interconnections between different levels, or nested systems, as central to analysis.

What might be the emergent properties for an international system?

We would argue that three types of emergent properties might be apparent. First, those associated with institutional structures. All international systems have developed sets of norms, rules and even supra-governmental organizations to oversee their interactions. Most accounts of international organization (for example, Claude 1965 [1956]) would point to a rapid acceleration in the levels of institutions in the international system since the start of the nineteenth century – from the loose-knit Concert of Europe to a world presided over by international law, and international organizations such as the United Nations and the World Trade Organization. For many complexity thinkers the deepening web of institutional arrangements would be unsurprising. These institutional properties would be close to the analysis of international systems provided by Wendt, and his view of changing international cultures would mirror this evolutionary pattern (Wendt 1999). However, most complexity thinkers would reject his view that a world state is *inevitable* (Wendt 2003).

Emergent properties can also be seen in relational terms. Waltz's discussion of polarity and the different character of international systems would apply here. We would seek, however, to expand the range of relations analysed to also incorporate economic, ideological, patriarchal and political forms of domination, exploitation and exclusion. Wallerstein's account of a capitalist world economy would provide a starting point for an analysis of systemic economic relations. The capacity to generate, propagate and impose ideological positions on the organization of society would also be included under this heading.

While systems can be analysed independently, they not only intersect with other systems, they are also in a constant state of co-evolution. So the activities of the British state with regard to criminal groups – for example, increasing border controls – might lead to a change in the criminal group – relying more on smuggling to isolated beaches. States have co-evolved as a result of their interactions with one another. As Charles Tilly (1990) has shown in his analysis of the European state system, one particular model of state formation appeared as the dominant form in Europe, subsequently spreading throughout the globe. These co-evolutionary processes are driven by feedback loops, which can either be negative (moving systems back towards equilibrium) or positive (moving further away from equilibrium).

As an example of positive feedback, states attempting to stem the flow of illegal drugs into their societies confront unexpected consequences to their actions. A key tactic has been to attempt to reduce the availability of illegal drugs. This has resulted in higher street prices for illegal drugs, meaning that criminal organizations are able to make much higher profits from the trade. This has brought about a much higher supply, as all along the supply chain there has been an increased incentive to become involved in the trade. State activities have brought about different outcomes from those intended (Bertram et al. 1996; Caulkins et al. 2005).

This set of interactions between systems means that the tapestry of international relations becomes very rich indeed. The upside is that the reasons that international relations are so unpredictable become apparent – international relations are not an independent realm where one set of actors' movements can be tracked and predicted like the orbits of the planets or the trajectories of billiard balls. What we call the international is a complex interweave of numerous systems nested, intersected and embedded in each other, all undergoing processes of co-evolution and linked by innumerable feedback loops. Which leads to the downside: how can it be possible to analyse this? The simple answer is that it isn't. All that we can do is attempt to capture snapshots of a constantly developing situation in the hope that it can reveal answers to the questions that we have, and illuminate the central features and interconnections in international relations. The study of complexity may provide an answer to the question of why international relations as a discipline has found it so hard to make progress, as this is a complex system with many subsystems interacting in multiple ways, and the developments in one can have impacts right across the system.

Although it provides no ultimate 'fix' for the problems of analysing a system as complex as international relations, the idea of fitness landscape does provide a framework within which complex interactions between systems can be examined. A fitness landscape is a constantly changing environment wherein there is the potential for the situation of actors to improve or deteriorate. The situation of actors may change as a result of changes within the actor (the mutations in genotype for Kauffman, or changes in component design for Fleming and Sorenson), or as a result of changes in other systems (or, of course, some combination of these). A move up the fitness landscape means that a particular actor is able to prosper more effectively in its environment; a move down the landscape means that the actor will find it harder to achieve its ends.

Various examples could be cited which would give an example of changes in fitness landscape. In terms of traditional competition between states, fitness landscapes can illustrate the ways in which states seek to gain an advantage or undermine the attempts of other states to gain advantages. In 1945 the United States exploded the first atom bombs, first on test ranges in New Mexico and subsequently on the Japanese cities of Hiroshima and Nagasaki. This radically changed the fitness landscape in ways that are still significant today. The position of the United States with regard to other states changed dramatically. It now possessed a weapon that meant that any attack on the United States by another state was virtually unthinkable – the United States could retaliate with a weapon of enormous destructive power. Its landscape fitness position had increased dramatically – those of other states, particularly those that were potentially opposed to the United States, such as the Soviet Union, were degraded. Other states confronted the situation wherein the United States could potentially use atomic weapons offensively, or could threaten their use to coerce a particular action. It was only when the Soviet Union demonstrated that it also had an atomic weapon capability that its landscape fitness position improved. The subsequent arms race comprised attempts by both sides to achieve new peaks in a fitness landscape, while attempts to change the technology, such as the multiple independently targetable re-entry vehicle (MIRV), and the Space Defence Initiative (or Star Wars), could be regarded as attempts by the United States to degrade the fitness landscape for the Soviet Union, by making their weapons comparatively less effective. Since 1945 a number of other states have attempted to gain nuclear weapons. The Non-Proliferation Treaty was an attempt to freeze the fitness landscape by, in exchange for an agreement by the non-nuclear powers not to seek nuclear weapons, the nuclear-weapon-possessing states agreeing to restrict development. However, some states, inside and outside of the agreement, have sought to improve their position by obtaining nuclear weapons capability.

This example shows how states, as complex adaptive systems, have attempted to increase their relative fitness in a number of ways, such as through developments in nuclear weapons, or by degrading the fitness landscape for others. Technological developments such as 'Star Wars' or the fixing of advantage in the Non-Proliferation Treaty were attempts to solidify particular sets of benefits for a key player, and indicate how the notion of fitness landscape, and the attempts to degrade the fitness landscape of others, represents an operation of power between complex adaptive systems.

Three main contributions of the use of the concept of fitness landscape can be identified. First, it provides a way of thinking about international relations. These can now be perceived as a set of relations which seek to make the most advantage of the particular characteristics of a complex adaptive system relative to other complex adaptive systems. These complex adaptive systems might be states, or they might be a variety of other entities. These relations between complex adaptive systems are not simply about a direct competition, but are also related to the specific qualities of entities, and their potential to provide a more effective fit with the international landscape. Some of these shifts might be a case of entities purposefully seeking to develop particular capacities, while others might be developments that happened accidentally, or were related to other changes. Secondly, it provides an alternative way of thinking about power. While particular capabilities and features of international actors might mean that they ascend or descend in a fitness landscape, the capability to degrade the landscape for other actors provides a distinctive way of thinking about the operation of power. Here it is the very context in which actors operate which is important, not simply an issue of capabilities or the use of force to coerce other actors to operate in a particular way. Thirdly, it provides a way of thinking about change. Here change can be analysed in a multidimensional way. Internal developments can lead to variations within an individual actor's position in the fitness landscape. However, there will also be changes between actors in the form of co-evolution as developments in one actor or the fitness landscape bring forth interrelated changes. Finally, actors can seek to amend the fitness landscape itself, with the intention of accruing benefits to themselves, but with unlikely end consequences. Putting these elements together allows the development of a dynamic analysis of international relations wherein both the actors and the environment in which they interact are not frozen in time, but are in a constant state of transformation.

A further element of system dynamics is provided by the concept of feedback. Jervis (1997: 125) describes feedback as: 'A change in an element or relationship often [altering] others, which in turn affect the original one.' Traditionally, international relations theorists have focused on 'negative feedback'. These are the actions that bring a system back into equilibrium. A central heating thermostat is the classic, non-social-science example of a negative feedback system. As a room cools a switch is operated in the thermostat to switch a central heating boiler on, which heats the room up again. Such systems are usually described as homeostatic: they always return to an equilibrium position. For realist theorists such as Morgenthau and Waltz the international system is homeostatic as they expect a balance of power (an equilibrium position) to always emerge. If the balance of power is disrupted, then negative feedback (such as war, or changes in alliances) will occur to return the system to a balanced position (Waltz 1979: 116–23; Morgenthau 1960: 167).

Complexity theorists retain an interest in negative feedback, but also point to the significance of positive feedback – those effects which take a system farther away from an equilibrium point. In the example of a central heating system, the equivalent would be the thermostat setting off a cooling system, which would make the room even cooler, rather than a heating system which would warm the room up. In international relations positive feedback has become associated with the term 'blowback', and an archetypal example would be the US funding of the mujahedin to fight the Soviet-backed government in Afghanistan in the 1980s. Some claim this led to the establishment of the Taliban government in Afghanistan, which was highly implicated in the plot to attack the USA on 11 September 2001 (Johnson 2002: xi–xii). The notion of positive feedback has also become linked to the patterns of climate change. There are concerns among scientists that as the earth warms, stores of carbon dioxide and other greenhouse gases will be released into the atmosphere from frozen peat bogs or the oceans, which will lead to even higher levels of greenhouse gases and even more rapid climate change (Heimann and Reichstein 2008). Positive feedback takes a system farther away from its equilibrium point, and the farther a system is from equilibrium, the more likely it is to display non-linear behaviour.

In terms of international systems a bifurcation point could result (in Waltzian terms) in a change in the system, or a change of the system. The end of the Cold War was a bifurcation point, with the collapse of the Soviet Union resulting in a change in the system, from bipolarity to unipolarity. Wallerstein argues that we are now in a non-linear period of international relations that will lead to a bifurcation point which will result in a change of the system – from the modern world-system to some kind of alternative (Wallerstein 2004: 104).

The implications of non-linearity, sensitivity to initial conditions and bifurcation are highly significant for the study of international relations. As Euel Elliott and Douglas Kiel argue: 'Nonlinear dynamics and the related sciences of complexity lead us to question the extent to which we may be capable of both prediction and control in social and policy systems' (Elliott and Kiel 1997: 68). Put simply, while perhaps theoretically possible, the features of complex systems suggest that it is very difficult to make predictions about what future trajectories the international system will take. During linear phases of stability (such as the Cold War) prediction may be possible, but during non-linear phases it is most likely that unexpected outcomes will occur, with large changes to or within systems, and unpredictable relationships between causes and events (for example, small events having major impacts, and major events perhaps little impact). In other words, the kinds of activities and expectations that pertain in the study of international relations may have to change. As Fritjof Capra (2007: 13) notes:

> We can still make very accurate predictions, but they concern the qualitative features of the system's behavior rather than the precise values of its variables at a particular time. Nonlinear dynamics thus represents a shift from quantity to quality. Whereas conventional mathematics deals with quantities and formulas, complexity theory deals with quality and pattern.

We can say what a system looks like rather than necessarily where it is going. This might be considered a considerable weakness of complexity approaches. However, we would argue that it might be more appropriate to accept that, with complex social systems, we have to expect the unexpected. While adopting theoretical positions that claim to have predictive capabilities is reassuring, the conclusion of complexity-based analyses is that predictions are extremely unlikely to be accurate.

Conclusions

In this chapter we have initiated our discussion of complex international relations by focusing on the international system. Complexity theorizing and international relations have both utilized the idea of system, but in theory and in practice the idea of system is radically different, and the purpose of this chapter has been to draw out some of these variations.

The key similarity between complexity approaches and the majority of international relations approaches to the study of systems is the claim that there is a value to studying the systemic level. There are forces at work that can only be analysed at a systemic level which a focus at the unit level will miss. While the study of the foreign policy of individual states is important, a focus at this level will miss some of the structures that operate at a systemic level. For Waltz there are forces which 'push and shove' the units. A complexity approach would describe these as emergent features of the international system – characteristics which surface as a result of interactions between the units.

The major difference between complexity and previous approaches to international relations is that the latter have utilized a mechanical notion of the ways that systems operate, derived from a Newtonian model of physics. A direct link is assumed between cause and effect, one that can be represented as a linear relationship. Existing approaches to the social sciences 'make assumptions of simplicity that fail to match the deep and multiple interactions that create complex phenomena' (Elliott and Kiel 1997: 77). By contrast, complexity approaches assume that the relationships between events may be hard to trace, that small effects can create large outcomes, and that at times of instability future events will be difficult to predict.

Realism has focused on the international realm as a homeostatic system, one that will move from non-equilibrium towards equilibrium. For complexity theorists it is important also to consider those forces which pull a system farther away from equilibrium. In other words, there are positive as well as negative feedback effects. Positive feedback effects would also allow for the study of change, as they lead to more chaotic (or non-linear) behaviour in a system, which can result in bifurcation and major system change. As Neil Harrison (2006b: 11) notes, 'complex systems are never homeostatic ... frequent and temporary equilibrium points are always distinct phenomena ... a fleeting event within a specific set of conditions, a point on a path of change'. We live in an international political context characterized by sudden, dramatic and unexpected changes, localized events with differentiated impact around the globe and also significant continuity. Complexity concepts allow international relations to move beyond hierarchical forms of theorizing by adopting a more flexible approach to the kinds of connections within and between each level of system. It also enables us to analyse different processes of relations and of change. For example, in using the notion of 'path dependency', we can understand the co-presence of different paths to economic, political and social development (Pierson 2000).

Realism draws attention to what it considers to be the timeless features of international relations, either, for traditional realists, because of the character of human nature, or as a result of the 'logic of anarchy'. For a system to have 'timeless qualities' would not be the characteristic of a complex system. Complex systems are affected by what Ilya Prigogine called the 'arrow of time'. Complex systems cannot return to a previous state, and developments within a system will be dependent on the order in which they occur. Ultimately, as Lars-Erik Cederman (1997: 53) argues, the properties of a system 'are a function of history, an assumption that defies deductive analysis'.

The study of history will be a key element of complexity approaches to international relations.

Waltz's neorealism attempted to isolate the international system as a sphere of analysis. His aim was to separate systemic causes from other effects. This might be a useful methodology in terms of deriving systemic effects, but (as many authors have argued) it leaves us with a vacuous account of international relations. A key contribution of constructivist approaches has been to see system and agents as co-constituted. The equivalent for complexity theorists would be the notion of nested systems, which overlap and impact on each other. However, we would argue that the international system is nested within a wider range of systems than constructivism suggests. In particular, the international system is embedded/nested within the environmental system, and its development cannot be analysed independently. Complexity theorists would describe this co-constitution as co-evolution – systems adapt to their environments and to other systems. Waltz (1979: 93–7) saw states just as units of the international system, which he regarded as undifferentiated – complexity theorists would regard states and system as in a constantly changing relationship, each developing in respect to the other. As Mary Lee (1997: 26) argues, 'social change cannot be truly explained without describing the co-evolution of all levels'. Thus there is no reason to expect that the core feature of the international system will be an eternal anarchy, or that it is valid to assume that the character of the units can be accurately (and timelessly) described as unchanging. In the next chapter we will demonstrate these claims through a discussion of the historical development of the international system, and will start to analyse how the international system can be depicted as embedded in a series of other, equally complex, systems.

4 · Emergent features in international systems

As we noted in the previous chapter, complexity approaches have provided analyses of systems which perceive them as self-organizing and displaying emergent features. This chapter will explore whether international systems can be described as complex.

Emergence and international relations

This section asks the question: to what extent is the international system 'organized', and can this be discussed in terms of self-organization and emergence? If the international system is viewed as a complex system then what features would we expect it to exhibit? Complex systems are usually perceived as: displaying emergent features – those that are apparent only at a systemic level rather than at the unit level; becoming more complex; experiencing periods of instability; and exhibiting linear and non-linear relations between their component parts.

This section will argue that these features can be perceived in the international system. Not only perceived, but that a complex approach aids in making sense of international relations. Two candidates in terms of organization become immediately apparent – relational organizations, in the sense of the structure of the international system, and institutional organizations (institutions, laws and norms), which have a long history, but have become increasingly significant since 1945.

Relational order That international relations can be described as complex is something of an understatement. James Rosenau (1996: 315–16) aptly drew parallels between the study of international relations and the complexities involved in landing planes on an aircraft carrier. But they are also complex in another sense of the word, and here one of the characteristics of complex systems seems to be particularly pertinent – a tendency to switch unpredictably between periods of stability and instability. The twentieth century would appear to be a paradigmatic example of such fluctuations, with a first half marked by violent global upheaval, and a second half (dependent on where one lived) marked by systemic stability. The start of the current century appears to be characterized by a return to global instability. If we want our theories of world politics to increase our understandings of world politics they need to be able to provide an account of such major upheavals. To what extent can a complexity approach shed light on such fluctuations?

Here there is clearly the possibility of drawing links between the notion of chaotic activity in complex systems and anarchy, as used by students of international relations. While 'anarchy' has been a defining quality in the study of international relations, this has been in the sense of a lack of sovereign power rather than in the sense of chaotic relations (Milner 1991: 70–1). It has been the character of relations (or order) within that 'anarchy' which has been a defining feature of the discipline. One of the most influential ways of seeing this order has been through the use of the term 'balance of power', the study of which, for some writers, is perhaps synonymous with the discipline itself.

However, the term has been used in many different ways. Ernst Haas (1953: 447–58), for example, identified eight potential variations. These ranged from descriptions of any distribution of power among international actors to a disposition of power where there was a degree of equilibrium among any combination of competing actors. For many there has been a tendency to see the balance of power as an equilibrium point in international relations. This view equates to equilibrium markets in economic theory and sociological models associated with Talcott Parsons (1951, 1960). In economic models there is an assumption that when markets are away from a position of equilibrium, a 'hidden hand' will steer them automatically back to that point. The balance of power often appears to operate in a similar way in realist analyses. State leaders, if they follow the national interests and attempt to maximize power, will automatically bring about such a balance. The danger is not the pursuit of power, but that states might act in ways (such as, for example, attempting to pursue collective security arrangements) that might bring about the collapse of a balance of power. From a realist perspective, a balance of power is more likely to result in peaceful relations between states because no one side would be tempted to take advantage of the other – they would be confronted with an equal level of power, rather than being able to exploit a superior position.

It is perhaps not surprising that the idea of a balance of power was such an influential one in international relations of the post-1945 period, given its focus on US interests and a tendency to be a little less interested in broader (in other words, non-European) historical examples. This limited focus was highlighted by Stanley Hoffmann's

(1977) famous description of international relations as an American social science. However, the end of the Cold War, and the apparent position of dominance of the United States, led to some questioning of the notion. For Charles Krauthammer (1991), the USA's predominant role was a 'unipolar moment'; though that 'moment' might last more than a generation, multi-polarity would 'no doubt' (ibid.: 23) come in time – other powers would rise to challenge the USA. Other authors questioned whether the balance of power was such an inevitable development. Surveying a range of historical accounts, William Wohlforth et al. (2007: 20) concluded that '7,500 years of the history of the international system shows that balanced and unbalanced distributions of power are roughly equally common. There is no iron law of history favouring either a balance of power or a hegemony.' Furthermore, they argue (ibid.: 20) that unipolar systems are not necessarily unstable. In all the cases they examined, balance-of-power systems were replaced by lasting hegemonies (ibid.: 229). Despite these arguments, Kenneth Waltz (2000: 30) maintained that, while balancing was not an absolute law of international relations, 'theory enables one to say that a new balance of power will form' (though it was not possible to say for definite when).

With the United States in a dominant position, attention now turned to thinking about the role of hierarchy in international relations, perhaps again affirming Hoffmann's assertion about the central concerns of the discipline. Hierarchy exists, David Lake (2009: 51) argued, where 'one actor, the ruler, possesses authority over a second actor, the ruled'. This was a significant variation from conventional realist theory, because by accepting the protection of the ruler, ruled states appeared prepared to give up sovereignty, and in particular reduce their reliance on self-help. This reduced the costs for the ruled and can be seen as part of the bargain for accepting the authority of the ruler.

To see hierarchy and balance as distinct forms of international order is rather puzzling, as the formation of competing blocs in a situation of balance can include the domination of alliance partners – the two Cold War blocs being the clearest example. There were clearly relations of hierarchy on both sides (for example, European countries' acceptance of large numbers of US troops on their soil). The major difference between that and the current international system is that it is now global and encompasses many states. The systems discussed by Wohlforth et al. encompassed the then 'known world'. Hence something significant has occurred in terms of the number of states and the territorial scope of the international system which might lead us to think that one state exerting a lasting hegemony over the entire system might be rather more different. In short, the international system has become more complex. With the break-up of the European empires, and then of the former Soviet bloc, the number of states has grown nearly fourfold (as indicated by membership of the United Nations) from just over fifty in 1945 to 192. However, it is not only in terms of the number of states, it is also types of states (e.g. colonial/post-colonial), and states that are more or less capable of exerting sovereignty over their territories. In a complex adaptive system, such increases in diversity are unsurprising.

Another way of considering the relationship between forms of order was suggested by Adam Watson. He argued that international order could be conceived of as a spectrum ranging between 'absolute independence and absolute empire' (Watson 1992: 13). At one end of the spectrum would be a system of sovereign states competing under anarchy – in effect Waltz's vision of international relations. At the other would be an empire where all other forms of competing sovereignty had been overcome – in other words, the demise of anarchy. Watson (ibid.: 13) did, however, consider the outermost points on the spectrum to be 'theoretical absolutes, that do not occur in practice'. Furthermore, systems were always in transition, oscillating between the two extremes, with a tendency for the 'gravitational pull of the pendulum' to be away from the extremes and towards the centre – 'a concert or multiple hegemony' (ibid.: 324). A similar argument is made by Michael Mann (1986: 537) when he notes a dialectical relationship between 'multi-power-actor civilisations' and 'empires of domination' that 'begins to look like a single world-historical process'.

Watson's analysis points to a variety of different forms of international order, and suggests that the character of order is in a constant state of flux. However, the concept of a swinging pendulum tends to suggest a smooth and predictable transition between different forms of order, and some scepticism might be expressed with regard to the notion of a swinging pendulum, which, from a complexity perspective, is excessively determinist.

A key factor in the development of international relations has been a consideration of the different forms of international systems. While the notion of the balance of power has been central in terms of post-1945 thinking about international politics, this represents the preoccupations of a particular time, the Cold War, when there was perceived to be a balance at work (however unbalanced the confrontation between the USSR and the United States was in practice). It also reflects the study of European history, particularly of the nineteenth century, when state leaders purposefully pursued balance-of-power politics. Students of the English School and others have widened the discussion through the examination of a larger range of historical international systems, and in these examples have drawn attention to a wider range of forms of 'order' in international relations, which leads to the conclusion that, historically, some forms of hegemony are at least as common as balance of power (Watson 1992; Wohlforth et al. 2007, Buzan and Little 2000). All these different forms, all the examples across Watson's spectrum, represent some form of order in international politics.

The international system therefore, in its simplest form as a collection of states, can be described as self-organizing. There is no authority outside of the system which has imposed order on the interactions of states, or enforced particular configurations of relations. Order, indicated by various forms of stability, has emerged from the interactions between state actors leading to features that are apparent only at a systemic level (balance, hegemony, suzerainty). These features of interstate relations equate very closely to the complexity notions of autopoeisis (or emergence) or self-organization, and suggest that the notion of the international system as a complex system is worthy of further investigation.

Beyond the apparent possibility of envisaging the international system as exhibiting features of self-organization and emergence, what else can complexity add to the discussion of different forms of international order? Perhaps the most significant contribution that complexity theorists could contribute to the analysis of different forms of relational order would be to stress the historical contingency of different forms of order. While the historical record is significant, it is not an absolute predictor of what future forms of order may consist of. Other minor changes in the interrelations of states, the character of states, and the interactions with other systems may generate features that push forms of international order in a particular direction. For example, intersection with the global economic system may mean that states are less likely to balance against states that they have close economic relations with. For example, Michel Fortmann et al. (2004: 363) argue that possible challengers to US hegemony such as China and Russia are too dependent on investment by the USA to 'hard balance' (that is to say, provocatively build up their military capability) its dominance. In other words, as a complex system, past behaviour is not a reliable predictor for what may occur in the future.

Hence some notions, as described by Haas, of the balance of power as a 'natural order' in international politics should be treated with some scepticism. The term 'arrow of time' has been used to describe the way that systems develop (Prigogine 2003: 56) in a non-reversible pattern. In other words, systems are in a constant state of change and patterns of relations between actors will not lead to the same results in different time periods, because the overall structure of the system is not the same as it was in the previous time period.

A second major contribution of complexity thinking would be to see international order as in a constant state of flux. Most analyses of international order, as we have seen, have tended to focus on issues of stability, and while stability may be a good thing in certain (more just and equitable) systems, in a complex system it is unlikely to be something that endures. The very detailed histories of international systems that have appeared would confirm that none of these orders has been in any sense permanent – even though certain actors have sought to maintain their position of dominance. The United States 2002 National Security Strategy would be a good example of such a desire. No state has been able to maintain a constant state of dominance in the international system, and the bipolar balance of power of the Cold War, despite the claims about its stability, did not persist. While Watson's account of change in international systems acknowledged this element of change, his notion of a pendulum indicates that he anticipated a direction – that there were forces that drew international politics back towards some more stable form of arrangement. This would be typical of negative feedback operating in a system to draw it back towards a more stable equilibrium. While for complexity theorists this is a possibility (and the mid-point of the pendulum swing might be described as an 'attractor'), it is also possible that positive feedback might draw the system away from the centre – and that indeed the swing of the pendulum is extremely erratic. So, for example, bandwagoning by states might be seen as a positive feedback – states seeking protection of a dominant state, or at least avoiding intervention from such a state, could increase the level of a state's dominance – pulling the system towards the extreme position of empire rather than towards the centre.

A third insight from complexity thinking would be that relations within a complex system are likely to be non-linear. Very small perturbations can result in very large changes within the system, and likewise major changes can result in very little change – for example, the impacts of climate change on global environmental governance systems, an issue that will be taken up in the next chapter.

The concept of fitness landscape can contribute to thinking about the ways that states interact, and how they can alter the environment for other states. States are not uniform actors and some have been better suited to survival than others. In his account of the development of states in Europe over the past 1,000 years Charles Tilly (1990) showed how one particular model of the state (where there was sufficient capital to finance war-making and sufficient coercion to maintain order) proved to be more successful than its competitors. Such a model of the state can be seen as one that moved up the fitness landscape compared to its competitors. The US model of governance could be seen as contributing to the success of that country – in terms of its ability to maintain its legitimacy and mobilize resources compared to the Soviet Union, though the Chinese government system may now be proving to have found a higher position on the fitness landscape. States can also be seen as deploying power to alter the fitness landscape. If states have the capability to affect the landscape this can act to improve their position compared to that of other states. The United States' key role in setting up the post-1945 international financial architecture in a way that suited its own interests compared to those of European states or of the Soviet Union is an example of the way that states can alter the fitness landscape.

In simple terms of relations between states the international system exhibits signs of being a complex system – emergent features become apparent in terms of different forms of international order. These are in a constant state of flux, and have been subject to periods of stability and instability. The pattern of relations shows no consistency, despite realist claims, suggesting that the arrow of time has an impact – it is not a Newtonian system where interactions display a continuity of outcome, but a system that is undergoing constant change. However, as will be seen in the next subsection, this complexity is not apparent only in relational order, but also in institutional order. We examine these issues before turning to a discussion of the ways in which the international system cannot be seen as independent of the other systems with which it interacts.

Institutional order Here we widen out our discussion to assess the possibility of also considering institutional features of the international system as emergent properties in international relations. By institutional features we mean those processes that have developed or have been implemented between states to regularize their interactions. This would include norms, international law and international organizations. While realist scholars have regarded these features as 'barely relevant' (Reinalda 2009: 5) to the study of international relations, they have been core to Liberal and English School approaches to the discipline. Our argument here is that these can also be seen as a form of self-organization and adaptation, and that insights into the ways in which this order has developed can be gained from deploying a complexity perspective.

The English School has been at the forefront of providing an account of the institutional features of international relations. Hedley Bull's account of an 'anarchical society' provided a development away from an entirely disordered or 'Hobbesian' account of international relations. Anarchy is a 'fact' for Bull (1977: 46), in the sense that 'it is obvious that sovereign states, unlike the individuals within them, are not subject to a common government'. However, the lack of common government does not necessarily equate to a lack of order. In 'international society', common interest, rules and institutions maintain a certain degree of order.

There are various accounts of the expansion of institutional features of international relations. The classic statement, in terms of international organization specifically, is Inis Claude's *Swords into Plowshares*. While certainly not a complexity theorist, his opening comments could perhaps come straight from a complexity handbook on international relations – 'the growing complexity of international relations has already produced international organizations; the world is engaged in the process of organizing' (Claude 1965 [1956]: 3). For Claude, international organization is a necessary feature of international relations, but not one without problems. While specific international organizations may 'come and go', international organization as a process 'is here to stay' (ibid.: 5–6). Claude was clearly aware that there were limitations in the way that international organization had developed – it had made little progress with regard to the 'coercive control of state behavior', but yet, writing in the middle of the last century, he argued that the world was in an era of 'continuous development of patterns and techniques for managing the business of the international community' (ibid.: 394–5). And the process that Claude describes could certainly be depicted in terms of 'continuous development'. International organization, despite various world-order proposals that had emerged through the second millennium, began with developments in the nineteenth century. The first of these was the Concert of Europe – a rather ill-defined series of meetings and conferences between the leaders of European states following the Napoleonic wars and proceeding more or less irregularly through the nineteenth century. The 'Concert' is perhaps best defined as an institution rather than an organization. It had none of the formal trappings that we might associate with an international organization, such as a charter, secretariat or system of organized meetings. By contrast, it provided a framework, in the sense of a series of norms and practices, whereby European leaders could meet to resolve issues that concerned them (or at least discuss them). Claude also describes the appearance throughout the nineteenth century of 'public international unions'. These were international organizations that appeared for the purpose of resolving technical issues relating to cross-border flows of trade, communications and people. The International Telegraphic Union, created in 1865, had the purpose of standardizing telegraphic systems so that telegraphic messages could be transmitted across borders. Prior to its creation individual countries had created their own telegraphic systems, which were incompatible with those of their neighbours. As a result messages could not be sent across borders, but had to be recoded if crossing country borders. Standardizing systems made cross-border transmissions possible. Hence the key role of international public unions was to resolve specifically technical problems in interstate activities. Likewise the International Postal Union was created to distribute revenue from mail posted across borders.

A final element of nineteenth-century international organization was the 'Hague System'. This relates to two (of an intended ongoing series) conferences, held in The Hague in 1899 and 1907. These conferences were significantly different from the Concert of Europe, in that their first intention was towards some degree of universality – delegations from forty-four states, including the majority of Latin American states, attended the 1907 meeting (although this universality did not extend to territories subjugated by European imperialism). Secondly, they were aimed at developing more durable means of maintaining peace, rather than reacting to specific problems, which the 'Concert' had tended to do. The Hague process, for example, created a Court of International Arbitration. Although having no recourse to force disputants to consult it, its mechanisms were used fourteen times between its creation and 1914, and it was the basis for the Permanent Court of International Justice (created by the League of Nations), and the International Court of Justice (founded as a part of the UN) (Calvocoressi 1987: 50).

It is a profound irony that at the second gathering of the Hague peace conference in 1907 it was proposed to hold a third meeting within a period equivalent to that which had elapsed since the 1899 conference, with signs that the process was becoming institutionalized.

By the proposed date (1915), the states of Europe and subsequently the globe were being sucked into the prolonged crisis, with order not being entirely re-established until 1945. This indicates that the development of institutional order is no linear process of growth. Despite the advances such as the great powers developing a role for management as indicated by the Concert of Europe, a move to regular meetings and universality in the Hague process and the appearance of a number of institutions with responsibilities to resolve technical issues, nineteenth-century international organization was not sufficiently robust to forestall the collapse of world order into the horror of the First World War. Subsequent to that global disaster was the attempt to re-establish institutional order through the League of Nations. Claude draws a distinction between the nineteenth century 'as the era of *preparation for* international organization', and the period after First World War 'as the era of *establishment of* international organization' (Claude 1965 [1956]: 36). While the League is generally cited to be a failure, it was a major development in the form of institutional order in that it combined negotiations between states, which had until then been on an ad hoc basis (as the Concert), with the permanent institutionalization of the international public unions. In other words, it was a permanent organization, with an institutional headquarters, a secretariat and a covenant that at least placed some obligations on states (in the preamble to the covenant the 'High Contracting Parties' accepted 'obligations not to resort to war'). That the League was humiliated by its incapacity to act against aggressor states such as Japan and Italy has long been part of the story of its failure. What is often overlooked in such discussions is the many positive contributions that were negotiated under the auspices of the organization: the creation of the International Labour Organization; agreements in the fields of economy, communication and transport, social health; creation of the opium committee to control the production and refinement of opium. Many of these policy areas were passed on to the United Nations.

More than certain competencies were passed on to the new organization. In structural terms the two organizations are more similar than different, the key differences being the veto power of the permanent members of the UN Security Council, and the powers given to the Security Council under Chapter 7 to draw upon and utilize the armed forces of the member states to react to breaches of the peace or international acts of aggression.

The most striking feature of post-1945 institutional order is the explosion in the number of organizations and the vast extension of international law. According to Joseph Camilleri and Jim Falk (2009: 160), the number of international organizations rose from 280 in 1970 to 3,456 in 1985 and 7,308 in 2003. Likewise, most discussions of international law emphasize the large increase in its scope since 1945 (see, for example, Wallace and Martin-Ortega 2009: 5–6). The term usually used to describe this phenomenon is evolutionary. However, we prefer to see it as one of increasing complexity – something not unexpected in complex systems.

In terms of developing a complexity-inspired approach to thinking about institutional order in the international system, Camilleri and Falk's *Worlds in Transition* provides a detailed and thoroughly argued analysis of human attempts to organize relations between different social groups. Their argument is that forms of institutional order have been the result of attempts to adapt to the environment (in the broader sense of the term). They argue that 'each succeeding epoch appears to have introduced a progressively more complex mosaic of social, economic and political arrangements, the net effect of which was to overcome a number of obstacles in the path of adaptation' (Camilleri and Falk 2009: 536). The human species is currently undergoing a transition, they argue, from 'modernity' to what they hope will be a 'holoreflexive era'. The term holoreflexive implies the appearance of a global consciousness that is both holistic and reflexive, exhibiting an awareness of the planetary aspects of human activities. Central to the holoreflexive enterprise is the need to develop the mechanisms that can lead to reconciliation between the human species and its many differentiated parts. Such a potential reconciliation 'lies at the heart of the holoreflexive enterprise' (ibid.: 559).

Modernity has reached its limits, they suggest, for a number of reasons. Primarily this relates to the breakdown of the European imperial project and its failure to provide effective and legitimate rule over the territories under its influence. However, there has also been a breakdown in sovereignty, with many states in the post-colonial world lacking the infrastructural resources to provide successful government over their territories. Added to this is the problem of limits to growth – partially due to limits imposed by resource shortages and also by 'the disruption of the delicate equilibrium established over a long evolutionary timescale between the human species and its biological and physical environment' (ibid.: 155–6). Related to the limits of growth that have appeared as part of modernity is a growing scepticism about the potential of science. The expectations regarding the possibilities that science could contribute to the improvement of the human situation gradually became replaced by concerns about the potential damage that human inventions could cause (for example, the atom bomb) and concerns over the impact of science on agricultural practices. Science, rather than appearing to be an omniscient and benevolent undertaking, began to appear both fallible and, at times, threatening. The appearance of these 'limits to modernity' has sparked a 'remarkable though still inchoate shift in intellectual orientation, cultural ethos, and organisational practice' (ibid.: 159). One response to these issues has been increased multilateralism, indicated by the increase in international organizations previously mentioned. Yet Camilleri and Falk are also hopeful that a response will be the emergence of a 'holoreflexive' epoch.

There is much to recommend this account of the development of institutional order, in particular the emphasis on adaptation as a stimulus to the development of international organization. However, in many ways it appears a liberal account of international organization supplemented by a side order of complexity. This is an account that stresses the progressive evolution and potential of international organization, and while it analyses at length the limits to modernity, it does little to discuss the exploitative character of other social systems. Where the analysis is less developed is in terms of intersectionality – while there is considerable discussion of international organizations in international politics, the relationship between this and a range of other systems is not developed – one particular example would be the failure to evaluate the relational order between states, as discussed earlier in the chapter. Furthermore, the intersections between institutional order and other systems, such as capitalism, gender and race, are not explored, with the result that exploitative systems are undertheorized. A key weakness that emerges as a result of this omission is that the power of states and other actors within the international system is not considered. Many such actors are potentially pulling in a rather different direction to that suggested by the possibilities of a holoreflexive epoch – though Camilleri and Falk (ibid.: 559) do indicate that they are aware of the existence of pressures operating against a more global consciousness.

As noted, the move to reconcile differences between different social groups is a key feature of the hoped-for holoreflexive epoch. Yet this reveals the project as a human-centred one. We would argue that a study of complexity pushes for more than a project to accept the human 'other' (as significant and difficult as such an undertaking is), but also for an awareness of human systems as embedded in and intersected with those of other species and of the biosphere more generally. A reconciliation is not only necessary within the human species, but also across the borders of species, and of non-animate systems.

What would a more developed complexity approach contribute to the discussion of institutional order in international relations? We argue that complexity can extend the discussion in four main ways.

First, we would argue that institutional order is an emergent feature. Institutional order appears to be a consistent feature of interstate relations and international systems in general. Through any historical period for which we have written evidence, and across all geographical areas where different organized groups have interacted, there appears to be some, albeit minimal, level of 'society'. There have been norms and rules, even of the basic kinds that have overseen relations between different actors (Bull 1977 is the classic statement of this viewpoint). Over time, these have become complex, with the current order perhaps being the one where norms and rules have become the most developed – the creation of international law, and permanent organizations which oversee the interactions of states, and to which states seem to have been prepared to cede some sovereignty in return for the benefits that they derive. These are systemic features which emerge from the interactions of the actors, and are a form of self-organization – they are not imposed from outside the system, and there is no sovereign body which imposes them. Rules, norms, organizations and laws are a mechanism to attempt to maintain some sort of order within the system, and are a form of adaptation to the problems that states confront in terms of their interactions and shared problems.

Seeing institutional order as part of a complex adaptive system suggests that institutional order can be envisaged as a form of organization in addition to and overlapping with the relational order described above – these are not conflicting processes, but ones that appear through the course of interrelations between states. Both are forms of self-organization – a tendency towards greater order and increased complexity which are features of complex adaptive systems.

Secondly, the development of forms of institutional order has not followed a linear trajectory. Rather, it has followed a punctuated and complex path of development. Periods where there has been cooperation have been punctuated by complete breakdowns in institutional order. Likening this process to a 'great experiment', Strobe Talbott (2008: 401) suggests that 'by and large, breakthroughs in the great experiment of nations learning to work together have come in the wake of explosions in the laboratory'.

We have already noted the vast expansion of international organization since the middle of the last century, and, particularly through the 1990s, this process appeared to be expanding more rapidly and in some instances growing in depth – e.g. the European Union (EU). However, this is no guarantee that this process of growth will continue, or the extent of international organization that has now emerged will persist. While 'society' and rules have existed across the range of previous international systems, they have always faltered, or ultimately been undermined by actors who fail to play by the rules. For example, a very intricate set of norms constrained conflict between groups in the Mexica empire, but this was swept aside by the Spanish intruders, who had a very different notion of how warfare should be carried out (for an account of the conquest of the Mexican empire, see Thomas 1993). Hence, rates of growth of international organization can vary enormously, and there is always the possibility that there may be an 'explosion in the laboratory'. Institutional order is not on a path of continual and progressive development. Periods of rapid growth of institutions could be followed by a period of complete dissolution. However, the historical record indicates that, while the character can be remarkably different, some form of institutional order has emerged in international systems.

Thirdly, institutional order exhibits intersectionality with other systems. Institutional order has emerged as a form of self-organization between states, and as a means of regularizing their relationships. Both the League of Nations and the United Nations were primarily seen by their founders as security organizations – their prime purpose was to prevent reoccurrences of the conflicts that had immediately preceded their formation. While this primary function has not been one that has been fulfilled with much success, institutional order has provided forums where other problems could be addressed. In so doing, the institutional order in international systems has intersected with a range of other systems. Here we briefly discuss two examples – the economic system and colonialism – while a third, the non-human world, will be the subject of the next chapter.

It is with regard to the global economic system that institutional order has developed to the largest extent. In particular, three powerful economic institutions oversee the running of the global economic system: the World Trade Organization (WTO), the International Monetary Fund (IMF) and the World Bank (see, for example, O'Brien and Williams 2010: 125–6). These three organizations have particular responsibilities in terms of attempting to maintain the smooth running of the capitalist system, and states have been prepared to endow these organizations with large amounts of power (particularly the IMF and the WTO). It is also interesting to note how these organizations have evolved as the world economy has developed. The IMF originated as an organization whose purpose was to provide short-term loans to countries undergoing short-term balance-of-payments problems, and was primarily seen as operating to maintain trade between developed economies. As a result of the Third World debt crisis, and in particular the exposure of banks from the developed countries, the focus of the IMF's activities has become increasingly the developing world, with the infamous structural adjustment policies being the price extracted for assistance with debt repayment.

Likewise, institutional order, in the form of the United Nations, has intersected with the colonial system, and in the process of delegitimizing colonialism has itself been changed. The United Nations was at the forefront of moves towards decolonization. In the organization's charter is a commitment by colonial powers to move towards the self-determination of non-self-governing territories (a euphemism for colonies), and it was on the floor of the General Assembly that an anti-colonial norm developed – codified in the 1960 'Declaration on the Granting of Independence to Colonial Countries and Peoples'. The United Nations was also significant in the provision of peacekeeping forces – frequently deployed to resolve or suppress issues left by colonialism (e.g. UNMOGIP, the observer force on the Pakistan–India border – deployed in 1949, and still there). However, the organization itself changed as a result of the large number of countries that gained their independence following the Second World War, and it underwent a transition from a Western-supporting organization to one where the majority of votes supported a Soviet position. Furthermore, as a result of the number of former colonies that had joined the organization, it also became a forum where issues of interest to developing countries could be voiced – such as the call for a New International Economic Order.

Finally, while institutional order is a form of self-organization, and arises from the interactions of states, this does not mean that this is a process that is devoid of power, or where power isn't utilized to embed positions of dominance. It is generally accepted that the world order post-1945 is a creation of the United States, and that this was primarily to enhance the economic and political power of the USA. A global free-trade regime is clearly to the advantage of that country which can produce more cheaply than any other (as the USA was in

1945). In this sense powerful states can mould the fitness landscape for others, through the creation of norms, laws and organizations which reflect their interests and priorities.

We have seen in this section that the tools we introduced in the last chapter can provide significant insights into the study of international relations. Thus far in this chapter we have remained within the confines of traditional topics in international relations, specifically forms of order in the international system. However, a further significant contribution that we have already mentioned, but wish to extend further, is the question of intersectionality. The next section does this through a consideration of the global food industry.

International relations and the global food industry: embedded systems

So far in this chapter we have considered the emergent forms of order, or self-organization, in the international system. In this section we discuss a second feature of complexity approaches, the nested and co-evolutionary character of complex adaptive systems.

We choose to look at food because, as we will argue, the development of a global food system has occurred in tandem with the system of states and the global capitalist economy. None of these features of the contemporary world can be explained independently of the others. Furthermore, the global food system can be seen as intersected with a large range of other systems, such as the biosphere or the individual human. We are quite literally 'what we eat'. We not only need food to stay alive, the food we eat also contributes to creating who we are. For example, Jane Bennett (2010: 40–1) cites various sources linking the properties of food as an 'actant' that has both physiological and psychological impacts on our individual systems. The global food production system is therefore one that intersects with a wide range of other systems, including our individual digestive systems, the colonial (and post-colonial) system, the system of states, the environment, and relations with other species.

Philip McMichael (1998) makes the observation that the international food regime is inherently both political and geopolitical – though this is perhaps, taking Bennett's comments into account, also a clear instance of where the 'personal is political (and geopolitical)'. Together with water – a whole interrelated topic, especially given the quantity of water embedded in food; see Evans (2009: 23–4) – food constitutes an essential of human survival. That an estimated 1.02 billion (FAO 2009) people in the world are undernourished is an indication of the imbalances of global power – given that, taking calorific value as an indicator, there is sufficient food to meet everyone's needs (Burke and Lobell 2010: 18). Furthermore, high levels of hunger are accompanied by very high rates of overconsumption of food in western Europe and North America (Pinstrup-Andersen 2002: 1201–2). Given this very obvious imbalance of power and, as we will see, the links between food production, the global economy and international diplomacy, it is perhaps surprising that this is a topic frequently overlooked by students of international relations.

Global food production has been analysed from a variety of perspectives. Kevin Morgan et al. (2006: 15–20) point to three ways in which global agricultural practices have been analysed: political economy approaches; actor network theory; and convention theory. Political economy approaches have largely been concerned with the study of commodity chains and the ways in which the processes of globalization have led to the disembeddedness of agricultural practices. These approaches have developed a historical (or food regime) account of the processes of food production, through colonialism, the Bretton Woods era and into the neoliberal period.

Actor network theory has tended to be more critical of the political economy approaches, arguing that they reify the expansion of capitalism, and see the development of the food industry as determined by the requirements of an expanding capitalism. For actor network theory, there is a need to take 'into account the full range of entities (natural, social, technological and so on)' (ibid.: 17). This 'range of entities' is involved in the development of food commodity chains, with differing forms of motivation and perceptions of the situation. Convention theory overlaps considerably with actor network theory, but here the focus is on the agreements that emerge between actors in their interactions. Convention theorists see these as emerging from coordination rather than from the simple application of power. With regard to the food sector, this requires the analysis of 'how differing food cultures mobilize particular convention types and how these types are woven together into a coherent cultural framework' (ibid.: 20).

All three of these approaches offer insights useful for building up a complexity approach to global agriculture. Political economy approaches have highlighted the inherent inequalities between actors, and the historical development of global food regimes, but there has been a tendency to depict relations between actors in deterministic terms, to understate disruptions and upheavals in food commodity chains. Both actor network theory and convention theory have been effective at bringing in the range of actors involved in food production and distribution systems, but, in contrast to the political economy approaches, tend to understate power relations between actors.

In a complexity-influenced discussion of the governance of the global food system, Abigail Cooke et al. (2009a: 2) point to a number of elements that a complexity approach can contribute. Unsurprisingly, they suggest that there may be a disparity between policy and outcomes, and that we should expect the unexpected. They also stress the significance of the activities of local actors for the processes of food production, and that 'the stakes are high' in terms of the possible impacts that can occur in a complex system for local communities and the environment. Complexity is 'the defining characteristic and most policy relevant feature of the global food trade' (Cooke et al. 2009b: 219). Likewise, Keith Hipel et al. (2010: 5) point to the non-linear behaviour of emergent features in the global food system. The food price 'spike' of 2007/08 is an example of such unpredictability – see Ghosh (2010) for a clear discussion of the crisis.

Hipel et al. (2010: 4) define the global food system as consisting of 'agricultural systems, food producers, processors, packagers and consumers, distribution networks, trade agreements, agricultural policies, markets and biotechnologies'. Our argument here is to see the interlinkages between these systems and a range of others. While we would perceive the implications of complexity being unexpected outcomes, we would also point to the intersectionality between the systems associated with the global food trade. While it is impossible to illustrate all the systems involved, the global food trade is embedded in a variety of systems, such as colonialism, the international system of states and the global economic system, and has co-evolved with these. The global political system has, in part, developed in response to colonialism and post- (or neo)colonialism, at the heart of which there has been the system of food production. Most discussions of the global food system are based on a misconceived dichotomy – that the North produces manufactured goods, while the South produces agricultural products, and 'development' involves the transition from one practice to the other. To the contrary, McMichael (1998) argues, the industrialized North was built on the agricultural exports of the South. Furthermore, agricultural practices such as the slave plantation were the precursor of the factory system. Similarly, the very high proportion of the world's agricultural exports that originate in the European Union and United States (WTO 2010: Table II.15) undermines claims regarding the primary sources of agricultural exports.

Our starting point is the negotiations within the WTO, an element in the institutional order of the international system. Negotiations as part of the Doha Round represent the coalescence of various systems – the system of states, post-colonial systems, global capitalism, interspecies relations and human–biosphere relations. Agriculture has been a major issue in interstate activity, particularly in terms of relational and institutional order. As an example of institutional order, the Food and Agriculture Organization (FAO) was created in 1945 to promote cooperation in the area of agricultural production and the alleviation of hunger. More recently, agriculture has become a major stumbling block in negotiations in the World Trade Organization, currently as part of the stalled Doha Round. During the Uruguay Round (1986–94) agriculture came on to the agenda for the first time as a significant part of negotiations. Prior to that, food had been deemed too difficult an issue to be part of trade negotiations. Under the Uruguay Round, major reforms of trade in agriculture occurred, though there was 'little liberalization' (Hathaway and Ingco 1996: 39). The Uruguay Round concluded with a commitment that states would undertake much wider agricultural liberalization in the subsequent round. However, by the start of the Doha Round in 2001, there was a growing concern among developing countries that the developed world had not followed through on the limited commitments that had been made. Put simply, the dispute is over the very high levels of subsidy given by the US government and by the EU to their respective farmers. The subsidies given by these two account for almost two-thirds of the farm subsidies given by OECD countries (Morgan et al. 2006: 28). So, while developed countries are calling for increased liberalization of agricultural production in the developing world, they have sought to maintain protection for their own agricultural communities. Per Pinstrup-Andersen (2002: 1203) describes this as 'negotiations to maintain as much trade distortion for oneself as possible while putting pressure on the rest of the world to liberalise', representing the attempts by powerful states to exert power by bending the fitness landscape into the form that they want in order to suit their best interests (also see Pritchard 2009: 302).

The context in which the breakdown of the Doha negotiations has occurred is one in which there has been a transformation in agricultural practices. The increasing complexity of food production and the emergence of a global food system have occurred in conjunction with the development of higher levels of social organization. According to Evans (1998), agriculture (in the sense of purposeful growth of useful crops) dates back approximately ten thousand years. And for the majority of those ten millennia the prime activities of the majority of the world's human population have been the production of food for immediate household consumption. However, over the last 500 years the pace of change has accelerated rapidly, such that we are now at a position where 'farms have become suppliers of raw materials within a transnational agrifood sector dominated by some of the largest, most technically dynamic corporations in the world' (Friedmann 1993: 30; see also Lang 2010: 88). A global food system has come into existence, passing through two distinct formations, or regimes, over the past 150 years.

That agricultural practices have changed over time is obvious when relations with non-human species are considered. One way in which food production processes have changed is in the industrialization of meat production. Through much of the pre-industrialized world, non-human domesticated animals tend to have been regarded as more important as a means of labour power than as a source of food. There is evidence, for example, that pigs were used for threshing and planting grain in ancient Egypt (Masson 2004: 36). In pre-industrial Britain, dogs and horses were also significant sources of power, and oxen were not eaten because of their importance in ploughing (Thomas 1983). According to Marvin Harris (1987), cattle were used in India as the principal means of ploughing, provided an important form of transport, and were deployed in various agricultural processes such as winnowing and flour-making. This reliance on animals as a source of labour power, however, came to a speedy and decisive end in Europe with the development of water, wind and steam power. Although pigs, sheep and goats may be kept as 'pets', and pigs are occasionally used as working animals (in hunting, for example), this is now extremely rare in the West.

This much closer relationship between humans and non-humans reflects a pre-Fordist model of the farm, such as might have been apparent in Britain and elsewhere in Europe from the thirteenth to the nineteenth centuries, with most farms being relatively small and mixed; and with a range of animals present, despite regional tendencies. Importantly, this small-scale farming occurred on relatively sustainable pastures. The regionality of the rural landscape was apparent in the different kinds of husbandry and different kinds of products – the keeping of different varieties of chickens, pigs, sheep and cattle, and the production of varied animal products such as the many different local kinds of cheese found in Britain and France. These reflected both geographical conditions and geographical constraints, with limited transportation possibilities and the perishable nature of animal foods. The seeds of the contemporary globalized animal food system were to be found in this period, and were tied to national interests and the domestic demands of the European dominant classes.

Food production systems changed rapidly with the spread of European colonialism. Initially, luxury food goods were the prime imports from the colonies, though over time these were displaced by 'new industrial commodities' (McMichael 1997: 636), such as sugar, coffee and tea, which were consumed by the proletariat in the European colonial centre. To these were subsequently added the products from the temperate settler colonies and post-colonies such as Australia, New Zealand and the United States, products such as grains and meat. These sets of interrelationships, suggest Harriet Friedmann and Philip McMichael (1989: 96), constituted the emergence of 'the first real inter*national* system'. The settler states developed representative governments which developed into a distinct model from the political control exerted by metropolitan centres over their colonial territories.

Friedmann and McMichael (ibid.) argue that in the period 1870–1914, the industrialization of agriculture and food and the development of independent liberal states were interlinked processes. They describe this pattern of organization as the first food regime, stabilized by British hegemony and characterized by large imports of agricultural products from the colonies into the European core. These processes can be seen as co-evolutionary: the food regime and a system of states, built on a European model, developed in tandem.

The rapid development of capitalism as a global system can also be seen as a parallel development. Jason Moore (2009: 5) makes the point that 'at base, every great wave of capital accumulation has unfolded through and upon a greatly expanded ecological surplus'. Hence it can be argued that close links can be drawn between the spread of European colonies and the pattern of agriculture production. Furthermore, this links back into capitalist development, as agricultural products provided cheap food commodities for the industrial working classes in the core. Complexity theorists would cite this as an example of positive feedback, the transfer of nutrients from the periphery to the core amplifying the power of the colonial centre.

Concurrently the practice of colonialism brought with it incredible changes in human relations with specific animal species. Countries such as Argentina and Brazil underwent 'cattleization' in order to satisfy the enormous demand for meat products and to exploit the potential profits to be made from the trade. In the United States, the

'Great Bovine Switch' (Rifkin 1994: 74–6) saw the replacement of buffalo with cattle through the sponsoring of the hunting of buffalo, which led to their virtual and almost instantaneous elimination from the western rangelands after thousands of years of successful habitation. This switch from buffalo to cattle was not only a colonialism of species, but a strategic undermining of the ways of life of Native Americans, whose fates were tied in co-evolved histories with those of the buffalo. The extermination of a major food source was a policy underpinning the forced resettlement of Native Americans on reservations (Hine and Faragher 2000: 317). Certain other wild species, such as prairie dogs, were also exterminated as pests (Nibert 2002: 45). Hence the impacts of the changes related to colonial practices of food production can be seen as rippling outwards through the systems of other species.

Landscapes were also transformed by agricultural practices. Plantation agriculture and the production of sugar, coffee and tea for export fundamentally altered the rural landscape of many regions of the global South throughout the nineteenth century, and long before it. The European colonization of the Americas would involve the development of an internationalized food system through ranching, which co-existed with the localized farming model in European regions. Extensive cattle ranching and sheep grazing on relatively unstable grasslands were the modus operandi of the farming system introduced by European colonization of the USA, South America, Australia and Africa from the sixteenth to the nineteenth centuries. This system involved particular forms of exploitative social relations. On the one hand, there was the use of slave labour, displaced indigenous peoples or exploited rural peasantries. On the other, landowning classes of sheep and cattle barons prospered, as did the exchequers of European nations through increased shipping wealth (Franklin 1999: 128–9).

As colonies drew in burgeoning immigrant populations, the ranching system, exploitative of both land and labour, became the model for an independent national system of production. Mexico provides a good example of the environmental impact of this system. Spanish conquistadors were followed by colonial pastoralists who assumed control of fertile agricultural land in the central highlands and began grazing sheep, shepherded by African slaves. By 1565, there were 2 million sheep in the region and by 1581 the indigenous Indians had been decimated by an epidemic imported by the settler community. Fields were turned into densely stocked pastures, which by 1600 had been transformed into thorn desert (Cockburn 1995: 33–4).

In addition to species changes, the colonial model of meat

production was enabled by technological changes such as the development of refrigerated shipping, which made it possible to ship meat to Europe from the USA, South America and Australasia (Franklin 1999: 130). Such ventures were particularly profitable in South America, primarily in Argentina in the eighteenth century, and in Brazil in the nineteenth (Velten 2007: 153). In addition, meat-processing plants were established in order to produce cheap meat products for working-class consumption, such as the famous Leibig spread, which was produced at the English-owned factory at Fray Bentos, in Uruguay (Rifkin 1994: 147). This enabled Europeans to consume greater quantities of meat, but in order to make best use of the potential market in Europe, the price had to be minimized by intensifying production and saving labour costs through increased mechanization. From the last quarter of the nineteenth century and through the twentieth, profitability from livestock farming has increased through intensification and market expansion as a complex, integrated and globalized system of animal food has developed.

The United States led the way in the mechanization of animal agriculture. By the 1920s, millions of diversified small family farms had been replaced by specialist, large, corporate enterprises. Important in this transition was the development and use of tractors, replacing mules and horses in ploughing and hauling. Technological innovation led to the development of a grain surplus in the USA, which in turn promoted the use of cheap grain by expanding meat producers (Nibert 2002: 102–3). Despite this, prior to the 1950s in Europe and America, most farms were family owned or rented and family run, rather than corporate, and many farming practices, though larger in scale, remained similar to those deployed a century before. From the 1950s through to the 1970s, one of the most important technological developments was the development of factory farming, which began with the confinement of chickens for both eggs and meat and was a means of significantly increased 'efficiency' and thus profit. Intensive farming maximizes land use through intensive housing, avoids labour time as animals are kept *in situ* and fed automatically. The saving of labour costs has been dramatic. For example, in the USA one person may manage up to 150,000 laying hens in an intensive system (Mason and Finelli 2006).

The first food regime broke down with the collapse of British power from the start of the twentieth century, and the global breakdown of trade resulting from the First World War. A second food regime was not established until after the Second World War, when the US model was diffused to the newly independent former European colonies as part of processes of modernization-theory-inspired development. McMichael points to processes of 'replication' and 'substitution'. The US model of farm ownership was replicated in the developing world, and traditional agricultural products were substituted by 'commercial cropping to provide agro-industrial inputs and luxury foods for affluent urban and foreign diets' (McMichael 1997: 640). The second food regime can be seen as the inverse of the first. Whereas British industrialization was built on the basis of the flow of cheap food supplies into the core, the second regime has consisted of the outflow of food commodities from the United States, and subsequently Europe, to the rest of the world.

Within agricultural studies there is considerable debate as to whether a 'third food regime' has now been entered, where footloose capital has the possibility of switching its production facilities at very short notice dependent on local conditions (for a discussion of the literature, see Bonanno and Constance 2001). Jan Douwe van der Ploeg (2010: 99) argues that this new food regime is built on a conjunction between the increased industrialization of production, the appearance of a world food market, and the growing power of 'food empires'. Three characteristics can be associated with this regime. First, a break between agriculture and geographic and seasonal conditions. One example could perhaps be the kiwi fruit, which, formerly as the Chinese gooseberry, became a global product. Initially pushed by the New Zealand government at a time when their farmers had a monopoly on growing the fruit, it was subsequently taken up by farmers in Italy, France, Spain, the USA and Chile (Bonanno et al. 1994: 10). A second feature is the interlinking of areas of poverty and wealth, so that high-value products such as mangetout are produced in parts of Africa and air-freighted to Europe and North America. Associated with these first two features is the breakdown of seasonality so that certain products such as strawberries, once a summer treat in the northern hemisphere, are available in the depths of winter. A third characteristic is increased complexity, which makes the global food system extremely sensitive to minor shocks, so that small perturbations can result in major upheavals (see Ploeg 2010).

Moore argues that each period of rapid expansion of capitalism has been the result of the availability of cheap food. In other words, the global expansion of capitalism is closely interlinked with the development of agriculture. The capitalist world differs from pre-capitalist formations in that peasant farmers have been forced off the land to be replaced by capitalist relations in the countryside. This led to an enormous increase in productivity and increased levels of production, thereby reducing prices. Indeed, 'the road to the modern world, it seems, has been paved with cheap food' (Moore 2010: 395). 'Yield honeymoons', as new crops from the Old World were introduced to the New World (e.g. sugar) and vice versa (e.g. potatoes), contributed to the rise of capitalism. These enabled vast increases in production at the cost of little input of capital. Each successive hegemonic wave has been built on an agricultural revolution, which occurred both domestically and internationally. 'Hegemonies are ecological projects, and each great power wove together internal and external agricultural revolutions in the drive to world primacy' (ibid.: 397).

We are now, however, maybe reaching the 'end of the road'. The possibility of obtaining a new 'yield honeymoon' requires an unexploited external frontier. While small pockets of unexploited resources may still exist, Moore argues 'their relative weight in the world-system is incomparably lower today than it was in 1873, or even 1973' (ibid.: 409). This has signal implications for the future development of the capitalist system. Central to Moore's argument is the drawing of a clear link between the development of capitalism, agricultural production and the relational order in the international system.

Moore's argument points to the ways in which nature has been commodified. Through techniques of genetic modification, capitalist relations have been introduced right down to the cellular level. This indicates the intersectionality of capitalism with the environment in a most direct fashion. Industrialized agriculture, including the production of genetically modified crops (often used for animal feed) and 'food' animals, has been seen as a solution to food poverty. However, Gabriela Pechlaner and Gerado Otero (2008), based on a discussion of Mexico, argue that the introduction of biotechnology has a negative impact on developing countries, particularly with respect to employment levels in agriculture.

There are further moves to 'democratize' diet, by encouraging Western intensive animal agriculture in regions of the South and, according to the Worldwatch Institute's *State of the World* (2004), citing UN Food and Agriculture Organization data, one of the most serious risks to the global environment is the expansion of intensive animal agriculture in Asia, South America and the Caribbean. Industrialized animal agriculture is, they claim, a driving force behind all of the contemporary and pressing environmental problems that we face – deforestation, water scarcity, air and water pollution, climate change and loss of biodiversity; in addition to issues of social injustice.

For levels of meat eating and meat production to have intensified across the globe from the mid-nineteenth century until today, on the scale that they have, the support of nation-states and international organizations has been requisite. In the aftermath of the Second World War, European states and the USA set out to reduce malnutrition and hunger among their own populations with the promotion of cheap meat and other animal products. Rising levels of meat and dairy consumption became associated with social progress, as meat was not only a historic marker of status in the West, but promoted as necessary for good health. This was also promoted internationally by the United Nations, which, in the 1960s and 1970s, emphasized the necessity of increasing animal protein production and making such food increasingly available in poor countries (see Rifkin 1994: 131). It is difficult not to conclude that such initiatives were strongly influenced by Western governments driven by the corporate interests of the multinational corporations based in their territories. Certainly, such initiatives ignore the fact that pulses and grains were the most common sources of protein across the globe, and that the ability of developing countries to feed their own populations successfully was significantly compromised by the replacement of staples such as corn, millet and rice with monocultures to supply the livestock feed industry. In the 1980s and much of the 1990s, the Common Agricultural Policy of the European Community/European Union also encouraged intensive animal farming through systems of grants and subsidies that explicitly favoured the equipment and buildings of intensive production rather than improvements to land on which animals might be raised (Johnson 1991: 181).

The extent of the deleterious environmental impact of agribusiness was detailed in the UN FAO report *Livestock's Long Shadow*, which concluded that animal agriculture is a greater contributor to global warming than the combined effects of all forms of transportation (Steinfeld et al. 2006). The increased deployment of Western agricultural models and the spread of Western food practices have significant implications for the environment in terms of undermining biodiversity, localized pollution, soil damage, rainforest depletion, and contributing 18 per cent of all greenhouse gases. The technologies of animal agriculture have made meat production incredibly profitable and also incredibly resource hungry and wasteful. Considering the resources involved in breeding and growing a single beef cow, journalist Michael Pollan argues: 'We have turned what was once a solar-powered ruminant into the very last thing we need: a fossil-fuel machine' (Pollan 2003).

Changes in the global climate system feed back into the food production system, contributing to the complex web of drivers of climate change. Estimating these changes is deeply problematic given the complex links involved. However, David Lobell and Marshall Burke (2010: 178) point to three interlinked areas which will impact on food production as a result of climate change. First, climate change itself; secondly, the response of crops to changes in the climate; and thirdly, adaptations in the global food economy. These three areas point to the interconnected character of food production within the biosphere and within the global economy. The possibilities of adaptation will also be closely linked to the activities of states as they try to ensure (with differing levels of capability) sufficient food for their populations.

It may be that with concern about climate change on the part of international organizations, and the incontrovertible evidence of the role of animal farming in contributing to greenhouses gases, impoverishment of vulnerable populations and different kinds of local and global pollution, national and international policy proclivities will shift. At the time of writing, however, the complex international system of animal agriculture seems set to expand.

To return to our starting point, a number of these systems intersected in the Doha discussions. The clash over agriculture reflects an attempt by powerful states to bend the fitness landscape to suit their own interests. The failure to achieve this, and the subsequent breakdown of the Doha Round, indicates the shifting power within the international system. State systems, particularly those of North America and Europe, were concerned to maintain their food security, while at the same time seeking liberalization of agricultural sectors in other parts of the world. The less-developed world sought greater liberalization of agricultural sectors of the North and had sufficient power to resist the pressure for greater liberalization on their part.

We have argued that there is a range of complex systems related to global food production which have co-evolved, and whose intersectionality has led to specific patterns of development. In other words, systems of states, global capitalism and the global food system have all developed complex and overlapping systems. There is not a linear causality in this history, but by considering these developments as co-evolutionary it is possible to see that none of these systems developed independently. In particular we focused on the co-evolution of the state system, global capitalism, the agricultural system and the biosphere. In short, it is not possible to understand developments in the international system, particularly those related to dominant powers in the system, without considering them within a related set of systems which includes global agriculture. Our intention has also been to indicate that food production systems are embedded within the environment. They are affected by and in turn affect the environmental system in which food production and trade occur. Thus we can see that there is a link between the system of states and the biosphere. It is this topic in particular, and the problems that international relations has had as a discipline in analysing environmental issues, that we turn to in the next chapter.

5 · Complex ecologism

In this chapter, drawing on the complexity understandings of systems as co-constituted and co-evolving that we have developed in the previous three chapters, we will suggest the need to account for changes in the biosphere resulting from human endeavours together with an understanding of the ways in which multiple and complex inequalities shape the environmental impact of different populations and raise regionally specific issues of insecurity for humans, other species and scapes. In order to theorize the environment as implicated in human systems and as fundamentally altered by them, we need to draw on various strands of thinking in 'green' political theory, or political ecologism. We will be developing elements of eco-socialism, ecofeminism and liberation ecologism in arguing that human relations to environments are characterized by social intersectionality and complex inequalities resulting from the interplay of complex systems of social relations such as colonialism, capitalism and patriarchy. Complexity approaches can help capture the patterns of these relations. So, the chapter draws on complexity in order to understand, first, the co-constitution of human communities and the 'natural environment', and secondly, that human relations with non-human species are shaped by persistent relations of power around gender, class, ethnicity, locality, and so on. This enables a move towards a posthuman international relations in which the embodied condition of the human species, and our co-constituted relations with other species and natural systems, frames our intellectual projects.

International relations, security and the environment

The term 'environmental security' has rapidly entered the lexicon of discussions about security, at academic, popular and policy levels. Increasing concerns about the environment, most evident in the issue of climate change, have combined with changing notions of what constitutes security. However, 'environmental security' is a much-contested concept. As Levy notes, 'both "environment" and "security" are flexible enough to mean almost anything one wishes' (Levy 1995: 37). There is no consensus on what is meant by 'security' and what is included under the term 'environment'. Global environmental change presents an incredible challenge for current approaches to security in the discipline of international relations, because, as Hugh Dyer (2001: 68) points out, it presents 'concerns which are qualitatively different from traditional security threats'.

Given this, it is unsurprising that international relations has had a problematic engagement with environmental questions. This is perhaps because a subject that is analytically state-centred (albeit with a focus on interstate relations) has difficulty in dealing with problems that transcend state borders. Despite a broadening of the security agenda, a more traditional approach to thinking about the ways in which environmental issues may impact global relations is apparent: environmental degradation as a cause of conflict. This focus on the environment as a source of conflict has not only been a concern to writers within international relations, it has been an issue discussed by politicians, the popular media and international organizations. A United Nations Environment Programme report, for example, cited environmental issues as being central to the conflict in Darfur (UNEP 2007: 8).

In a review of the literature on environment and security, Nicole Detraz (2009) suggests that three main approaches can be identified: environmental conflict, environmental security and ecological security. This typology usefully distinguishes quite different approaches that have previously all been included under the umbrella term of environmental security, and is summarized in the table below.

A clear example of the environmental conflict literature is Michael Klare's discussion of resource wars. Access to resources is 'becoming an increasingly prominent feature of American security policy' (Klare 2001: 6). Wars of the future 'will largely be fought over the control and possession of vital economic goods – especially resources needed for the functioning of modern industrial resources' (ibid.: 213). For many, the US and British invasion of Iraq would seem to present a clear example of such a resource war. Paul Wolfowitz's comment that 'economically we just had no choice in Iraq. The country swims in a sea of oil' (quoted in Kaldor et al. 2007: 1) would appear to confirm the invasion as a clear instance of 'petroimperialism' (Jhaveri 2004).

While retaining a focus on access to resources, other authors have provided a more nuanced account of the relations between resource availability and conflict, at both a state and sub-state level. Michael Renner (2002: 6) argues that, in 2001, about one quarter of the approximately fifty violent conflicts in the world had 'a strong resources dimension'. Renner draws attention to the point that it is not only

TABLE 5.1 Environment and security

	Referent/Level of analysis	Perspective	Source of insecurity	Key examples
Environmental conflict	State	Realist	Environmental change, or resource depletion	Klare
Environmental security	Individual or sub-state community	Liberal	Environmental change/ degradation, or resource depletion	Eckersley, UN
Ecological security	Biosphere	Ecological	Human activity	Dalby

resource scarcity which can prompt conflict; resource wealth can also provide a significant contribution to conflict. Conflict diamonds are a notable means by which conflict in Africa has been financed (Lujala et al. 2005), while in Colombia control over cocaine production has been a major source of finance for both sides in the civil war. Philippe Le Billon (2005: 23) argues that 'natural resources have become the economic mainstay of most wars in the post-Cold War context'.

It is, as Julia Trombetta (2008: 592) has observed, the environmental conflict notion which has 'captured' policy-oriented discussions of environmental issues. John Reid, former British Defence Secretary, warned of the increased risk of violent conflict related to environmental change (Russell and Morris 2006), while the potential links between environmental change and conflict were discussed by the United Nations Security Council in April 2007. Jon Barnett (2001: 71–91) provides a detailed discussion of the ways in which the Clinton administration incorporated environmental security issues into the national security policies of the United States.

Detraz utilizes the term environmental security to encompass the literature more influenced by the discussions of human security. As Eckersley notes, these analyses reflect the new 'expansive security discourses' (Eckersley 2009: 90). This literature focuses on the individual or immediate community at risk from environmental change or degradation. One clear example of this has been the development of the notion of 'human security'. The term originates in a 1994 United Nations Development Programme report, *New Dimensions of Human Security* (UNDP 1994). Since 1994, the term has entered both popular and academic discussions of security, though within academia it has been a source of considerable controversy (see, in particular, the debate in *Security Dialogue*, 35(3), 2004). In *New Dimensions of Human Security*, the environment was included among a list of seven issues that required addressing to ensure human security. While the human security literature provides a welcome relief from the state-centred character of much of the analysis, the focus frequently remains on threats from the environment to humans. Such approaches have been positively appraised as a 'human-centred perspective' within policy forums (Annan 2005). Yet they can also be criticized on these same grounds in terms of a failure to consider the wider biosphere and the impact of human activities within that broader context. In addition, human security, often with a focus on the global poor, has been insufficiently attentive to cross-cutting forms of social inequality – for example, the feminization of poverty.

Ecological security, by contrast, refers to those analyses which focus 'on the negative impacts human behaviors have on the environment' (Detraz 2009: 351). We consider the work of Simon Dalby to be an example of such an approach. Dalby (2002b) has been critical of elements of theorizing within the environmental security field, and has raised important questions about conceptualizing environmental problems in security terms. While he goes as far as to suggest that we should consider whether to abandon the notion of 'environmental security' altogether (Dalby 2009: 4), he ultimately draws back from this. He argues that human beings have changed the 'circumstances of life' in ways that mean that the environment we are attempting to secure is one which is increasingly artificial. Human ways of life have modified our environment to the extent that we have remade the environmental context of our own existence. Dalby (ibid.: 97–104) uses the geologically inflected term developed by Paul Crutzen, 'the anthropocene', in order to capture this. Dalby's account is influenced by certain kinds of political ecologism and draws on some complexity approaches. This 'ecological security' approach represents a significant improvement on 'environmental security' and, certainly, on approaches emphasizing 'environmental conflict'. While sophisticated, this analysis still underplays the political significance of social difference. Complex systems of power in the social world are cross-cutting and intersected. While Dalby considers the problematic effects of carboniferous consumer capitalism, and relations between rich and poor regions and peoples, in his analysis, he scarcely considers gender. Our articulation of complex systems developed below deploys the feminist concept of social intersectionality in trying to capture the range of multiple, complex inequalities that shape human relations with 'the environment' and resultant environmental insecurities.

Despite this range of approaches to environmental security, specific interventions can be seen as problematic, and this raises questions about the application of 'security', however broadly defined, in analysing both environmental problems and associated risks for human populations, and intra-human vulnerabilities. International relations, with its tradition of state-based analysis, has difficulties in dealing with the global character of many environmental issues. The globalized character of some environmental problems needs to be fully appreciated, while the differential impact of problem effects in the context of profound and persistent inequities is also recognized.

Global warming is the clearest and most pressing example of a global environmental problem. Other environmental issues may not be so 'global' in impact. Land pollution is often localized; humans pollute land where they bury industrial and consumer waste or locate industrial processing. However, the international trade in commercial and industrial waste, and the practices of dumping waste in international waters and on other countries, adds a global dimension. The pollution of seas is global, as almost all seawater is connected; as is air pollution, carried over considerable distances by prevailing winds (Yearley 1996: 33–4). The loss of species biodiversity has also come to be defined as an environmental problem for the maintenance of healthy ecosystems, and the extent of this collapse has been labelled the 'sixth extinction' (Leakey and Lewin 1996).

This said, most authors argue that the impacts of global climate change will have greater impact on the South. Stephen Devereux and Jenny Edwards argue that the effects of global warming will be 'globally stratifying'. Those countries where drought is already a problem are likely to become drier. These same countries are more dependent on agriculture, where the possibilities for diversification are more limited. It is likely, they argue, that 'the prevalence and depth of hunger will deteriorate in those countries and population groups where food security is already significant' (Devereux and Edwards 2004: 28). This has historical precedent – as David Goldblatt (1996) argues, the exploitation of the South's environment commenced during the colonial period and has continued since the end of the European empires. In this sense the 'North' has exported much of its environmentally damaging industrialization, making the notion of environmental security on a national basis nonsensical.

In addition, the extent to which gender inequalities differentiate human causes of environmental changes and their effects is absent from most accounts in the environmental security literature. Ariel Salleh argues that the impact of gender inequalities is absent from the notion of ecological footprint that has been used in an essentialist way, as it differentiates humanity only in terms of Northern or Southern location (Salleh 2009: 11). This ignores the gendered qualities of paid and unpaid work and of transport and energy use and the feminization of poverty. Collectively, as Meike Spitzner notes, these inequalities mean that both the causes and the consequences of global warming are gendered (2009: 218–22). An exception here is the work of Ursula Oswald Spring (2007, 2008a, 2008b), who has suggested a conceptualization in terms of 'human, gender and environmental security' or 'HUGE'. Oswald Spring promotes a 'broad' understanding of gender in terms of vulnerability rather than, as she suggests (somewhat simply), the more traditional approach of inequality. A key strength of this work is the placing of gender on environmental security agendas and, of equal significance, an attempt to mainstream issues of intra-personal violence as systemic and structural in terms of vulnerability (of elders, women and children) in situations of environmental and other conflict. However, there are a number of drawbacks with the HUGE formulation. First, the conceptualization of gender conflates the specific vulnerabilities of adult women and elders and children of both sexes. It is insufficiently complex and, we would argue, does not see these differences as intersectionalized – that is, as radically differentiated through the cross-cutting, qualitatively and quantitatively impacting effects of inequities and differences of age and cultural context. In an undifferentiated model of 'patriarchy' it does not account, for example, for regional systemic formations of gender exclusion (Walby 2007). Secondly, the notion of gender security as vulnerability does not draw together the links between the vulnerabilities of communities (of indigenous minorities, for example) and those of non-human animals, and the co-dependencies of these communities with/in 'natural' systems. The use of the term 'security' may certainly have helped with policy mainstreaming, but it is framed by a static and homogeneous analysis of gender relations and carries a risk of statism associated with mainstreaming generally. These problems of social difference – of region, location, gender, age, cultural specificity, species, and so on – require a complex systems approach.

Furthermore, and ironically, territorial states are in many ways foundational for securitization approaches, but as Dalby (2002c: 5) notes, charging states with responsibility for the environment may well be a case of foxes guarding chickens. States have been drivers for modernization, putting in place infrastructure dependent on carbon fuels and high levels of resource use, in large part by establishing a capitalist system (Latouche 1993). The fundamental question is whether states, and the international organizations of which they are members, can construct new physical and institutional infrastructures which move us away from an ever-expanding use of resources. Much of what we have seen in terms of the internationalization of environmental policy involves an assumption that economic growth can be compatible with ecological sustainability and 'there is a techno-institutional fix for the present problems' (Hajer 1995: 32). The politics of ecologism implies radical departures from our currently normative economic, political and social practices in wealthy Western/Northern states, and has been extremely pessimistic concerning the ability of states to deliver change

(Sachs et al. 1998). Robyn Eckersley (2004: 241), however, is confident that a decline in territorially based governance accompanying globalization, coupled with a radical institutional reform, will make possible the consideration of ecological concern. She suggests a move from liberal democracies to 'ecological democracies', where those collectivities subject to ecological risk must be involved in or represented in decision-making that may involve or generate ecological risk. Yet it is most uncertain that globalization has actually reduced the power of states, and international political organizations remain limited in both authority and power. In addition, as we will see in Chapter 6, there are significant difficulties in the representation of non-human beings and things which would form part of Eckersley's eco-social collectivities. We seem far from the realization of ecological democracy. Currently, reforms undertaken by states and supranational institutions tend to be processes in which environmental questions are subsumed under a bureaucratic rationality of resource managerialism (Luke 1999). The logic of capitalist development, albeit linked with 'sustainability', is foundational for environmental policy initiatives (Clack and York 2005). State-derived security, as Mark Neocleous (2008: 185–6) suggests, is a 'gift' that we might like to return.

In addition, this statist focus has resulted in a tendency to associate issues of security with military solutions. Daniel Deudney has argued that the use of the term 'security' links the environment too closely to questions of national survival. Such an association may lead to inappropriate policies, especially the prioritizing of military solutions over diplomatic methods (Deudney 1990: 465–9). There is evidence that the leaky nature of environmental insecurities has also led organizations concerned with transnational security to take non-military threats seriously. NATO had a team of researchers employed from the late 1990s with the task of ascertaining which environmental matters might contribute to international conflict (as discussed by Dalby 2002a: 97). A report produced by a group of retired US military personnel concluded that 'climate change can act as a threat multiplier for instability in some of the most volatile regions of the world, and it presents significant national security challenges for the United States' (CNA 2009). Some suggest, therefore, that we have witnessed a 'greening of the military', wherein security organizations are increasingly deployed in realizing environmental goals (Matthew 2002: 118). Yet there may be unintended consequences of this link. Extending the notion of security to the environmental sphere, according to Brock (1997: 21), might 'actually broaden the range of arguments for justifying military action'. Hence a link to security might have unexpected and undesirable consequences: the prioritization of coercive solutions over diplomatic approaches to environmental issues, and the legitimization of other forms of intervention.

Finally, the environmental security literature tends to reproduce a dualistic understanding of human relations to 'the environment' in which 'we' humans are either threatened by or pose a threat to 'nature' (Barnett 2001: 67). Such a dualism becomes apparent in the typology advocated by Detraz, in which either the environment is a threat to the state (environmental conflict) or the individual (environmental security), or the biosphere itself is under threat (ecological security). As Andrew Dobson (2006: 180; emphasis in original) has argued, this *'idea of a boundary has always existed'* and is arguably 'crucial to our self-conception as human beings'. For Bruno Latour (2004: 53), 'the terms "nature" and "society" do not designate domains of reality: instead they refer to a quite specific form of public organization'. Latour argues that we need to adapt current institutions to give a voice to a single collective of humans and non-humans. Likewise, Rob Walker (2006: 189) argues that politics itself is constituted by 'a profound rupture between man and nature'. In other words, there is an ontological issue which the environmental security literature highlights most profoundly. Dualism underestimates the complex interlinkages in the biosphere by focusing on the security of one referent rather than allowing an analysis which permits the examination of the complex and overlapping processes that constitute environmental problems. The term 'environment' itself is a catch-all category which homogenizes the diversity of non-human life and encompasses a multiplicity of incredibly varied non-human plant and animal species. Such an understanding of the 'environment' and the distinction of the human species from it is a product of Western histories and sensibilities (Soper 1995). Human modifications of our habitat(s) are shaped by histories of social relations, economic practices and formations of political power. These problems of dualism, an inability to take on board a range of multiple intersected inequalities in the analyses of 'environmental issues', and of a tendency for the reproduction of the status quo through managerialist understandings of human relations with 'nature', can be seen very clearly below as we consider the case of environmental governance in the European Union.

Securitization and environmental governance in Europe

The European Union (EU) is lauded by some as pushing for some of the most radical initiatives in addressing the causes and consequences of environmental problems. This section considers the nature of current environmental policy in the European Union. We will argue that discourses which underpin EU environmental policy are blind to issues of social inequality and that policies for mitigating environmental problems assume that both the members and regions of Europe and the populations therein are all equally placed. While there is a rhetoric of environmental threat and securitizing initiatives, the strategic framework for EU policy stresses adaptation to changed circumstances and is inadequate for rising to the challenges of global environmental change that we have so far discussed.

The EU has, and only very recently, begun to prioritize environmental policy. Since 2005, climate change has entered the mainstream of EU politics, being debated regularly at meetings of the European Council (Jordan et al. 2010: 3). Despite this very recent 'green turn', the EU, at least in its policy statements, seeks to lead the world in responding to environmental problems such as climate change. Between 1990 and 2000 a dramatic shift was seen to take place, with the European Commission claiming in 2000 that tackling climate change was the central and overriding policy challenge the EU faced (Oberthür and Kelly 2008). Some have made strong claims for European leadership on environmental policy – for example, asserting that EU intervention effectively 'saved' the Kyoto Protocol after the withdrawal of the US administration's support under George W. Bush in 2001 (Bretherton and Vogler 2006: 110). The EU has been seen as playing an important role in the international arena on environmental policy in terms of pushing for time-bound targets, implementing what are seen as 'novel' policy instruments, such as carbon emissions trading, and promoting guiding norms such as the precautionary principle (Jordan et al. 2010: 7).

Yet despite such initiatives and assertions, in concrete terms, such as levels of carbon dioxide emissions, the EU seems to be heading very much in the wrong direction (Helm 2008: 214). The EU is a fairly large emitter of carbon dioxide, for example (contributing 10.5 per cent of global emissions in 2006; EEA 2008). There is something of a disjuncture, therefore, between apparent commitment and policy on the ground. In addition, for member states, the EU has become a key focus for environmental policy, with most policy made by it, or in association with it. Thus, from 2000 we can speak of the successful 'Europeanization' of environmental policy (ibid.: 7).

In the EU environment action programme, *Environment 2010: Our Future, Our Choice*, four priority areas are identified: climate change; nature and biodiversity; environment and health; and natural resources and waste. This is the latest development within the framework of the 6th Environmental Action Programme, which was adopted in July 2002 and runs until 2012. The programme promoted the integration of environmental protection requirements and sustainable developments across other areas of policy-making (such as competitiveness, employment, health and quality of life). The EU has made climate change the most pressing of its concerns, yet if we consider this framework document, alongside the concerns and strategies articulated in the 2009 White Paper *Adapting to Climate Change: Towards a European Framework for Action*, we find that policy is structured through conceptions of environmental securitization, and proposes responses that are less radical, on closer reading, than they may at first appear.

The 2009 paper sets out a framework to reduce the EU's vulnerability to the impact of climate change in the context of the United Nations Framework Convention on Climate Change (UNFCCC) and sets out the parameters of EU policy beyond 2012. There are two key policy responses to climate change emphasized:

> Firstly, and importantly, we must reduce our greenhouse gas emissions (GHG) (i.e. take mitigation action) and secondly we must take adaptation action to deal with the unavoidable impacts. The EU's recently agreed climate change legislation puts in place the concrete measures to reach the EU's commitment to reduce emissions to 20% below 1990 levels by 2020 ... However, even if the world succeeds in limiting and then reducing GHG emissions, our planet will take time to recover from the greenhouse gases already in the atmosphere. Thus we will be faced with the impact of climate change for at least the next 50 years. We need therefore to take measures to adapt. (European Commission 2009: 3)

The references to the UNFCCC make acknowledgement of the human causes of environmental damage, in particular of global warming. Our need to adapt and mitigate is clearly set in the context of environmental risks and threats – of what is broadly considered a radical notion of environmental security. Yet the European Commission also considers that environmental risks challenge the security of European member states and the Union itself in more traditional ways:

> Failure to adapt could have security implications. The EU is therefore strengthening its analysis and early warning systems and integrating climate change into existing tools such as conflict prevention mechanisms and security sector reform. The effects of climate change on migratory flows should also be considered in the broader EU reflection on security, development and migration policies. (Ibid.: 15)

The frame of environmental policy is thus a rather conventional notion of securitization from external threats, both human and 'natural'. Europe stands as an entity that may be secured in this discursive regime, and one whose social fabric is at risk.

The notions of 'mitigation' and 'adaptation' themselves are taken from the Intergovernmental Panel on Climate Change (2007). 'Mitigation' is 'anthropogenic intervention', as in the above example, to reduce the stresses on the climate system by reducing emissions. Adaptation is rather vaguer and is taken to mean an 'adjustment in natural or human systems' in response to actual or expected effects of global warming (Hulme and Neufeldt 2010: 6). We might, then, perhaps expect, given the level of political rhetoric and the burgeoning policy documentation, that assertive and concrete policy initiatives might be necessary in response to what is clearly perceived as a threat.

However, in its incarnation in EU policy, adaptation seems to mean that minimal change is required. For example, while a shift in patterns of investment towards the realization of a low-carbon economy is seen as necessary, this is conceptualized in the very conservative terms of: 'promoting energy efficiency and the uptake of green products' (European Commission 2009: 6). In this literature, citizens are cast as consumers of both 'environmental goods' such as air, water and food 'free of pollution and contaminants', and potentially of 'greener' products:

> People demand that the air they breathe, the water they drink and the food they eat is free of pollution and contaminants; they want to live undisturbed by noise; and they want to enjoy the beauty of the countryside, unspoilt coastlines and mountain areas. They also want a world that is not threatened by climate change.
>
> A healthy environment is essential to long term prosperity and quality of life and citizens in Europe demand a high level of environmental protection. Future economic development and increasing prosperity will put pressure on the planet's capacity to sustain demands for resources or to absorb pollution. At the same time, high environmental standards are an engine for innovation and business opportunities. Overall, society must work to de-couple environmental impacts and degradation from economic growth. Business must operate in a more eco-efficient way, in other words producing the same or more products with less input and less waste, and consumption patterns have to become more sustainable. (European Commission 2001)

Undergirding this notion of the environmental consumer is a notion of a pure environment free from threat, and the language in which these claims are framed is one of 'risk' and, in particular, of 'threatened' public environmental goods. Yet, despite periodic acknowledgements that environmental problems such as various forms of pollution, and in particular global warming, are caused by patterns of human behaviour, the description of the problem and the proposed solution articulate a dualist conception of the environment and 'society'.

Certainly, the non-human cannot take centre stage, for: '[p]riority should be given to adaptation measures that would generate net social and/or economic benefits' (European Commission 2009: 8). This effectively subsumes environmental goals within other policy priorities. We have suggested earlier in this book that questions of social (in)justice are closely tied to the nature of environmental problems, but adaptation measures do not address the pressing issues of social inequality in relation to sustainable behaviour, practices and institutions. Rather, 'adaptation' very much means business as usual. Particularly emphasized is that:

> Adaptation should be mainstreamed in all of the EU's external policies. In trade policy adaptation should be incorporated, notably through the liberalisation of trade in environmental goods and services and in the elaboration of Free Trade Agreements (FTAs). There is a huge potential for green trade which can contribute to enhancing growth and creating jobs. (Ibid.: 15)

The key trajectory, then, is the 'greening' of both business and of consumer behaviour:

> Working with the market through business and consumer interests will contribute to more sustainable production and consumption patterns. Business should not simply be penalised for failure but schemes should be introduced to reward good performance. Consumers need useful information to allow them to choose environmentally benevolent products, thus driving the market. (European Commission 2001)

The notion that environmental change will bring with it increased inequalities is acknowledged only very generally:

> Adaptation will require solidarity among EU Member States to ensure that disadvantaged regions and regions most affected by climate change will be capable of taking the measures needed to adapt. (European Commission 2009: 6)

Remarkably, the differences in wealth, resources and other indicators of social inequality do not feature at all in the Commission's planning.

There is no discussion of differentiated targets for implementation of mitigation policies and little, if anything, said on the need for a differentiated understanding of, and planning for, adaptation. Rather, all states are responsible for delivering the policies for mitigation that the EU has already attempted to implement, and those that do not deliver as they might are castigated without reference to the economic, social and political placement of EU members:

> ... much of our wastes still go to older and less well managed facilities, partly due to the failure of Member States to properly implement Community waste legislation. The impacts of waste management and waste transport are, therefore, still problematic in many areas of the Community. (European Commission 2001)

Furthermore, the statist framing of policy trajectories is explicitly and uncompromisingly liberal, and some alliance between environmental social protest and liberalization serves to shape the future composition of the Union:

> Environmental protest was a feature of the resistance to the old regimes in the Central and Eastern European Candidate Countries. This awareness needs to be built on by showing that environment and economic development are not mutually exclusive. Rather, the message needs to be passed that the Candidate Countries have the chance to construct a modern and prosperous society that maintains unspoilt landscapes and countryside. (Ibid.)

Environmental policy in the EU exemplifies all three articulations of the notion of 'environmental security' with which we began this chapter. First, at the level of rhetoric alone, there are some elements of the 'ecological security' approach outlined by Dalby. In the language of threat and risk, there is also some acknowledgement that it is we humans as a species that are insecure, and we have made other species and even planetary life insecure through our economic and social practices. In the analysis of the threats to European societies and 'natural' spaces, there are elements of a more traditional securitization approach that carries the language of 'environmental conflict'. Finally, the more common notion of 'environmental security' is invoked in a policy analysis which sees human communities as threatened by environmental change and resource depletion and offers statist and supra-statist solutions to the problems raised by these developments.

As we have seen in the critiques of environmental security, guaranteeing security for particular populations is tricky as environmental problems are international in scope, or at least move across national and regional boundaries. They also exacerbate existing disparities between rich and poor regions, states and communities and are resistant to technological fixing (Luke 1999). Most significantly, however, as we have seen, they constitute a significant challenge to prevailing social norms, both in the West and increasingly elsewhere across the globe. The key trajectory of environmental policy in the EU is summarized in this statement:

> Climate change is a significant challenge to modern society. It must be met at international level with concerted action and long-term planning. If tackled in the right way, our efforts to limit climate change are likely to generate significant opportunities and benefits for business as well as side benefits in terms of reduced air pollution. Industry will be helped to innovate, develop new products and services and win new markets on a global scale. But most importantly, success will help ensure that future generations inherit a viable environment and sustainable society. (European Commission 2001)

Herein a 'viable environment' and a 'sustainable society' are not most important – they are by-products of the greening of capitalist production and consumption. There is, therefore, in our view, a radical disjuncture at the heart of environmental policy in the European Union. On the one hand, there is the acceptance of considerable threats to our own and other species, and rhetoric of significant concern and evidence of action which presses for change. On the other hand, European Union environmental policy is literally, for the most part, enabling 'business as usual'.

We suggested that we need a new political framework, and it is to this that the second half of this chapter will attend. Complex ecologism provides a politics and an analytics that take account of our imperative need to care for the biosphere, together with an understanding of the ways in which multiple and complex inequalities shape the securities of different populations. The environmental security approach is significant for the way in which it has prioritized the issue of the global environment, yet the way it has centred on the role of the state, and seen the environment as something 'out there' from which security can be provided, has led to limitations in the way of seeing human/non-human relations and theorizing international environmental politics. Complex ecologism stresses the embedding of human systems within environments. It implies that the alleviation of environmental crises involves, not the provision of security, but rather a reorienting of human activity, which will reduce the risks for all systems within the biosphere. We do not need business as usual. Rather, carboniferous consumer capitalism and social injustices and inequalities are what might fruitfully become less secure in the realization of a sustainable society, in Europe and elsewhere.

We consider that two moves are required in order that international relations produce an understanding of environmental questions which is neither foundationally dualist and state-centric, nor contains some essentialism of 'the human'. First, we need an approach that understands the embedded situation of the human species in networks and scapes populated with non-humans. Secondly, we need an approach that can account for different kinds of power relations. We favour a social ecologism that takes account of both our imperative need to care for the biosphere and an understanding of the ways in which multiple and complex inequalities shape the securities of different populations. For this, we consider that an understanding of difference and inequalities as intersectionalized is necessary.

Complexity, difference and ecopolitical theory

Over the course of the last three chapters, we have argued that concepts from complexity theory can be deployed effectively to further the study of international relations. Complexity theory allows for differentiated systems, with various layers and levels of emergent properties and powers, and does not assume that relationships between levels are fixed or hierarchical in character. In addition, there is the presumption that systems interrelate, overlap each other, may exist within each other and are co-constitutive. There is no presumption of stasis, but rather the notion that systems are constantly making and remaking themselves. This understanding of ecosystems as complex systems has already underpinned some of the stronger work on environmental security (see, for example, Dalby 2009: 78–104). However, the foundational concepts for such theorizations have not been drawn through in such work in terms of understanding the overlapping and interactive qualities of human and non-human systems, and the co-constituted qualities of intra-human systems of social domination.

Into this general theorization (or meta-theorization) of systems as complex, we need to integrate the analysis of relational systems of intra-human power and inequality, and an understanding of the systemic relations of the diversity of human populations with/in non-human systems. In doing so, we now turn to elements of political ecologism. Albeit that typologies often oversimplify and caricature the work of individual theorists, we can consider four approaches to understanding human relations to the natural environment. What they have in common is a radicalism that demands fundamental changes in social, economic and political institutions and processes, and a fundamental recasting of human relations to non-human nature.

Deep ecologism already adopts a systemic approach to understanding the organization and patterning of both social and natural life. All processes are connected and human intervention in natural ecosystems cannot be without impact. Arne Naess (1989) suggests that living beings of all kinds are 'knots' in a biospherical field of relations. Such webs of relationships are incredibly complex and need to be understood as vast systems that interlink us with a variety of species and scapes. The net or web of relations is of paramount importance, and no 'system' is discrete, as Robyn Eckersley puts it:

> The world is an intrinsically dynamic, interconnected web of relations in which there are no absolute discrete entities and no absolute dividing lines between the living and the non-living, the animate and the inanimate, or the human and the non-human. (Eckersley 1992: 49)

This reflects the understanding of some complexity theorists that social, political and economic practices are ecologically embedded (Capra 2002). In addition, a strength of deep ecologism is that it understands human society as structured in particular relations with the 'natural world', a system of relationships termed 'anthropocentrism'. Western society is human-centred in its organization and has a dominant world-view in which non-human natures are conceptualized in terms of means to human ends. Anthropocentrism is usually considered to be the most deep-seated form of domination and, for some, it accounts for other kinds of social domination (Fox 1986). Yet humanity, given all its differences of power, wealth, abundance and consumption, is embedded with/in environments with different relationships and impacts. Eckersley, for example (and following Naess), deploys anthropocentrism in a way that marginalizes human diversity and relations of intra-human power – for example, by using the term 'human-racism' to critique those who do not subscribe to her understanding of the intrinsic value of non-human life forms (Eckersley 1999: 38). For the anarchist Murray Bookchin, the exploitation of humans by other humans is the key to explaining the human exploitation of the natural environment, and that, therefore, all humans are not equally responsible for environmental destruction (Bookchin 1980: 62, 1990: 44). Social ecology (and certainly not only that associated with Bookchin's contribution) is clearly aware of the social causes of environmental destruction, understanding that: 'human society is fractured by race, class and sex. It is not right to hold the poor or people of the South responsible for developments by the rich white North' (Mellor 1992: 106). We want to retain this notion of social relations with 'the environment' as systemic and exploitative, but also to understand human relations with the environment as socially intersectionalized – that is, existent in a context of overlapping relations with other systems of social relations, such as those based on class, gender and ethnic hierarchy.

In feminism, the theorization of multiple differences and inequalities has been difficult and contested. Some of those attempting to understand the cross-cutting of multiple social inequalities (of ethnicities, class, and so on) with gender have used the term 'intersectionality' to emphasize the ways social differences and dominations are mutually constitutive. The effects of, for example, 'race' for gender are not simply an overlapping of inequalities. Gender relations, through intersection, change the properties of 'race' (McCall 2005; Phoenix and Pattynama 2006). Surprisingly, even feminist- and Marxist- inflected accounts which have drawn on complexity theory (such as Byrne 1998; Nowotny 2005) have not used it to account for the intersection of complex relations of social domination (albeit with notable exceptions – for example, Walby 2007). The uses of complexity in social theory have also often been unashamedly anthropocentric in conceptualizing the social as exclusively human (Luhmann 1995). Yet, as we have argued in previous chapters, complexity is a framework in which the operation of interrelated social and 'natural' systems might be captured.

What are often called 'social' ecologisms have accounted for the interplay between human domination of nature, and our various kinds of systemic domination of each other (Bookchin 1990: 44). For many, environmental exploitation is the direct result of 'intra-human domination'. As we have seen, a key insight of complexity approaches is the notion of self-organization – that order can arise without a specific orderer. Here there is a considerable overlap with key anarchist contributions to the study of political ecology. In the work of Bookchin in particular, the analysis of various kinds of social hierarchies and forms of institutionalized social domination is key, and Bookchin's understanding of these as co-constitutive is highly compatible with a complexity understanding of social systems. Bookchin's contribution in turn was highly influenced by the work of Peter Kropotkin. Both Bookchin and Kropotkin are interested in contemporary scientific debates, at least in part because they consider the relationship between natural systems and social forms, and in our view they develop understandings of the world that are compatible with complexity approaches. In Bookchin's case, complexity is specifically referenced and critiqued; interestingly, however, it is Kropotkin who might be read as more clearly a proto-complexity theorist.

In addition to his work as a political theorist and revolutionary, Kropotkin was a geographer and a biologist. His experiences in eastern Siberia and northern Manchuria led him to challenge the ways in which Darwin's theory of evolution had been interpreted. Kropotkin argued that the metaphor of the survival of the fittest had become the central way in which evolutionary theory had been explained. The focus on the competitive aspect of evolutionary theory overstated one aspect of evolution, ignoring in particular the significance of cooperation within species. Kropotkin claimed that 'sociability is as much a law of nature as mutual struggle' (Kropotkin 1987a [1902]: 24). Starting with an examination of non-human animals, Kropotkin claimed that 'natural selection continually seeks out the ways precisely for avoiding competition as much as possible' (ibid.: 72). He noted how few animal species exist by directly competing with each other compared to the numbers that do practise mutual aid, and that those who do are likely to experience the best evolutionary prospects. Given this history, it is therefore unlikely that humans, 'a creature so defenceless ... at his beginnings', should have flourished so successfully without cooperation (ibid.: 74). Drawing upon the work of contemporary anthropologists and the observations of Darwin himself (Darwin 1871), Kropotkin argued that from the earliest times human beings were social rather than individualistic. Studying the development of medieval cities, Kropotkin remarked on the notable similarities between them, despite the different circumstances in which they occurred, each the 'varying result of struggle between various forces which adjusted and re-adjusted themselves in conformity with their relative energies, the chances of their conflicts, and the support they found in their surroundings' (1987a [1902]: 154). Complexity theorists would see this as an example of co-evolution – systems developing as a result of interactions with their environment. Moving on to his own time period, despite attempts by the state to eradicate all forms of mutual aid, Kropotkin found many examples of sociability. The appearance of labour unions is one key example, including the frequent examples of cooperation between unions during times of hardship. Mutual aid has been, Kropotkin argues, a feature of human existence that has widened its reach, ultimately potentially to the whole human species, while at the same time being refined (ibid.: 234).

There is much in Kropotkin's analysis that could be equated to the central complexity concepts that we have discussed in Chapter 2. The notion of mutual aid appears to be an organizing force across a range of species, as a 'factor of evolution' – it is not specifically a human attribute, but one which has enabled a range of species to flourish. This would equate closely to the notion of self-organization in complexity theory. Self-organization points to the tendency of units to interact with each other to produce ever more complex systems. These interactions produce emergent features, which can be seen in Kropotkin's works as the appearance of ever more complex forms of social organization, involving cooperation between the individuals concerned. *Mutual Aid* stressed the process of evolution as one where successful adaptation and exploitation of evolutionary niches are secured by species' propensity for cooperation and solidarity (van Duyn 1969: 21). This is very similar to 'symbiogenesis', a notion used extensively in complexity biology (see, for example, Margulis and Sagan 2002; also Gilbert 2002). Hence both 'mutual aid' and complexity theory see the possibility of order without a sovereign body, and which can be spontaneous and progressive. The core of Kropotkin's work was a critique of the state of nature as perceived by Hobbes, and he noted that 'the Hobbesian philosophy has plenty of admirers still' (1987a [1902]: 75). Life in various forms was not a war of all against all, and while conflict was apparent across the animal world, there was also a story to be told from a perspective of cooperation.

In addition, Kropotkin's political theory follows trajectories of changes in social relations, institutions and processes through a historically evolutionary model in which societies move through stages and points, acquiring increased complexity and diversity (Miller 1984: 182). His intention was not only to show the interrelation between social and ecological changes, and the continued significance of 'mutual aid', but also to set out the co-evolved properties of systemic relations of social domination. For example, Kropotkin provides a historical account of the emergence of the modern political system from the medieval period in Europe wherein there is a coalescing of military elites with new forms of judicial authority, and a breaking down of 'primitive village communities'. This political system is also a product of the dynamics of feudal class relations and is a class-based structure that is seized by the emerging bourgeoisie with the development of capitalism (Kropotkin 1987b [1911]: 17–21). The development of capitalism as a system is co-constituted with the development of modern political institutions and relations. Thus the co-evolution of social/natural systems in Kropotkin's account is not without politics. Rather, Kropotkin also maps a range of sets of oppressive relations and institutional systems. These insights are compatible with a complexity understanding of social relations as both multiple and systemic.

Many of Kropotkin's ideas are elaborated in the work of Bookchin, who has been instrumental in linking anarchism to green social and political thought. In his best-known work, Bookchin gave an account of the emergence of social hierarchies. These emerged with, first, the oppression of women, proceeding to the exploitation and oppression of other groups of humans, socially stratified according to age, 'race', class and sexuality (see Bookchin 2005). The notion of overlapping and intersected forms of social domination that are systemic and co-constituting is clearly compatible with a complex systems analysis of social domination. In addition, Bookchin's understanding of the hybridized and amorphous nature of contemporary political systems embedded firmly in the social fabric and constantly in the processes of arranging and rearranging social life – maintaining themselves – can be given a complexity reading (ibid.: 191–200).

Humans as a species have developed to an exceptional degree such that they have produced a 'second nature', a 'uniquely human culture, a wide variety of institutionalized human communities, an effective human technics, a richly symbolic language, and a carefully managed source of nutriment' (Bookchin 1990: 162). This is a development out of 'first nature', or 'nonhuman nature'. An important distinction that has emerged between human and non-human nature is hierarchy, 'institutionalized and highly ideological systems of command and obedience', which are an 'exclusive characteristic of second nature' (Bookchin 2005: 24). Hierarchy is not a defining feature of second nature, but one that has emerged historically. Earlier, organic societies were non-hierarchic, and characterized by usufruct and complementarity, or mutualism, where care was taken for all members of society, without attributing particular status to differences between its members (ibid.: 26). Over time, hierarchic relations emerged related primarily to gender, age and lineage, developing into the range of hierarchic distinctions that typify the contemporary world. Our current malaise is a result of an evolutionary history containing two competing logics – that of spontaneous mutualistic ecological differentiation, and that of social domination (Light 1998: 7).

In some ways, complexity theory is a latent presence in Bookchin's work. Similarly to Kropotkin, he considers that nature is unified despite its diversity, and species exist in relations of mutual interdependence and cooperation (Bookchin 1986: 26). The concept of co-evolution runs through both *Mutual Aid* and *The Ecology of Freedom*, and Kropotkin's representation of 'life' in terms of multilevelled and nesting systems, or 'federations' of life forms, informed both Bookchin and a range of contemporary social theorists (for example, Haraway 2008: 42). *The Ecology of Freedom* outlined an evolutionary model of human social development. Bookchin suggested that social hierarchy emerged in the early Neolithic period with the establishment of rudimentary forms of government and the development of warrior groups to protect and extend territory. In his descriptions of evolutionary patterns and pathways, Bookchin considered that: 'The universe bears witness to an ever-striving developing – not merely "moving" substance, whose most dynamic and creative attribute is its ceaseless capacity for self-organization into increasingly complex forms' (Bookchin 2005: 458)

Drawing on Lynn Margulis, Bookchin argued that there are symbiotic relations in 'nature' between systems of land, sea and atmosphere, and forms of evolutionary cooperation/co-adaptation (see Margulis 1981). We participate in the evolutionary process, co-evolving with our environments and other species. However, while complexity science is not teleological, Bookchin's use of it is very much shaped by his Enlightenment narrative, which tells of an evolution to a higher level of complexity and consciousness culminating, not just in ever-increasing diversity, but in a state of 'free nature' in which intra-human hierarchies are dissolved and the domination of the environment is no more. Bookchin certainly seemed to be influenced by complexity thinking in terms of the language and concepts he used, but he was critical of systems thinking in general. In a critique of Fritjof Capra, he stated that 'theories of indeterminacy and probability in physics are rendered coequal with human autonomy and social freedom without the least regard for the fact that the human domain is marked by a staggering complexity of social institutions, wayward individual proclivities, diverse cultural traditions, and conflicting personal wills' (Bookchin 1990: 151). In short, the social world is different.

Bookchin was also concerned that complexity theory does not entail a particular political project when he observes with reference to Prigoginian systems theory that 'a system of positive feedback allows for no concept of potentiality' (ibid.: 192, n.15). In many ways, this concern is well founded, as the ambiguities and different trajectories in scientific complexity theory have meant that it has been appropriated by kinds of social and political theorizing (such as postmodernism) to which Bookchin is so implacably hostile. Yet some complexity positions have been usefully deployed by those analysing the politics of domination and arguing for change. Various contemporary political ecologisms see human communities in a complex network of relations with non-human nature – relations characterized by reciprocity and interdependency, and also, importantly, by exploitation and domination. Complexity theory can help us to consider intermeshing multiple systems as both analytically distinct, while also being mutually constitutive. The domination of non-human nature is a system of exploitative relations that overlaps and interlinks with other systems of power and domination based on gender, capital, ethnic hierarchy, and so on.

We would concur with Bookchin that the social world is different, but, because human systems are embedded in non-human systems, his separation between 'first' and 'second' natures is problematic. What is needed is a conception of different systems of social domination that are complex and intersected, with the possibility of capturing the scales and levels of different kinds of systems – what we have suggested in Chapter 1 can be seen as a 'differentiated complexity'. Here, the notion of 'panarchy' can help us to draw in ecosystems, political, economic and social systems, alongside a notion of local, specific human cultural systems. Panarchies are living systems, conceived of as internally dynamic and historically non-static structures which develop mutually reinforcing relationships which are co-constitutive and adaptive. It is not only panarchies involving human systems which demonstrate decision-making properties; rather a huge variety of non-human animals make collective decisions and engage in individual decision-making behaviour with a cumulative systemic effect (Holling et al. 2002b: 72–87). These self-organized interactions do not result in stability. Rather, systems may be vulnerable – ecosystems may be undermined by human endeavours; political systems may be vulnerable owing to the collapse of natural systems on which populations depend for resources. Also, systems in interaction are themselves complex systems with their own emergent properties (Holling et al. 2002c: 411). This allows for qualitative and quantitative differences between 'natural' and 'social' systems, in particular, because the self-organizing properties of intra-human systems outstrip those of natural systems (Westley et al. 2002: 104–5). While social and natural systems may be structured by similar processes, social systems have properties of consciousness and reflexivity. They also reproduce and develop formations of social power, which, like capitalism, patriarchy and so on, are usefully understood as complex adaptive systems.

In the work of anarchist social ecologists such as Kropotkin and Bookchin, the notions of emergent order and the embedding of social and political systems within 'natural' systems are foregrounded. What is perhaps most significant in terms of their placing in the anarchist tradition, however, is their analysis of social and political systems. Patterns of hierarchy and domination usurp, distort and reconfigure human relations, but also, particularly for Bookchin, structure our co-existence with non-human natures. Complexity theory, with its notions of coexisting, interrelated, multilevelled and co-constituted systems, enables the capture of the ontological depth of relational systems of social domination (of class, race, ethnicity, gender, and so on) and their interaction or intersection. It usually also assumes the co-constitution and co-evolution of social with natural systems. Complexity reinvents our understanding of systems, such that we might speak of panarchies, configurations both social and natural, which are dynamic, non-linear and unpredictable. Despite the strengths of this kind of social ecologism, we think that the theorization of different but intersected intra-human hierarchies needs further elaboration. Murray Bookchin may well have considered his ideas to 'be' social ecology in its entirety, but there are a range of other perspectives that can be considered as specific variants of social ecology and have contributed importantly to the understanding of different kinds of relational systems of domination (such as those associated with capitalism, colonialism and patriarchy), and their co-constitution with non-human systems.

Marxist theorists have drawn on Marx's own conception of the dialectical relation between human society and 'nature', and his understanding of natural limits on production and of, to use Marx's term, human 'species being' (Benton 1993; Dickens 1992). Developing these concepts, systemic analyses of capitalism have been deployed in order to understand environment–society relations. Peter Dickens (1996) suggests, for example, that the nexus of environmental exploita-tion is the social organization of labour power in capitalist societies around the production of goods for the market. Further, a complexity reading of Marx has been developed by David Harvey (1996: 187) in suggesting that local actions (for example, the exploitation of work-ers) reproduce the capitalist system and its emergent properties (for example, class relations, resource depletion) and give rise to various system contradictions (from social movements to environmental col-lapse). For various theorists, contemporary developments in capitalist relations mean 'nature' becomes increasingly internal to the dynamics of capital accumulation as biotechnology is harnessed to overcome 'natural' barriers (for example, by manufacturing hybrid seeds which develop into sterile plants; Castree 2001: 191). Thus Harvey (1996: 187) suggests that we now have what he calls 'constructed ecosystems'. Such conceptions are crucial for understanding the ways in which nature is produced/reproduced, but these processes are also constituted through complex coalitions of formations of social domination in addition to capitalism.

Also Marxist-influenced is 'liberation ecologism', which has brought the conceptual apparatus of post-colonialism to bear on debates around social difference and human–environment relations. Ramachandra Guha (1997a) has referred to this kind of thinking as a 'social ecology of the poor' and makes a convincing case that Mohandas Gandhi's philosophical critique of modern Western development is both implicitly and explicitly an early articulation of such a post-colonial ecologism (see Guha 1997b). Contemporary environmental difficulties are embedded in the social relations of (post-)colonial capital, but those specific problems differ both from those experienced in the North, and across the regional formations of the global South. For some, this means that we can grasp the articulations of social nature only according to geographic specifics (Peet and Watts 1996: 14), while others consider various human communities in the context of diverse natural systems and also within the global system characterized by relations of post-coloniality (Guha 1989). The latter is compatible with complexity analytics because specific social/natural formations are understood as produced by a range of interrelating social and natural structures and processes, and because these localized systems of environmental exploitation and human injustice have impacts beyond the region in which they are located, and have global effects.

These Marxist and Marxist-influenced perspectives do consider the important differences between Northern and Southern regions and states, and the structuring of global capitalism on human–environment relations is an important analytic underpinning much of this work. In addition, they have important things to say about the ways in which discourses of racialization and naturalization are co-constitutive of the practices and institutions of the colonial past and post-colonial present (see Arnold 1996: 140–60; Gregory 2001: 100). However, they have very little indeed to say about the gendering of such discourses, or about gender inequalities and the complicating qualities of the ways in which these intersect with those of capital, 'race' and place. Indeed, some are strongly antagonistic to feminist political ecologisms, which are considered forms of reverse sexism (Pepper 1993: 148) or positions which essentialize gender differences (Martinez-Alier 1997: 36). While post-colonial and socialist ecologism is not fully intersectionalized in its analysis, ecofeminism provides a version of social ecology in which the domination of nature is interrelated particularly with gender, but also with a range of other forms of systemic inequalities; it is to this intersectional social ecologism that we now turn.

'Ecofeminism' is composed of a variety of different kinds of theorizing, reflecting a range of feminist positions and influences but which usually considers that the gendered division of labour structures relations between society and the environment, and that discourses suggesting the domination of 'nature' are interwoven with those which marginalize certain social groups. Historian Carolyn Merchant (1980) has made a strong case, for example, that the ideas associated with European modernization from the seventeenth century involved the objectification of the natural world, as a prerequisite for the commercial exploitation of natural resources and the social exclusion of women. One of the key thinkers and activists in liberation ecology, Vandana Shiva (1988), argues that the West has imposed its ecologically destructive and gender-dichotomous model of modernity on the rest of the globe. Political economist Maria Mies (1986) considers that the gendered division of labour is at the core of the linked exploitation of women by men, Southern countries by wealthy Northern global powers and the natural environment by human society.

However, these theorists have not used a multiple systems model of intersectionality, but have often reduced and confined a range of dominations to a theory of patriarchy (Cudworth 2005: 119–27). For example, Karen Warren argues that a 'patriarchal conceptual framework' (1994: 181) accounts for a plethora of oppressive 'isms' (1997: 4). While Val Plumwood sees gender, nature, race, colonialism and class as interfacing in a 'network' or web (1993: 2), she retains a conflationary approach where different dominations are characterized by 'a unified overall mode of operation, forming a *single system*' (ibid.: 79; our emphasis). Others appear to articulate a multiple systems perspective, but for Mies (1993: 223–6) the dominations of colonialism, gender and nature appear as systemic effects of capitalism, and for Mary Mellor (1992) the domination of nature emerges, almost by accident, as an outcome of complex social intersectionality. In some ecofeminist accounts, a full range of intersected differences is not accounted for. Oswald Spring (2008a), discussed earlier, does not account for the social/natural impacts of global capitalism, for example, whereas in other accounts, such as that of Mies (1986), this is key. Ariel Salleh has emphasized that a 'triangulated' political ecologism would integrate the analysis of gender relations, North–South relations and those of capital into an understanding of human relations with 'nature' (Salleh 2009: 3–5). However, ecofeminist analysis would be enhanced by understanding systems of social domination (such as patriarchy, capitalism and the domination of the natural world) as analytically distinct but overlapping, and deploying complexity concepts in articulating how they are interrelated, co-constituted and multilevelled (see Cudworth 2005).

In spite of the various shortcomings we have identified here, these political ecologisms see human communities in a complex network of relations with non-human nature – relations characterized by reciprocity and interdependency, and also, importantly, by exploitation and domination. We take from deep ecology that there is a social system of human domination, but consider that this takes historically and geographically specific formations. Such domination is linked to multiplicitous intra-human formations of domination, outlined in various ways by the different kinds of social ecologism. It is here that complexity theory can help us to consider intermeshing multiple systems. We conceive these systems as analytically distinct, while being also mutually constitutive. The domination of non-human nature is a system of exploitative relations that overlaps and interlinks with other systems of power and domination based on gender, capital, ethnic hierarchy, and so on. This is what we call 'complex ecologism'.

A perspective of complex ecologism enables us to consider systems of social power relations, ecosystems and various levels of systems and structure in the social world that give rise to a multiplicity of local, regional and global configurations. In what ways might such an analytics and politics be incorporated into the study of environmental issues in international politics?

Complex ecologism and international relations

A complexity-inspired approach to environmental issues in international relations would constitute a distinct form of analysis compared to 'environmental conflict' and 'environmental security' approaches. It would also be undergirded by a fully intersectionalized social ecologism. Such an approach gives priority to developing an understanding of social, political and economic relations as impacting beyond the human and as taking account of a range of intra-human inclusions and exclusions that are also embedded in our relations with non-human species and 'natural' spaces. While human and non-human systems have distinct features, ultimately they are co-constitutive, overlapping and intersected. Rather than seeing a separation between the human and the non-human, complex ecologism sees the human world as embedded within the natural world, with the variety of human social systems intersecting with those of other natural systems – what Haraway (2003) would call a 'socialnatural' world.

There are a few attempts to deploy complexity in 'ecological security approaches'. Neil Harrison, for example, identifies 'four principal concepts of complexity adapted to ecological systems: adaptive agency, self-organizing emergence, authority and openness' (2006d: 55). There are two major difficulties with Harrison's application of complexity concepts: dualism and the eliding of power relations. Harrison discusses the concept of agency entirely in relation to the subjectivity and adaptation strategies of human beings, in the context of environmental change. The agency of other species that are supposedly co-evolving with those human agents is absent. Second, in his discussions of self-organization and emergence, he stresses the bottom-up interconnections and processes – for example, in environmental policy-making. In Harrison's interconnected, non-linear systems, natural and social systems are analytically separate and the politics of complex ecologism is absent – there is no understanding of power in the social world here, or its impact on non-human systems.

While 'ecological security' firmly places the analysis of political, social and economic relations within the global environmental system, and pays attention to regional differences, it does not account for the full range of complex social inequalities that shape human relations with, and within, environments. The contribution of a complex ecology approach is the potential to analyse intersectionality and multiple power relations. As discussed above, a variety of different sets of power relations have been analysed by political ecologists. These represent the operation of different sets of systems, such as patriarchal, capitalist, ethnocentrist, and so on, which can have an impact on each other, and have implications for the environment. We would argue that, while these can be considered as distinct systems, the development path of each has implications for other systems. This allows for the development of multiple levels of analysis, drawing the focus away from the state, to supra-state levels (including the biosphere) and sub-state levels.

Complex ecologism provides a means of overcoming the weaknesses in the range of environmental securitization approaches critiqued in the first half of this chapter. By moving away from a state-focused framework, and considering a panarchy of interlinked systems, environmental 'problems' can be considered at global, regional and local levels. The biosphere itself is a system co-constitutive with other human and non-human systems. Envisioning human systems embedded within a wider range of systems overcomes the duality inherent in the majority of approaches to understanding environmental issues within international relations. The environment is not 'out there', but instead constitutive of, and reactive to, human systems. Human systems are embedded within a number of non-human systems, with the consequence that developments in one system may have implications elsewhere in the panarchy. Thus, as a simple example, increased carbon dioxide levels as a result of increased industrialization can be linked to species migration in local ecological systems. Likewise, global temperature rises can increase energy use (often in gender-differentiated ways), impacting across economic (oil prices), political (interstate relations) and ethnic systems (relations with the Middle East).

The interlinking of complex systems also allows the analysis to shift from a focus on security to one on insecurity. Complex ecologism understands interactions and changes in complex human/natural systems as resulting in multiple risks, hazards and uncertainties that international politics must navigate. A significant feature of current global environmental issues is that many of those most in a situation of risk are not the authors of the causes of that risk. Environmental risk situations faced by individuals, communities and societies are frequently the consequences of complex power interrelationships among differentially stratified human beings in various geographical locations. More-developed societies have been effective at exporting their pollution, gaining the benefits of industrial production without the inherent environmental costs. The populations of small low-lying islands in the Pacific, whose societies are put at risk from rising sea levels, are not the beneficiaries of large-scale industrialization.

Finally, by focusing on the intersection of power relations operating in and between different systems, and the creation of risk that is associated with relations between systems, the possibilities for a mitigation of risk throughout the panarchy become the key issue. The move from 'security' to 'risk alleviation' implies that the focus of attention is on the restructuring of risk-creating activities, rather than attempts to secure protection for specific groups. Breaking the link between this as a state-focused issue and instead concentrating on an analysis focused on intersecting systems removes the focus on particular social groups, and reorients the analysis towards both a concern for the wider biosphere and social justice. As many others have pointed out, work on environmental change in international relations theory has tended to modify existing approaches by including the environment in pre-existing frameworks, such as securitization (Dalby 2009). Perspectives such as 'ecological security', which attempt a radical questioning and transformation of that framework, are still shaped by it. We need to move beyond securitization.

We have argued that complexity theory enables a number of important theoretical moves. It enables the capture of the ontological depth of relational systems of social inequality and their interaction or intersection. It is a transdisciplinary approach that most usually assumes the co-constitution and co-evolution of social with natural systems. In understanding systems, both social and natural, as dynamic, non-linear and unpredictable, however, environmental 'issues' and 'problems' can be analysed as having multiple causes and consequences from which no species can be 'secured'. We live in a matrix of multiple risk. The politics of social ecologism (broadly defined and including insights from Marxist, feminist and post-colonial approaches) suggests that the way to face hazard may be to take concrete steps to regulate the uneven flow of resources from poor to rich, institutionalize and normativize the practices and ideals of social justice. In addition, those developments should take account of the complex relationships of interdependency between human communities and the 'natural environment'. Yet while this might suggest a policy agenda for the attempted control of risk, our complex ecologism suggests something more. Carboniferous consumer capitalism and the injustices of gender relations and colonialism need to become less 'secure', and this would entail a reconceptualization of dominant economic relations and social practices and a reinvention of our political world.

If we abandon established approaches to 'environmental questions', rejecting the application of mainstream political conceptual repertoires such as securitization and governance, what kind of an international relations might we be looking at? The politics of complex ecologism requires the interrogation and undermining of contemporary forms of social relations, both within and across species. It also requires that we understand international politics very differently. Let us move on, then, to consider what questions are raised by a decentring of 'the human' in our notions of politics. In the next chapter, we will argue that the past, present and future of international relations are posthuman.

6 · The politics of posthumanism

The term 'environment', as many critics have pointed out, is inadequate in that it reproduces a dualist understanding which sets the 'human' apart from other species, natures and entities and is grounded in the assumption that humans are not animals, or are an animal of a very special kind indeed. We have argued that by incorporating 'the environment' into the study of international relations as an 'issue' raising questions for security or governance, the separation of the 'human' from other species, natures and entities remains fixed, and the discipline continues to be anthropocentric. In order to move beyond anthropocentric international relations, we need to add to the mix of complex systems theory and the politics of complex ecologism proposed in the previous chapters. We also require a more adequate comprehension of the ontological depth of the political world. For that, this chapter will argue that we need to be critically posthumanist.

Theorizations of international relations have been little concerned with the vast variety of other, non-human populations of species and 'things'. This has meant that scholarship has been narrowly focused and does not actually reflect the ways in which human social and political life is neither exclusively social nor exclusively human but bound up with non-human beings and things. In this chapter, therefore, we are particularly interested in exploring what happens to the study of politics if:

> we took the 'stuff' of politics seriously, not as a shorthand phrase for political activity but to signal instead the constitutive nature of the material processes and entities in social and political life, the way that things of every imaginable kind ... help constitute the common worlds that we share and the dense fabric of relations with others in and through which we live? (Braun and Whatmore 2010: ix)

This chapter argues for a decentring of 'the human' in our scholarship. While some view this as scholarship in and of a 'new' reality in a technological age (Badmington 2004; Barry 2001), we concur with those who suggest that 'our' human condition was ever populated with, by and in other worlds of beings and things (Latour 1993, 2005a).

The imperative of posthumanism is not just the desire to more ac- curately capture the complexity of the world, it also has a political incentive. Like Cary Wolfe, we would hope that posthumanist scholar- ship might contribute to 'an increase in vigilance, responsibility and humility' that might accompany living in a world that is not understood humanocentrically' (Wolfe 2010: 47).

We further suggest that a *critical* posthumanism is required. For Katherine Hayles, the posthuman can be defined as a privileging of 'informational pattern over material instantiation' (1999: 2). What this means is that in some accounts, the posthuman world-view sees no essential differences between human bodily existence and com- puter simulation, between organisms and cybernetic mechanisms, as humans and other animals are seen primarily as information processing machines (also Haraway 1991). This has resulted, as we will later argue, in some rather weak and slippery theorizations of the contemporary nature of social and political life (see, for example, Thrift 2010). We would not go so far, for while many 'things' are hybrids, composed of a variety of social and natural elements, there are important physical boundaries that distinguish humans and non-human animals from machines, and indeed, that also distinguish non-human animals from other non-human animals given 'this vast encampment' of 'the Animal' (Derrida 2002: 339). We need to take analytic account of both differences and distinctions as well as the ways in which beings and things (including ourselves, of course) are co-constituted.

There are also persistent differences and social inequalities in human social relations and human relations with 'nature'. The concept of the 'posthuman', as it is currently articulated in the humanities and social sciences, tends, almost despite itself, to underplay the signi- ficance of the embodied condition of our species. This is because it makes much of examples of close interactions between the human mind and forms of technology. In addition, the persistence of forms of social power and domination disappears. When we contend that theorizations should be critically posthuman in quality, we mean that they need to understand our human condition as embedded in, and constituted with, relations and practices with other species. For ex- ample, as we argued in Chapter 4, what we eat and how it is grown, manufactured, exchanged and consumed is deeply political, and can be understood in terms of multilevelled systems of institutions and process and relations of capitalism and colonialism. In addition, a criti- cally posthumanist analysis must also acknowledge forms of power and domination over non-human beings, in the case of the international politics of food, for example, in terms of relations of species, in addition to those of capitalism and colonialism.

The category 'human' itself is a human invention, a social construct linked to formations of power that both set the 'human' apart from other species and also constitute discourses of forms of intra-human domination. Sets of historically situated discourses, be they religious or secular, reproduce the separation of man from matter – 'the anthropological machine', as Giorgio Agamben describes it (Agamben 2004; see also Merchant 1980). The power relations and dominant social, economic and political institutions of Western modernity have been constituted by and through constructions of social inequality, of class, race and gender (Shiva 1988). However, these social categories of difference and domination have also been cross-cut by prevailing ideas about 'nature' and the separation of the human from it.

We have spent time in this book attending to relational and, to a lesser extent, institutional constitutions of power. Thinking beyond the human, however, also means that we understand political power as embodied. To this end, this chapter will add a Foucauldian notion of biopower to the discussion of complex systems in order to examine the ways social relations are inscribed on to and embedded in human and other bodies. Both humans and non-human species may be subjected to certain forms of biological control or manipulation with political implications. This understanding of power as embodied has important implications for the study of established preoccupations in international relations, such as warfare (see Sylvester 2004). Posthuman international relations, then, means not *only* thinking about non-human species and scapes and the interlinking of human and non-human complex systems. Posthuman international relations *also* means thinking differently about the human and about the political.

More and less critical posthumanisms

... As the archaeology of our thought easily shows, man is an invention of recent date. And one perhaps nearing its end.

If those arrangements were to disappear as they appeared, if some event of which we can at the moment do no more than sense the possibility – without knowing either what its form will be or what it promises – were to cause them to crumble, as the ground of Classical thought did, at the end of the eighteenth century, then one can certainly wager that man would be erased, like a face drawn in the sand at the edge of the sea. (Foucault 1971: 387)

Emphasizing the historically situated and socially constituted understanding of the human and of the humanistic understanding of the human condition is a preoccupation of much of Foucault's work. The humanist rendering of the 'human', he asserts, is largely dogma, owing much to pre-Enlightenment superstitions (Foucault 1984: 44). The category 'human' is a social construct linked to formations of power. This insight is crucial in most definitions of the 'posthuman'. Katherine Hayles (1999), for example, considers that the notion of the 'posthuman' indicates the extent to which narrow definitions of what it means to be human have lost credibility. Historically, however, our social world and our understandings of it have been defined and understood as 'human centred' or anthropocentric, and as 'exclusively human' (Midgely 1996: 105). The term 'posthumanism' has entered academic and popular discourse as a descriptor for critical perspectives on our human-centrism (see Badmington 2004). Critics of exclusive humanism argue that we should approach the world from a 'posthumanist' perspective and seek to understand more about the diversity of species and non-human beings of which our world is constituted (Gane and Haraway 2006: 140).

In turn, the category human has always been differentiated – some humans are 'more human' than others. This has had implications for the treatment of certain categories of humans who are 'natured' and thereby seen as closer to nature or 'less civilized'; for example, with the 'naturing' of 'race' (Anderson 2001), or gender (Merchant 1980). The social constitution of the 'human' has certainly impacted on non-human species and lifeworlds, usually regarded and utilized as means for the satisfaction of human ends. It is this socially constituted division between human/animal, nature/culture which is the object of critique for most posthumanist thinkers – undoing these (and other) binaries of Western dualist thinking.

The term 'posthuman', as we have already indicated, is flexible, ambiguous and contested. It has been associated, particularly in popular culture, with contemporary technological developments that have been seen to transform social worlds and the condition of 'the human'. 'Posthumanism' has operated as a somewhat inaccurate collective descriptor for a range of discourses and claims about the constitution and construction of minds and bodies (both human and non-human) and of nature and artifice. This chapter considers various understandings of the posthuman and posthumanism and locates our approach, drawing on some of the more critical perspectives.

Posthumanism as transhumanism Posthumanism has sometimes been understood as being synonymous with transhumanism – that is, the ideology that emphasizes the possible good of a future in which humans are able to acquire 'posthuman capacities' and extend their life and health spans, their capacities for happiness and their intellectual capabilities (Bostrom 2003). Here, posthumanism implies the physical and/or intellectual extension of human beings utilizing available technologies and further developing technologies for that purpose. It is the desire for, and the acknowledgement of, the possibility of selective human transcendence. This is also often linked to a utopian futurology, seen, for example, in Hans Moravec's (1988) vision of a new society populated by more or less artificial beings, from robots to intellectually and physically enhanced and modified humans.

There are dystopian responses to such understandings (Caygill 2000), and some have argued that they represent a tangible threat and challenge to the still incomplete projects of liberal humanism and, fundamentally, undermine human dignity (Fukuyama 2002). While neither utopian nor apocalyptic futurology is very convincing, what is more certain is that this ideology of transhumanism is blind to the inequalities surrounding the production and deployment of new technologies, and is prone to the fantasy of transcending the human through disembodiment (Hayles 1999). In addition, as Andy Miah (2007) points out, transhumanist faith in enhancement technologies seems framed by the very Enlightenment conviction in human progress that has been the subject of more critical posthumanisms. As such, despite the appropriation of the term posthumanism by transhumanist advocates (Bostrom 2003, 2008), transhumanism is distinct and ultimately itself a form of humanocentrism. As Wolfe puts it, the disembodied and transcendent fantasies of those such as Moravec or Bostrom are best seen as 'an intensification of humanism' rather than an element of a project problematizing human-centrism (Wolfe 2010: xv).

Biophysical and political posthumanism In sharp contrast, biophysical, philosophical and political posthumanisms centre on the relationships between human beings, other species and the whole other worlds of 'nature'. Biologists such as Lynn Margulis and Dorion Sagan (1986: 214) have argued that 'there is no physiological basis for the classification of human beings into their own family'. The category human is a reflection of the anthropocentric framing of taxonomy and, following Darwin, they suggest that we must normativize the category 'Great Apes' as inclusive of human beings. Such a notion undergirds some philosophical and political projects in contemporary animal rights

(Cavalieri and Singer 1993). In this view, we are simply another kind of animal, interlocked in webs of relations at different ecosystem levels. And that animal has actually never been human at all.

A well-known example of what we might think of as biophysical posthumanism is the work of earth systems scientist James Lovelock. In Lovelock's model, humans are utterly embedded in the multitude of systemic processes that make up the 'mega system' of the planet. Lovelock's fame was made by his development of the concept of Gaia: the idea that earth's multifarious living forms act as regulators that control conditions on the planet by a series of chemical feedbacks (Lovelock 2000). When first developed in the sixties, earth system science was derided as 'unscientific' but is now accepted by many biologists and physicists as an accurate description, and this has become the basis of most contemporary climate science. Lovelock literally sees our future as posthuman in the sense that he thinks that the severity of the stresses humans have caused in the earth's system(s) mean that we have critically endangered the survival of humans and a vast number of other species. Lovelock has certainly become increasingly apocalyptic in his predictions over the years. A 'pitiless' change in our environment is now inevitable, he argues. For Lovelock, the earth's system is currently in incredible difficulties owing to its 'infection' by the pestilent species *Homo sapiens*, which, in the short geological blink of an eye that is the last two hundred years, has overseen mass species extinctions, depleted biodiversity and destabilized the climate. We have reached a new condition, 'polyanthroponomia', wherein human overpopulation is so extensive that we cannot *but* harm the planet (Lovelock 2009). Lovelock is clear that there is now no reversing climate catastrophe, and we face a future in which there will be but pockets of humanity left alive. While this science is fiercely independent, Lovelock is on dubious ground when speaking of human social development where population growth is fetishized (Lovelock is an adherent of Malthusianism, and in this is decidedly anti-humanist), market organization is our only collective mechanism, and the rural English landscape is romanticized as the soon-to-be-lost world. Given this, some have disengaged the science from such a socially conservative and economically liberal politics, and successfully linked earth systems science to left, green and anti-colonialist political projects.

Fritjof Capra (1996, 2002), for example, has linked deep ecologism to ideas emerging from complexity approaches in the sciences. In this analysis, we become part of a multitude of various levels of natural and social systems, in which we humans exploit other species and scapes as resources. Capra has drawn on the work of Manuel Castells in looking at the ways systemic relations of capitalism are co-constituted with biological systems. Simon Dalby (borrowing from Crutzen; see Dalby 2009: 11–12) uses the concept of a new geological age, the 'anthropocene', in which we humans have remade the 'circumstances of life' of both our own existence and those of all other species, with serious consequences for the survival of many life forms. These human-induced changes mean that the environment is increasingly artificial – we have remade the environmental context of our own existence. Dalby's account is influenced by certain kinds of political ecologism, and he considers our current predicament to be constituted through collective human activity that has been structured by carboniferous consumer capitalism, and relations between rich and poor regions and peoples. In such understandings, humanity is understood as locked into systemically exploitative relations to non-human lifeworlds, and also as socially intersectionalized. This kind of posthumanism is close to the complex ecologism we advocated in Chapter 5.

This understanding of 'humanity' as a fundamentally socially and culturally constituted category, and of humans as existent in webs of relations with other species, has been foregrounded in the range of work within animal studies across the humanities and, more recently, some of the social sciences. From philosophy, literature, art history and cultural studies, to sociology and politics, disciplines are delimited by human exclusivity. According to Wolfe (2010: 1) we need to develop modes of social and cultural inquiry that reject the classic humanist divisions of self and other, mind and body, society and nature, human and animal, organic and technological. This philosophical posthumanism enables different kinds of readings of the cultural, the technological and biological, and also a rethinking of established social forms of difference and exclusions. According to those such as Ralph Acampora (2006) and Wolfe (2003), we need to pay attention to human animality as well, and understand not only that we are one (animal) life form among a multitude, but also that, crucially, our biology and evolution are co-constituted with and by this multitude. What Wolfe and others emphasize is that it is not so much 'the human' which is a difficulty, but the human-centric understanding of the human as the unique individual striving in the world, and not embodied and embedded in complex biotic lifeworlds. We would very much endorse Wolfe's understanding.

The posthuman and the hybrid Less politically committed than these posthuman perspectives coming from ecologism and animal studies, but perhaps more engaged in some ways with established notions of 'politics', are a range of positions within science and technology and cultural studies that want to move beyond an 'outdated' understanding of the human in our current social, cultural and material context of technoscience. While Margulis may argue that we have never been human, and Acampora might stress the animality of the 'human' condition, Latour is keen to point out that we have never been purely human or 'animal'. In arguing that we humans have 'never been modern', Latour (1993) describes modernity in terms of two interlinked but seemingly inconsistent processes: 'purification' and 'hybridization'. Purification involves the construction of a realm of 'nature' and the scientific study thereof, the world of 'things', separate from the social or the cultural world or the world of the self and of 'subjects'. Hybridization involves mixtures of nature and culture. We modern 'humans' consider that the real world of nature and the discursively constituted social world of ideas and beliefs are 'pure' – that is, distinct and exclusive. We are, however, pretending to be modern; in the real natural/cultural world all kinds of hybrids of natures and cultures are produced. In this sense, we have never been modern, but rather we are 'a-modern'; the separation of nature and culture never was. In cultural studies, and social studies of technology, there have been attempts to develop the notion of the posthuman drawing specifically on this hybrid ontology.

Many theorizations about the posthuman abound with ideas of boundary-crossing between humans, other animals and, in particular, machines. Hayles's important contribution posits the 'posthuman' as a descriptor of our contemporary historical epoch. She makes clear historical distinctions between different understandings of the human condition. For example, she defines 'the human' in terms of a historical epoch associated with the Enlightenment tradition of liberal humanism, wherein the human individual is taken as the basis of most understandings of what it means to 'be' in the world (Hayles 1999: 34). The 'posthuman' is historically distinct, defined as an epoch in which 'computation ... is taken as the ground of being'. This means that humans, non-human animals and machines are generally understood in terms of codes and signs and, rather than being seen as distinctly different, they are conceptualized as (relatively) seamless things. As Hayles makes clear, the scientific discourse of the 'posthuman' is one which is very much bound up with notions of complexity, in the study of artificial intelligence and, more recently, artificial 'life'. However, she does tend to oppose embodiment and posthumanism, and her historical trajectory of development is not altogether convincing (see Wolfe 2010: xv).

A more common position is to understand boundaries as almost always blurred. In an early use of 'posthumanism' heavily influenced by the feminist work of Donna Haraway (1991, 1996), Judith Halberstram and Ira Livingston (1995: 3) suggest that, given the social constitution of both humanity and animality, we embodied humans are best seen as part of a 'zoo of posthumanities', in which any differences between species groups is minimized. The political theorist Jane Bennett (2010) has also emphasized the need for more horizontal ontologies. Bennett argues for a 'vital materialism' which recognizes the role of non-human forces affecting and configuring situations and events. Drawing on thinkers such as Spinoza, Thoreau and Adorno, Bennett's argument about the animism of all things, to different degrees, resonates with the complexity understandings of Capra (1996) and of neuroscientists Maturana and Varela (who argue for a dispersed notion of cognition – for example, 1980, 1987). The Spinozist notion of animate matter has also been foundational for systems-inflected political ecologism, in particular deep ecology (see Naess 1973; Eckersley 1992).

In vital materialism, there is a tendency towards the production of lists of animate 'things' we might think about. For Bennett, this involved a dead rat, a plastic bottle cap, a plastic workman's glove, a stick of wood and some oak pollen, an unexpected encounter with which led her to catch 'a glimpse of energetic vitality in all these things' (Bennett, 2010: 5). Other lists include 'the Web; the AIDS virus; oil-devouring cars; hurricanes; neutrinos; the climate; genes; psychotropic drugs, be they legal or illegal; the great apes' (Stengers 2010b: 4), 'a shoe, a ship, a cabbage or a king' (Lin 2006: 147), metals (Barry 2010) or differently placed plastic bags (Hawkins 2010). However, such lists tell us very little about the nature of vital materiality or, indeed, very much else. An adequate understanding of social natures and the hybrid constitution of the social/natural/technological must be cognizant of the *detail* and *specificity* of the political, social and physiological differences between species, the social and political constitution of human power and the important differences between living and non-living matter.

This is not to say that for thinkers such as Bennett or Stengers there are no differences between different species and 'objects', but rather it is a problem of human exceptionalism that insists on making 'the most drastic cut between those beings who "have ideas" and everything else' (Stengers 2010b: 7; also Bennett 2010: 11). A difficulty is that specific kinds of embodied difference are not sufficiently accounted for. The point, for Bennett, is to 'minimize' the differences between subjects and objects with this notion of a vitality which runs through both human and non-human matter. The end in view is the development of a more environmentally aware and cautious politics. However, the elevation of the 'shared materiality of all things' (Bennett 2010: 13) is a rather blunt instrument in securing this end. Whereas Bennett insists on the notion of assemblage (following Deleuze and Guattari 1987) in order, for example, to describe the multiple animate bodies of which an individual human body is constituted, we consider that the complexity notion of nested, overlapping or intersected co-evolved system(s) is more helpful. The latter allows us to differentiate and distinguish as well as examine the specific sites and forms of relation between the multiple organisms of a human body. It also presumes a contextualizing array of systemic contexts in which a body might emerge.

Haraway's (1991) notion of the cyborg pushes this understanding of the hybrid quality of life farther, in arguing not just that 'things' are 'assemblages' – that is, composed of various influences, processes and material qualities – but that they are constantly shifting. In this liquid world, it is difficult to talk of fixed entities, such as humans or 'animals', or to understand humans as being in clear relations to different forms of social power. This is unacceptable for many, such as Vandana Shiva, who, for example, analyses the globalization of bio-technology in terms of plants and animals becoming 'instruments for commodity production and profit maximization' (1988: 29); and the 'predation' of one class, 'race', gender and species on others wherein the 'dominant local' seeks global control (ibid.: 105,122). Conceptions of unequal power relations around class, 'race', gender and 'nature' are implicit in Shiva's analysis, and contemporary forms of hybridization, while involving physical interpenetration across species, do not easily contest power, but often remain embedded in the social networks of domination based on species, gender and racialized difference.

Heavily influenced by Haraway and more focused on explicitly political questions is Chris Hables Gray, whose previously discussed *Cyborg Citizen* (2001) has become a cult 'manifesto' for those drawn to postmodern cultural studies. In addition, these perspectives do fruitfully engage with the Foucauldian notion that the human body is the site for political struggles. We would argue that all bodies, human and non-human, individual and collective, might be so conceived.

There is, then, a wide range of perspectives associated with the notion of the 'posthuman'. Common to them is a critique of humanism as a guiding normative framework for understanding the social/natural world, and all are preoccupied with the consequences of developments in technology, albeit that they are often ambiguous on the desirability of biological interventions. Critical cultural posthumanists such as Hayles, Haraway and Wolfe, political ecologists such as Capra and Dalby, and philosophers such as Acampora and Calarco are considerably different from normative transhumanists like Nick Bostrom. While Bostrom wants the human to transcend the boundaries of limited physical embodiment, posthumanism emphasizes the extent to which the liberal humanist subject is undone by a consideration of both the embodied condition of the human animal, and of life beyond the human. As Wolfe (2008) suggests, posthuman work undertakes two related tasks. First, it challenges the ontological and ethical divide between humans and non-humans that has been the philosophical linchpin of modernity. Secondly, it engages with the challenge of sharing this planet we inhabit with 'non-human subjects'.

A sufficiently critical posthumanism must draw in the insights about human-centrism, human power and social justice provided by elements within political ecologism and critical animal studies. We may never have been human, but our social relations have been human-exclusive. Any attempt to transform international politics in a posthumanist direction must have questions of political power and relations with non-humans at its core. We understand political systems as dependent on natural systems involving multiple species, as co-constituted with them, and as affecting and affected by them. How would adopting a critical posthumanism alter the way we approach, understand and conceive of matters of politics?

Reinventing politics

Allowing space in political life and political analysis for non-human beings and things is radically transgressive for the tightly circumscribed discipline of politics and its smaller sibling, international relations. There is a profusion of complex materials, systems and processes through and with which we humans live. We consider that a post-human approach to politics involves the recasting of key debates around the subjects, actors and objects of politics, the public/private divide in Western liberal societies, different levels of political activity and institutional arenas, and notions of change in political systems.

Who, or what, is the political subject? The history of political theory has ascribed political will and agency to humans alone (or, often, to very limited groups of humans). Even those contemporary thinkers with challenging and radical notions of the nature of decision-making in democratic political institutions consider that (human) speech is the medium of politics (Habermas 1996). While in animal studies writers of different persuasions and perspectives have understood various animal species as 'agentic beings' (Bekoff 2002; Haraway 2008) there has been more resistance to the notion of animals as possessing any kind of agency that we might understand in terms of relations of political power (Carter and Charles 2011).

Even political theorists with environmental credentials have cast both technologies and 'natures' as outside of political life – as the objects of political attention rather than political agents with affect and causality (for example, Rose 1999; Dobson and Bell 2005). Those theorists who have experimented with radical notions of 'environmental democracy' have experimented only so far, and tend to conceive of politics as a human-exclusive sphere of activity and democratic decision-making that is separate from the objects over which democratic deliberation takes place (see Dobson and Eckersley 2006).

Drawing on Latour, however, Bennett (2004) contests this humanocentrism with her notion of 'thing power'. For this, she draws on Latour's notion of an 'actant', which can be a human or non-human source of action (Latour 2004: 75). This enables us, says Bennett (2010: 9), to see agentic capacity as distributed, and as distributed differently, 'across a range of ontological types'. This said, these differences need to be flattened out and difference needs to be understood horizontally rather than hierarchically. This does in many ways link with the kinds of complexity thinking we have come across in the sciences. For microbiologists like Margulis and Sagan, for example, we are conglomerates of matter that has been recycled into 'walking, talking minerals' (Margulis and Sagan 1995: 49). For Lovelock we are all co-constituted by multiple matter, living and dead, for '[w]e live in a world that has been built by our ancestors, ancient and modern, and which is continually maintained by all things alive today' (Lovelock 2000: 33). The problem with 'thing power', however, is an over-comparison of the liveliness of beings and things in an attempt to decentre the human. In minimizing the importance of distinction, Bennett loses sight of the important differentiations of species and other things, and in particular of the notion of the persistent power relations that reproduce the human-centred institutions and practices of our anthropocentric world.

Drawing on Spinoza, Bennett asserts that the agency of things is not an individual property but a property of heterogeneous assemblages (2010: 23). In describing an electric grid as an assemblage of vital material, however, and in her use of the term 'emergent properties', Bennett is actually close to the notion of a complex system (see ibid.: 24–8). Such systems – or, for Bennett, non-human assemblages – can act, by which she means they can have an impact or effect on humans and non-humans. Following on from this, she argues that human agency has never been separate from the non-human world, but always intermingled and co-constituted. The causes of events are emergent properties, in Bennett's account, from assemblages of non-human and human. But herein lies a recurrent problem in Bennett's work – a conflation between the idea of the properties and powers of beings and things and the idea of agency.

This problem of non-human agency haunts the work of animal studies scholars. In much work, Latour's notion of an 'actant' makes its presence felt and there is a very loose and broad conception of agency in which all kinds of varied 'actants' exercise their being in the world. This notion is influenced by the kind of vital materialism seen in the work of Bennett. In the social sciences, agency has been attributed to beings with desires, intentions and wills. This definition does not apply to many things (such as metals or plastic bags) but it applies to some non-human species, and certainly seems relevant to many mammals. Many non-human species have been found to have a sense of selfhood (see Bekoff 2002, who discusses a wide variety of 'wild' mammals, insects and birds and domesticates, such as dogs). They can exercise choice and communicate with humans and other species (however much the content may be open to interpretation) as fellow agentic beings. Many domesticate non-human animals, as Leslie Irvine (2004) suggests, may have the capacity to be self-willed actors, however constrained their lives.

However, as Bob Carter and Nickie Charles (2011) have recently argued, agency should not be understood as a capacity or property that humans and/or other animals possess. In the case of mammals, much has been made of the idea that sentiency can confer a capacity to act. However, while sentiency certainly confers awareness and shapes the capacity to *act*, it does not confer *agency*. Rather, as Carter and Charles suggest, agency is socially structured – options for actors/actants are shaped by social relations. Carter and Charles draw on the work of Margaret Archer (2000: 261), who argues that a defining characteristic of agency, as opposed to action, is that it is plural – agents are collectivities and actors are singular. Individual actors might reflect on their embodied situation and they might also recognize commonality.

However, to engage in anything beyond this primary agency, another emergent property is needed – the political influence associated with, for example, social movements. Archer (2003) speaks of the relationship between our individual selves and (human) identities and the wider social forces that shape us as the 'internal conversation'. Carter and Charles (2011) build on this insight. They consider that animals can be seen as agents to the degree that they share life chances and are affected by their social location. Secondly, they argue that considering this social location is of prime importance. Non-human animals, for example, are 'highly disadvantaged' in an anthropocentric distribution of resources. Carter and Charles further argue that humans have far greater agency owing to their capacity to communicate and engage in the reflexivity that language allows. Language enables humans to change the world and their own place in it to such a degree that there is a fundamental asymmetry in the agency of human and non-human animals. We are not convinced, however, that we understand enough about forms of communication in other species to preclude animal agency. We do not need language as an enabler of agency, but we urgently need to take account of the placement of non-human beings and things in the network of power relations.

Without an explicit inclusion of social systems and their emergent features and powers, we lose the ability to properly integrate the ways social and political structures constrain actions in relation to networks of power relations of domination. The understanding of agency suggested by Archer is useful primarily because it emphasizes how agency is systemically constituted. The retort of those such as Bennett, Latour and Haraway might be that unless we allow for the agency of things and of human–non-human assemblages, we cannot decentre the human in political analysis. Bennett has rightly argued that the human/non-human dichotomy in political thought has not helped many of the political demands of humanism – the successful articulation of human rights claims, for example. Conversely, there are serious questions to be raised about Bennett's assumption that distributing agency will be effective in unsettling humanocentric politics (2010: 36–7). If we look to different historical models, distributing agency and responsibility for action across species has not been disruptive for humanocentrism. For example, Erica Fudge shows the ways in which, unlike in early modern England, in continental Europe non-human animals were understood as culpable for their 'crimes' and to be capable of receiving justice (Fudge 2006: 109). Such concepts and practices happily co-existed with the hierarchy of the Great Chain of Being!

Archer, Carter and Charles suggest that for actions to involve agency there must be collective endeavour and common positioning. Bennett's appeal for the agency of the earthworms, whose importance for human life was so emphasized by Darwin, does not convince. In Chapter 5 we argued that there were important differences between ecosystems and human systems (such as political systems). Bennett (2010: 98), however, asserts that: 'There are many affinities between the acts of persons dragging their belongings to their new homes in the suburbs [she alludes here to "white flight"] and the acts of worms dragging leaves to their burrows or migrating to a savanna-forest border.'

It is interesting that she does not detail exactly what these 'many affinities' might actually be! We do not need to assert the agency of earthworms in order to argue that human action, behaviour, social organization and so on are utterly dependent on and co-constituted with complex relations with other beings and things. Such a phenomenological approach to political agency (see Coole 2005) conflates the properties, capacities and powers of beings and things with the notion of 'agency'. This vastly underplays the socially and politically constituted systemic power of humans.

We would do better to concentrate on the way in which co-constitutive properties and powers are manifest in configurations of social and natural systems. We do sympathize with the efforts of those such as Bennett to decentre humanist political theory and ask questions about the nature of political action. A further step beyond the agency of beings and things is to consider what citizenship and representation might be in the posthuman political world. What questions does this raise for our particular version of posthumanism, which resists the elision of ecosystems with intra-human systems?

From polity to cosmopolis – a posthuman public?

Are you ready, and at the price of what sacrifice, to live the good life together? That this highest of moral and political questions could have been raised, for so many centuries, by so many bright minds, *for human only* without the nonhumans that make them up, will soon appear, I have no doubt, as extravagant as when the Founding Fathers denied slaves and women the vote. (Latour 1993: 297; emphasis in original)

Bennett argues that political systems might best be seen as 'a kind of ecosystem' (2010: 100). Combining Spinoza and (following Latour) the pragmatist political philosopher John Dewey, she asserts that 'endeavoring bodies' with interests (in avoiding harm, in their own protection) draw together in publics. Whether human or non-human, we join in political action as affected and affecting bodies. Latour has argued that the powers and properties of non-human 'objects' call for a public space that is profoundly different from what is usually recognized as 'the political' (Latour 2005b: 15). Latour (1993) reminds us that the actions of human agents always result in unexpected outcomes and that, in this sense, human intentionality and will is over-egged as a defining character of agency. This implies also that the capacity of social structures to shape the world is incredibly compromised. The certainties of humanism have always been problematic and contestable, and Latour (2004) is right to suggest that we have never been properly autonomous and self-sufficient beings.

In his view, a more fully democratic space recognizes that our collective public is not a body of human representatives of human interests but a cosmos. Bennett develops these notions, arguing that we need to loosen the tie between the human use of language and political participation in order for democracy to engage with non-human affected bodies (see 2010: 106–7). But what form this 'loosening' might take she cannot tell us. Others (such as Latour and Stengers) have attempted more detail, and we shall investigate this below.

In Chapter 5, we made a sustained critique of the ways in which 'environmental' questions and problems are engaged by established institutions in international politics. Nation-states and international organizations respond to the way we have harmed non-human matter by incorporating the 'environment', the non-human lifeworld, into existing modes of the political – securitization and governance. A political perspective of complex ecologism, however, does not understand 'the environment' as 'out there' but as 'with' and 'in here'. A key difficulty is that the spatial boundaries of the nation-state deal poorly with non-human relations and our entanglements with other beings and things. Thom Kuehls (1996) has argued that such entanglements with biological life and non-human lifeworlds produce a topology that cannot be contained or understood within the current frameworks of nation-states and international system. For Stengers (2010b: 7), such political institutions are deeply problematic – we cannot reduce the inclusion of non-human worlds in politics to an account of the role they would play in political association and public life as currently constituted. This is because the very framing of those institutions was developed by mobilizing the category 'human' – our idea of what politics is, as such, is human exceptionalist.

However, there are ways in which contemporary politics might be made more open to the vital materiality of 'things'. This might be glimpsed in the failures of current political arrangements to attend to the properties and powers of non-human beings and things. Andrew Barry (2010), for example, considers the relations between fields of scientific and technical expertise, corporations, governments and citizens in the case of the Baku–Tbilisi–Ceyhan oil pipeline in the early 2000s. This is an incredible development that would bring oil from the Caspian Sea through Azerbaijan, Georgia and Turkey, avoiding both Russia and Iran. Barry traces the national and international political debates concerning the 'informed material', the technologically enhanced metal coating material for the pipeline. 'Failures' with and debates concerning safety around this material led to debates in which the impact of material was brought to the forefront. Barry sees this as a 'more than human politics' (cf. Whatmore 2006) of the action and dynamism of non-human assemblages (Barry 2010: 110). This illustrates the point about action and agency very well. Political debates in established political institutions can be attendant to the dynamic properties and powers of materials. These have affected politics in the sense that the powers of these materials have forced themselves into human political debate. However, as Barry also notes, the debates around the materiality of the pipeline were also framed by what we would call systems of relational power, in particular those of capitalism.

The politics of beings and things also contests the unstable and untenable notions of private and public and of micro and macro in the Western political model. Environmental policies, even in their limited form in liberal and capitalist societies, impact on the life of the home and the life of the consumer. Plastic bags in supermarkets become defined as environmentally problematic, while they continue to assert their utility in domestic spaces (Hawkins 2010). What we do in our homes becomes constituted as political, as a 'matter of concern' (Latour 2005b).

Andrew Dobson and Derek Bell (2005) have argued that contemporary practices to facilitate and promote an 'environmental citizenship' have been disruptive of the Western political distinction between public and private spheres. Western environmentalism used the political slogan 'think global, act local' from the early 1980s, but that 'local' is often on a micro scale. For Dobson and Bell, environmental politics is the politics of everyday life, and questions of the 'common' or 'public' good are not articulated and struggled for in public arenas but are part of everyday practices. Noortje Marres (2010) has argued that imperatives to 'green' the home by public authorities ultimately amount to a deprivatization as we are instructed to 'save the planet' by recycling packaging, using low-energy light bulbs and washing clothes at a lower temperature and with 'greener' detergents (ibid.: 177–8). The boundaries are further blurred by the notion that private practices are considered in terms of their public effects – from local water pollution to climate change (ibid.: 179). This may be an endorsement of Phil Macnaghten's (2003) claim that concern about environmental problems must be grounded in personal experience and policies attempting to 'green' the behaviour of citizens cannot be distanced from everyday life if they are to succeed. The 'private' sphere of the home has come to be seen as a key location in which the transition to a low-carbon economy might be realized by governments. Marres (2010: 179, 183) notes, for example, the commitment of the mayor of London to 'green the home' and that of the then prime minister, Gordon Brown, in 2007 to build carbon-neutral homes.

This boundary-blurring between public and private is certainly not unique to 'green' politics, and a variety of feminist scholars, for example, have drawn attention to the ways in which local and national states and international organizations engage with the reproduction and recasting of gender relations through policy initiatives which profoundly affect the life of the home (see Enloe 1988, 2000; Sylvester 1994; Tickner 2001). The policy-oriented engagements above can be read as an exercise in 'green governmentality'. Here, citizens and states remain unreconstructed and environmentalism simply becomes a policy discourse among many others. As we have suggested in the previous chapter, the technocratic management of 'the environment' as a policy 'issue' is minimally disruptive to our social and political arrangements and does not take on board the ways in which we are co-constituted with other beings and things. At this point, it is apposite to return to where we began this book, with Latour, and his notion of 'attachments'. For Latour, if we take our entangled condition with non-human beings and things seriously, then we are driven to reinvent the public. This calls for a very different notion of the political and of political institutions and relations, at all levels.

A parliament of beings and things? In the previous two sections, we have considered questions of political agency and the boundaries of the public sphere. This section considers the sites of politics, the specific institutional forms that might enable the non-human to be brought in. Bennett (2005) has suggested that we might see ourselves in 'parliament with things', but articulating what this might mean more practically is a difficult task. As Latour (2004: 68) has noted, our notion of a political assembly is predicated on the language of humans and the muteness of 'things'. This has profoundly shaped our idea of political representation. While humans are held to be able to articulate views about the world, interests and 'wants', non-humans cannot and are thus held not to have interests, opinions and 'wants'. For Latour, the natural, technical world of non-human beings and things is represented not by politicians, but by professional experts, by 'science'. Science represents not the 'wants' of beings and things, however, but 'facts' about them. Politicians, on the other hand, also represent, but are seen to represent views, claims and desires (see ibid.: 148). For Isabelle Stengers (2000: 84) this raises the problem of authority – there is power in both these kinds of representation, the representation of human wills and the representation of 'facts' about non-human worlds.

Undergirding these ideas is the notion that political representation is an artifice. As Latour (2004: 68) claims, it is a misrepresentation to say that 'the people' speak for themselves – they elect others who claim to speak in their name. In countering the charge that the process of elections in liberal democracies involves some kind of 'speech' for the human voters, Latour suggests that science does a better, more accurate job of representing 'things' than politicians do of representing the views of their constituents (ibid.: 170–1). What both Stengers and Latour propose is the idea of being the representatives of 'things' in the same assembly as the parliaments which claim to represent the wills of the 'people' – they want closer integration between scientific expertise and politics. Stengers is happy to have scientists represent things by virtue of close encounters with 'the represented' through the experiment. For Latour (1999), this is insufficient, and as a solution he suggests public 'trials by force', by which he means the staging of public interrogations, situations for mutual engagement between politicians and scientific experts, and publics. Scientists do not just carry out experiments and articulate facts, they have to play politics – they have to win an argument and carry a debate.

While Latour is right to argue that scientific facts and arguments are socially constituted and that this can be understood as a political process, there remains the problem of representation – whether of humans or non-human beings and things. It takes us back to the question of the political subject and the notion of agency. When we look at the detailed examples used by Latour (1999, for example), we come to the difficulty of the slippery notion of actant, which elides properties and powers with agency. In detailed descriptions of experimentation we find that yeast, for example, has agency, because of the given effects of its properties and powers in an experimental context. Science may be attentive to the being of things and may represent it. However, as the debates in science indicate, there are different opinions on 'facts' and the representation of the being of non-humans is itself deeply political.

All is not lost, though, with Latour's model of reinventing democracy. We endorse the critique of the artifice of representation, although we consider that Latour's conception of representing non-humans is horizontal – there are incredible differences in properties, powers, affects, interests and even standpoints that fundamentally affect the politics of representing the 'non-human' in all its incredible variety. Yet what Latour cautions is a more attentive process of democracy, and this might make hearing about the politics of things a possibility.

Stengers (2010b: 28–30) argues along similar lines in reworking the notion of 'diplomacy' as a way of embedding the notion of an 'ecology of practices'. Diplomacy, she says, does not, even in its current ethically dubious and unpopular guise, involve the need for a shared language, but rather the need for translation. The qualities of flexibility and the skills of negotiation and sensitivity to context required for successful diplomacy are also necessary for a politics which involves the articulation of interests of non-human life. Diplomacy is unpopular, Stengers reminds us, because it is seen as artificiality, yet this is essentially what all forms of politics are. In the politics of diplomacy, we are required to act with deliberation – to slow down, to engage in an encounter with others who may well have other interests. A condition for diplomacy is what Stengers calls 'a *culture of hesitation*' (ibid.: 30; emphasis in original) which values symbiosis, divergence and obligation. This, she says, opens up possibilities for engaging with non-humans politically. How this might actually be done is another matter. James Brassett and William Smith (2010) have argued that the difficulties of deliberation are further exacerbated at the level of international politics. While there have been many arguments for the democratization of global governance and an increase in deliberation involving 'global civil society' (Bohman 2007), opening up international organizations to such deliberation is contested and difficult. This is particularly so because of the way in which international political institutions and processes reflect systemic imperatives of relational power, such as that of capital (Dryzek 2006). In opening up the international political arena to deliberation, it is interesting to see those similar problems of engagements through representation by elites (comparable to the professional scientists of Latour and Stengers) surfacing. For example, Brassett and Smith emphasize cultural interventions by NGOs (2010: 425–30; also Bohman 2010).

The debates in the animal studies literature indicate the terrible difficulties involved with 'knowing' both the being and the possible wants, interests and desires of other species. It is very difficult to know what different species might want, and to determine which beings have interests and wants, and which, if any, do not. The question becomes even trickier if we consider the representation of non-human *systems*. Certainly, governments and international organizations are increasingly interested in the articulation of the powers of things and their integration into public policy. This has taken a variety of forms – reflecting concerns of local and national governments. At a localized level in the UK, for example, there have been attempts to minimize the waste of drinking water (with its tendency to leak from pipes) or to restrict the use of certain chemicals in household and industrial products. The most interesting international example would be the difficult politics of managing climate change through carbon trading schemes. For Foucault, there would be nothing remarkable in this aspect of contemporary politics. Since the eighteenth century, governments have been preoccupied with the control of the world of 'things' in terms of what we might now refer to as securitization (see Foucault 2007). For the final section of this chapter, we will draw on Foucault's notion of 'biopower' and argue that this provides a way of linking the political manipulation of matter to a system of relational power based on intra-human domination and its intersection with the human domination of non-human beings and things.

Embodied power and posthuman politics

As we saw in Chapter 2, many uses of complexity in the social sciences are not able to account for the forms of power exercised by groups of humans over other humans, or by humans over the lifeworld. When John Urry discusses the forms of power in a global age, he is not concerned with the interests which influence the ways in which power might be exercised. This, he suggests, is precisely the point. A complexity approach sees power as 'something that flows or runs and may be increasingly detached from a specific territory or space' (Urry 2003: 112). Power is not to be seen as a possession and is not exercised through interpersonal threat, manipulation or persuasion. Power here is nebulous, diffuse and, most importantly, indifferent. Running through the pages of this book has been a very different understanding of power – the notion of relational systems of social domination that shape social life from local patterns to global systemic features. In Chapter 5, we proposed the ontology of complex ecologism that might be able to consider different intersected patterns of multilevelled relational power between humans and non-human beings and things. In addition, we have suggested that these systemic relations are constitutive of institutionalized sites of political power. We have used complex systems analytics in order to understand these different kinds of systems.

In doing so, we have made use of the work of José López and John Scott on the idea of 'social structure'. Here, they make a dis-armingly simple but highly useful distinction between what they call 'institutional structure', 'relational structure' and 'embodied structure' (2000: 3–5) to capture different facets of the organization of social life. These terms, in our view, are useful to distinguish between *different kinds of system*, those based on sets of institutions and their related procedures and practices (a system of government or the UN system, for example), those based on patterns of social relations (around class, gender, ethnicity, and so on) and those involving the embodiment of social relations and the control of social bodies (such as populations of a particular species, for example). Following López and Scott, we see institutional, relational and embodied aspects of social organization as co-present. A critically posthuman approach to international relations entails three kinds of systems: institutional, relational and embodied.

International relations has made much of the study of an inter-national system wherein the elements are different kinds of states at different levels of political organization, which relate to both one another, in group formations, and to international organizations and both local and international 'civil society'. In Chapters 3 and 4, we provided a consideration of *institutional systems*, and argued that inter-national politics can be understood not only in terms of systems, but of complex, multilevelled and non-linear systems. We also considered questions of power and argued that various *relational systems* of power underpin social and political institutions. In Chapter 5 particularly, we argued that such systems both privilege the human and at the same time are intersected by other complex forms of intra-human relations of social domination based on class, gender, ethnic hierarchy, region, and so on. Being shaped by the environment in which they find themselves, such systemic relations of capitalism or patriarchy, for example, assume various local specific forms; thus we can identify subsystems and sub-subsystems and so on, each with its own distinct level of organized complexity.

In addition, such relational power is *embodied* and it is to the power of embodied systems that the rest of this chapter is devoted. By the embodiment of power relations we mean that, following Foucault, social relations are inscribed on to and embedded in human and other bodies. This is rather a different take on embodied power to the vital materialism of those such as Bennett. Foucault's biopower contains both a micro- and a macro-level understanding of the regulation of bodies, because it considers individual and collective regulation of bodies through social institutions and practice. Both humans and non-human species may be subjected to certain forms of biological control or manipulation with political implications. Relational and institutional systems can be seen in embodied practices – from the eating of a McDonald's burger to a disciplinary discourse on 'healthy eating', which may or may not be successfully inscribed on a population 'at risk'.

In understanding relational, institutional and embodied power as interrelated but also distinct systems, we also take on board the idea (apparent in both complexity theory and in Foucault) that the organization of power is continuously dynamic and shifting. For Foucault, power is never an accomplishment but a constant process of recombination, and this is compatible with a complexity notion of dissipative systems and autopoiesis. However, while we would argue that a Foucauldian notion of biopower is compatible with a complexity framework, it is not sufficient without it. In Foucault's work, we have discourses operating through institutions and practices, but we do not have a sense of the multilevelled qualities of institutional, relational or embodied forms of power. Foucault's method involves an excavation of the detailed historical processes that reveal the operation of specific sites of power. What we are particularly interested in, and what complexity enables, is theorizing the links between and across such sites and the co-constituted qualities of embodied layers of complex social relations and practices. In turn, as we have argued in previous chapters, physiological systems are themselves embedded and implicated in wider bio/social systems. This embedding is of great importance to any theorization which looks at the co-evolution and adaptation of social/natural systems. What we will specifically take from Foucault, therefore, is the notion of the physicality of power relations, and their attachment to institutional power (what we would call institutional systems), and it is to the elaboration of this in the concept of 'biopower' that we now turn.

The posthuman politics of biopower Foucault is interested in the ways complex networks of power relations impinge on the individual physical body and the 'social body'. First, disciplinary power operates at the micro level – Foucault discusses, for example, the ways in which power operates to regulate the spatiality and temporality of the human body, and alters the body's actual movements (Foucault 1979: 136–8). This leads Foucault to discuss the governance of bodies in terms of the *political* technologies of the body' (ibid.: 26). The operation of biopower here centres on the individual body, primarily conceptualized within the medical model (Foucault 1978: 139), but, and more important for our purposes, it focuses on the species body, in terms of population control policies, for example, and conditions of health and variance in longevity (ibid.: 140). A good illustration of the way relational systems are embodied are feminist theorizations which outline the powerful array of disciplinary practices that produce what Foucault would call 'docile bodies' (Foucault 1979: 138). We discipline our bodies; train them, to make them socially acceptable. For example, bodily modifications such as dieting can be seen as gendered forms of embodiment (Bordo 1993: 90).

Secondly, biopower is used as a macro-level concept in order to understand how these disciplinary regimes of the body reproduce normal, productive bodies that fit well with the systemic imperatives of capital. The latter can be clearly seen in Foucault's writings on government, where he argues 'government' is a process of disciplining a population through 'biopolitical' control (Foucault 1976: 42). So, Foucault's biopower is concerned with both the implication of individual bodies in the procedures of social institutions and also the ways in which 'social bodies' are controlled, organized and distributed in social and physical space (Turner 1996: 161).

For Foucault, the nature of modern politics itself is the exercise of biopower, as the control of certain kinds of human populations in certain ways is a key feature of the organization of social life (Foucault 1978: 102). Its institutionalization represents, for Foucault, 'nothing less than the entry of life into history' (Foucault 1984: 264). The concern for the health of the 'social body' gave rise to all kinds of policy decisions and strategies around 'madness', sex, crime, and so on, and a range of disciplinary institutions, practices and professions (Foucault, respectively 1973, 1980, 1979). Biopower can be evidenced in these institutions and practices as individual bodies and selves are placed, ordered and regimented. These social institutions are relational, and are embedded in wider (or, perhaps, ontologically deeper) systems of power relations. In Foucault's case, the social relations of capitalism are the primary mover (1979), although the structural imperatives of race are also considered (2003), as is sexuality (although, interestingly, gender relations do not feature; 1980). In our view, this understanding of the politics of the lifeworld is more useful than many of the ideas of Latour and Stengers when it comes to opening up politics to the world of the non-human. Foucault also sees science as crucial in articulating claims about life, but emphasizes the extent to which these are already very much bound up with the mechanisms of political power (see 2007, in particular).

In Foucault's account, biopower is linked to the concerns of states with security. Alongside the disciplining of individual bodies, biopower is seen as forms of intervention and control that have 'the power to *foster* life or *disallow* it' (1980: 139). In later work, Foucault is specifically concerned with the way in which forms of 'pastoral power' combine with disciplinary power in attending to the health, stability and security of whole populations and 'societies'. This biopower is significant – at once 'an individualizing and totalizing form of state power' (2003: 332).

Michael Dillon and Luis Lobo-Guerrero (2008: 267) develop Foucault's notion of biopower as power exercised with 'species life as its referent object'. They focus on contemporary biopolitical security 'experiments with novel ensembles ... which seek to enact "natures"'. In the contemporary world, they consider that the object of biopolitical security, 'life', has undergone 'profound transformation' (ibid.: 269). This is in terms of technological interventions upon and physical alterations of non-human natures and human bodies and populations. Human security is here recast in terms of physical risk, including that from transformation by chronic illnesses (rather than infectious diseases) and genetic engineering, wherein 'life becomes a matter of continuous mobile recomposition' (ibid.: 289). Here, as for Urry, power seems a slippery, fractured and uncertain property. Dillon and Lobo-Guerrero do attempt to provide some understanding of power as a process of control and regulation in which life (for example, in terms of human health) is encouraged to self-correct by adopting 'best practices'. Modern states and international systems of states promote such best practices in terms of health schemes and poverty reduction strategies (ibid.: 291), and this promotion of 'life' is a regulatory and disciplinary exercise of power. Clearly, this notion blurs distinctions between micro and macro levels of 'politics', as we noted in our discussion of the 'greening' of private space in liberal states, above.

The notion of biopower explicitly links power to the biosphere. It is this kind of move which is necessary in order to enable us to theorize about international relations beyond the human. For example, environmental questions are subsumed under a bureaucratic rationality of resource managerialism by various nodes in the institutional system of international politics, be they local, national, regional or 'global' levels of governance (see Luke 1999). Robyn Eckersley (2004) has raised territorially based governance as a key problematic in terms of understanding environmental risks and accounting for diverse engagements of humans with non-human species and scapes. As Eva Lövbrand and Johannes Stripple (2006: 234–5) note, the climate is itself an international political space, which is fundamentally shaped by local, national and international politics. The contemporary features of the 'carbon cycle' are tied in to a logic of nation-states operating territorially. Yet, while we concur that the climate is indeed a political space, and that the institutional systems of states seek and fail in their attempts to reterritorialize and 'manage' it, climate is also a space shaped by relational power. The climate is shaped by relations of capitalism, colonialism and other regimes of power and domination. Evidence suggests that various kinds of global environmental change have qualitatively and quantitatively different impacts than in previous decades, owing to the intensity and scale of human activities, resulting in a potential collapse of both human social systems and natural ecosystems (McNeill 2000).

Social systems, including those of political institutions and relations, are shaped by different forms of power: relational, institutional and embodied. Human power relations are fundamentally interested – that is to say, the interests of individuals and collectivities organize political power. What we have seen from the different forms of political ecologism is that various kinds of analytics and politics might be adopted. Our ontology is one which considers the impact of various intersecting kinds of human domination and relational power – capitalism, patriarchy, colonialism, alongside our social relations of domination over natural systems and non-human species and scapes. Indeed, political, social and economic elites have attempted to legitimize, often successfully, highly iniquitous patterns of land use and resource allocation, exploitation of seas, soils and waterways, alongside the constitution of iniquitous social arrangements in which certain human populations are oppressed, exploited or marginalized.

A posthuman international relations for earthlings

What draws together different kinds of posthumanists, be they vital materialists, political ecologists, complex ecologists or Foucauldians, is the idea of the politics of life, be it human or non-human. 'We', the living, for example, are embedded in a carbon cycle that international politics seeks increasingly to regulate. Our embodied and embedded condition in a world of multiple species and systems which operate at multiple levels from domestic relations in the home to the regulation of the temperature of the planet raises deep problems for politics based on the fictive constructs of nation-states.

Yet in the contemporary world, nation-states are multiplying and many are strengthening. Even in the face of anthropogenic climate change, the politics of states assert themselves in regional and global policy, for as Lövbrand and Stripple (2006: 218) note:

> ... the 1997 Kyoto Protocol to the Climate convention opens up the inclusion of land-based carbon sinks as a way for states to comply with their emission reduction targets. In less than fifteen years, the international climate discourse has rearticulated global carbon flows as 'national sinks'.

Vital materialists such as Stengers (2010a) argue that we cannot have a politics that is not attached to a cosmos – we need to articulate a 'cosmopolitics' to reflect our more-than-human condition. The complexity theorizing of Edgar Morin (2008), whom we met in Chapter 2, suggests a similarly cosmological understanding of the co-constituted lifeworld of social and natural systems. We would not disagree, but we do think these are utopian texts.

The world of politics, national and international, is an artifice, just as Latour suggests. It cannot capture the cosmological reality of life on this planet, and attempts by institutions of human governance to regulate life, since the eighteenth century in particular, have remade a world in deeply problematic ways. Kuehls (1996) has argued that the space of ecopolitics must be beyond sovereign territory. Currently, it is not, and we are faced with the biopolitics of nation-states and the international institutional system of states attempting to regulate life with such problematic consequences. The notion of bio-regionalism, developed in the 1970s, remains a pipedream; notions of 'environmental citizenship' poorly describe the identities of human citizens, and the speaking, human political subject remains a foundational discourse of 'the political'. We have not yet made much headway in developing theories, let alone politics, *for earthlings*.

Perhaps if international relations – a discipline so preoccupied with territory and borders – can move more firmly into explaining international politics in terms of systems, preferably complex ones and not just institutional ones, it might better grasp the politics of the world in which we live. That world is not divided into territories in which bounded societies of humans live under singular political authority and in the context of discrete 'natural environments'. Posthuman international relations, then, would be concerned with the study of the politics of international systems. In Chapters 2 to 5, we argued that complex systems thinking alone is insufficient. We also require a critical politics. International relations has demonstrated, at least at its margins, the growth of critical positions, and these have also often been an antidote to state-centrism. This has been particularly driven by feminist scholarship, for example, and the attempt to broaden the actors and 'populations' of study – to women, of course, and also more recently to children. The realization of an international relations which better appreciates the ways in which our world is teeming with multiple human and non-human lives, relations and formations of being represents a more fundamental challenge.

We have argued that a complexity approach to international politics that takes into account the worlds beyond the human species requires an understanding of social, political and economic relations as impacting beyond the human and as co-constituted by elements of non-human and human systems. This chapter has also contended that theorizations should be *critically* posthuman in quality. By this we mean that they need to understand our human condition as embedded in, and constituted with, relations and practices with other species that are shaped by power. Critically posthumanist analysis, therefore, must also acknowledge forms of power and domination over non-human beings. We have also argued for an appreciation of the different kinds of social systems – relational, institutional and embodied. Both relational and embodied systems have made their presence strongly felt in this chapter. In terms of relational systems, we argued for a political position which attempts to account for social intersectionality and various kinds of power relations, particularly those of human domination over the non-human lifeworld. This chapter has endorsed one of the key insights of posthumanist theorizing – our condition as embodied creatures, co-constituted with myriad other beings and things. The embodied condition of both humans and non-human species must be recognized as a site of power relations. This embodied power has been under-theorized in international relations. This chapter has suggested that we might need to rethink our very conceptions of politics in the light of our posthuman being in the world. That task, however, is one for another book! The task at hand here is to integrate the insights of embodied power and complex ecologism into our understanding of international systems as complex, and make our case for posthuman international relations.

7 · For a posthuman international relations

> Where international relations is supposed to be and where it's not supposed to be. To be or not to be: that is a question of powerful surreptitious stealth versus power officially scripted. Both exist side by side, mimicking each other, hiding together sometimes or shouting loudly at one another, often out of kilter. International relations where it's not supposed to be is not some understudy to international relations where it's supposed to be. It's not waiting in the wings for the superstars to get ill. No. It has its own missions, parties, techniques, destinations and drivers. It's there, giving off a whiff of smelly cheese as it passes. That's enough to put most people off, but international relations where it's not supposed to be also has investigators and devotees. (Sylvester 2004: 58)

The purpose of this book is to argue for a posthuman international relations. This is, no doubt, an international relations where, in Christine Sylvester's words, it's not 'supposed to be'. For many, it will give off an unappealing aroma. We hope, though, to encourage others to investigate its potentials. In this final chapter we will assess some of the implications for the discipline of taking a posthuman approach, make some brief comments on the policy implications of living in a complex world and consider avenues of further research.

Implications of posthuman approaches for the study of international relations

A posthuman approach to the study of international relations has a variety of implications, epistemologically, ontologically, methodologically and ethically. We start with some of the implications that acknowledging complexity has for the study of international relations. As we have argued, many studies of international relations have attempted to follow a means of studying the social world derived from Newtonian physics. The central characteristic of such an approach is to perceive the world as operating like a gigantic calculating machine. The outcomes from this calculating machine are regular, repeatable and predetermined. The model here is Pierre-Simon Laplace's (1902 [1840]: 4) 'intelligence sufficient vast' to be able to 'embrace in the same formula the movements of the greatest bodies in the universe and those of the lightest atom; for it nothing would be uncertain and the future, as the past, would be present to its eyes'.

Three characteristics of complex systems in particular are significant in terms of challenging the Newtonian model of the social world: complex systems are non-mechanical and unpredictable; complex systems require a historical understanding of phenomena; and the study of complex systems involves a rejection of subject–object differentiation.

Complex systems are non-mechanical and unpredictable A key feature of complex systems is that they can behave in both linear and non-linear ways. In a linear system we would expect there to be a constant and predictable relationship between cause and effect. For example, if I throw a ball twice as hard, I might expect it to go twice as far. Most models of the international system expect such a constant relationship between variables. For Kenneth Waltz (1979), there was the expectation that there would be a regular relationship between the number of great powers and the characteristics of international relations: a bipolar system will exhibit greater stability than a unipolar system. The democratic peace theory, seen as coming 'as close as anything we have to an empirical law in international relations' (Levy 1988: 662), likewise points to a supposed regular linear relationship in international relations – democracies don't fight each other. In non-linear systems such regularities are less reliable. There is no predictable pattern in terms of the relationship between events, and there is no expectation that the same events will result in the same pattern of results.

Ultimately, a complex approach to the study of the social world suggests that there are very definite limits to how much predictability is possible. This is, of course, a less comfortable viewpoint, in particular for a discipline that originated in an attempt to put controls on the operation of the social world – to find and put limits on the occurrence of warfare. This may indicate why complexity theory has, thus far, made little impact on the discipline (or where it has, it is primarily in terms of actor-based modelling approaches). It is much more reassuring to be able to offer predictions and to suggest that there may be obvious connections between policy and outcomes. Complexity theory suggests that while complex systems can exhibit linear behaviour, this may be the exception rather than the rule, and that prediction based on linearity is successful by coincidence rather than by correlation. As Patrick Baker (1993: 133) observes, 'order is always transitory. The pattern of interaction is repeated and then without warning, a change occurs.' It is more reassuring to seek order and predictability, and this may explain the persuasiveness of approaches that suggest that this is possible. However, as Cristoforo Bertuglia and Franco Vaio (2005: 242) indicate, 'a linear tool, even if substantially inadequate to describe natural and social phenomena, with the exception of a very limited number of cases, erroneously appears to be more useful and more correct than a nonlinear one, because the latter does not allow us to make predictions, whereas the former does'. Complexity theory suggests that, although less comfortable, the possibilities for prediction-making are limited. Certainty is, of course, a good thing, but 'if it is a false certainty, then this is very bad' (Morin 2008: 97).

Complex systems and 'time's arrow' A second element in Newtonian social sciences is the attempt to stand outside of history and to seek timeless laws. In Newtonian physics processes are reversible – in other words 'laws governing behavior work the same in both temporal directions' (Ulanowicz 2007: 29). This notion of reversibility, together with a mechanical view of the world as described in the previous section, has been carried over into the analysis of the social world. However, such reversibility is not a feature of complex systems; instead they are the subject of what complexity theorists describe as 'time's arrow'.

Time's arrow has been described by the physicist Ilya Prigogine (2003: 56) as 'the irreversible succession of events'. Complex systems are in a constant state of flux, and are 'active and creative' (Gulbenkian Commission 1996: 61). In other words, complex systems do not remain in a 'constant state' where the interactions between the parts can be modelled as if their features were fixed. They are constantly changing and, in particular, over time have a propensity to become more complex. Complex systems develop in an organic fashion in that the interactions between the parts, and the character of their interactions, become increasingly multifaceted. In this process, systems and agents change in ways that are not reversible. As James McGlade and Elizabeth Garnsey (2006: 3) observe, 'It is ... difficult, if not impossible to study [a complex system's] properties by decomposing it into functionally stable parts.'

Complicating matters further, in complex systems, feedback mechanisms are seen as central to the understanding of systems development. Also, complex systems are seen as being very susceptible to minute changes in initial conditions. In other words, very small fluctuations in starting circumstances can result in major changes in terms of the development of the system. The classic example of this is, of course, Lorenz's notion of a butterfly flapping its wings in Brazil resulting in a tornado in Texas, though it might perhaps not be too difficult to think about similar examples from the realm of international politics.

These characteristics of complex systems have considerable implications for the study of the social world. We have already argued that complex systems exhibit unpredictability. We would also argue that because of their actively creative features, it is the development of social systems which should be studied. This would be a distinctly different approach from that of, for example, Waltzian neorealism. Waltz sees the international system as essentially unchanging because of the determinant features of anarchy, which conditions states to act in certain ways. Complexity theorists would argue that while international systems may be stable for a certain period of time, autopoiesis would be likely to result in changes in their character. The central contribution that students of international relations can make is to study the development of that system, its self-organizing characteristics, and its relations to other human (such as capitalism, colonialism, patriarchy) and non-human (other species, the biosphere) systems. Sensitivity to initial conditions, and the very large potential impacts of very small events, also suggests that causal analysis is a rather uncertain undertaking in the analysis of complex systems. Ultimately, a historical approach is the only means to understanding the development of complex systems.

Complexity theory and subject–object differentiation   As noted in the previous section, a feature of complex systems is that small events can have a large impact. This extends to the role of the researcher, and the impact that pursuing a particular line of inquiry might have. Based on a Newtonian world-view that saw the world as external to the observer, many of the social sciences have maintained a view of a strict distinction between subject and object. This strict distinction between subject and object started to break down in the physical sciences in quantum mechanics, where in the famous two-slit experiment the result of the experiment was found to depend on what was actually being measured. As the physicist Werner Heisenberg (quoted in Law and Urry 2004: 395) observed, 'what we observe is not nature itself, but nature exposed to our method of questioning'. Subject–object differentiation has come under considerable criticism in the social sciences and in international relations. Initial scepticism came from a Critical Theory perspective, noting that our values direct and colour our observations, and from a poststructural perspective, where the focus has been on the analysis of discourse.

A complexity approach would acknowledge (in common with Critical Theory) that values play a role in the research process, though (contrary to poststructuralism) there is an external world of which we can have knowledge (however contingent that knowledge might be). Where subject–object differentiation breaks down for complexity theorists is in the interconnectedness and overlapping of systems. By carrying out research and measurement, students of international politics impact on the subjects of study. As noted by Bertuglia and Vaio (2005: 268), complexity approaches imply 'the idea that an observer cannot be detached from the real situation that [s]he is describing. The act of measuring in itself perturbs the state of what is being measured, which leads to the abandonment of the idea that we can obtain a totally objective description of a reality detached from the observer and in itself objective.'

What this suggests is that the act of study is neither neutral nor without impact. Our research can cause 'perturbations' in and beyond the systems that we are studying with unpredictable results. Hence, as Alexander Wendt (2006: 217) notes, there is an ethical element to our undertakings: 'If IR scholars are irreducibly participants in the super-organism that is world politics ... then we have ethical responsibilities to the other subjects of those politics in measuring them, responsibilities which we do not necessarily have if facts and values can be clearly separated as in the classical worldview.' Small actions, then, can have a larger impact, and though we would disagree with John Law and John Urry (2004) that in carrying out research we are 'enacting the social', which sounds far too purposeful and determinist, our actions as students of international politics are not without potential (though unpredictable) results. The Newtonian notion of a distinction between subject and object breaks down from a complex perspective because of the overlapping of complex systems and the possibility that action can occur at a distance.

Why posthuman international relations?

As we have seen, there are some serious implications in the development of a posthuman/non-Newtonian approach to thinking about international relations. Such an approach, we argue, has benefits to offer in thinking about global politics, though it also has what might be considered to be limitations. Here we advance some reasons for adopting a posthuman style of analysis.

The unpredictability of international relations Central to the development of rationalist theory in international relations has been the claim that theories can be verified by their ability to make statements that can be confirmed by future events. But these attempts to produce a predictive capacity in international relations have been plagued by the uncooperative character of events. To a certain extent the discipline of international relations has never recovered from the failure to predict the end of the Cold War. Through the 1970s and 1980s it was a shibboleth of the discipline that the bipolar system was stable and enduring. However, the Soviet Union disappeared, virtually overnight. In the early 1990s there was much talk of Japan becoming the next global hegemon, and very little discussion of the growing significance of China. The impacts of the attacks of 11 September 2001, for some the defining international event of the current century, were not predicted. Significantly for the study of international relations, given their international impact, the attacks were carried out by a non-state actor. These unexpected, and probably unpredictable, events suggest that an approach to studying international relations is needed that has at its core a view of the world as unpredictable.

To be in the prediction business is not useful for international relations, and, we would argue, not possible. It may also be inherently harmful. Starting with a perspective that it is possible to predict future events, to foresee what the likely results of our actions will be, potentially gives policy-makers a greater confidence about their actions than is warranted. Starting out from a perspective that the future is intrinsically unknowable, that in implementing policy decisions we need to allow for the unexpected, that greater caution is needed, and greater preparedness to respond to unexpected developments, might lead to more effective decision-making.

An account of systems As we saw in Chapter 3, a key feature of the discipline has been the attempt to develop a systemic theory of international relations. The character of the subject itself, given its global character, seems to imply the need for a way of thinking about global politics that can theorize the interactions between a range of units. However, systems thinking in international relations has been plagued by a number of problems. The posthuman approach to thinking about systems draws on thinking from a number of disciplines in developing a much more dynamic account. In particular, the concept of the complex adaptive system provides a much more effective way of thinking about how systems develop and how they interact and co-evolve with other systems. The focus in the analysis of complex adaptive systems is on change rather than the stasis of, for example, neorealism. Self-organizing systems will develop as a result of interactions at the unit level, and are subject to change as the character of the units and their interactions change. Neither the character of the units nor the outcome of their interactions is a 'given'. Complex adaptive systems also operate in an environment of other systems and adapt as these interactions develop. As systems come into contact with other systems their character will change. Powerful actors may have the capacity to affect the fitness landscape in which other actors operate, forcing them to adapt to changing circumstances. Hence it is possible to interpret change from both within and outside of particular systems.

A way out of the level of analysis problem Posthuman international relations doesn't so much offer a solution to the level of analysis problem as transcend it altogether. In David Singer's (1961: 77) initial formulation, the level of analysis problem was one where there were 'manifold implications' to the choice of what level (system, unit) of analysis was chosen as the focus. International relations could be studied at one of a number of levels of analysis, but the level chosen, and for Singer there always was a choice to be made, would introduce distortions. The problem was choosing the level of analysis that introduced the lowest level of distortion for a particular area of study. The level of analysis problem subsequently reappeared as the agent–structure debate, spawning its own enormous literature.

The perspective from a complex adaptive systems approach is somewhat different. The system level is emergent from the interactions of the units and hence, while perhaps a *different* level of analysis, it is not a *distinct* level of analysis. It is different in that we can distinguish between system-level features and unit-level features. Indeed, given that there are emergent features at the system level, an analysis simply of unit-level interactions will be incomplete. But it is not distinct as it is the interactions at the unit level which lead to system-level features. Hence, to see system and units as separate is problematic. For Edgar Morin (2008: 85), the issue was that 'not only is the part in the whole, but the whole is in the part'. In order to understand the unit level we also need to understand the systemic level. Thus international systems can be understood, as we argued in Chapter 3, as a form of self-organization, emergent from the interactions of unit-level actors. These in turn are also systems with emergent features. In turn, systems take as their environment all other systems, and will, if they are to persist, have to develop dependent on the exigencies of those relations.

Questions of causality The Newtonian basis of much international relations theorizing has developed from a view of the world that perceives the possibility of determining the ultimate causes of particular events. A feature of this form of theorizing is the possibility of saying 'if x then y' (all other things being equal). In a detailed discussion of causality in international relations, Milja Kurki (2008) has argued that the discipline has had a very limited notion of what causality entails. Both sides of the 'divided discipline' (in other words, positivists and post-positivists) have envisaged causality in Humean terms, whether they have supported causal analysis of that kind, or whether they have rejected it. Such a perspective has a limited view of causes that regards causal analysis as the study of regularities that are observable, deterministic and efficient (ibid.: 6). This view of what constitutes a cause is closely linked to Newtonian approaches to physics and, as Kurki argues, will be of limited application to the study of the social world. However, as she argues, even those who reject causal analysis base their idea of what this constitutes on the Humean account of causality. In its place Kurki draws on philosophical realism to advocate the importance of 'deep ontology' in 'reclaiming causal analysis'. By this she means seeing causes as 'real non-conceptual "naturally necessitating" ontological entities, structures, relations, conditions or forces that produce outcomes or processes' (ibid.: 295).

Complexity theorists have a slightly different approach to thinking about causality. While, as will be apparent from the discussion so far in this book, we would reject a Humean approach, and concur that a wider discussion of causality is valuable, in the analysis of a complex world it becomes very difficult to talk about causes. As with the level of analysis/agent–structure debate, complexity theorizing suggests attempting to transcend these issues.

Neil Harrison (2006b) argues that there are four reasons why the Humean account of causation is not suited for the analysis of complex systems. First, it applies only to closed systems, whereas a keystone of complexity analyses is the analysis of open systems. He notes that 'in an open system, a cause may have different effects at different times due to changed conditions. Therefore, it is not surprising that no general laws of world politics have been found' (ibid.: 12). As David Harvey points out, 'in nature's open milieu the constancy of causal sequences – the empiricist's guarantor of nature's "iron-clad laws" – breaks down' (Harvey 2009: 25). Secondly, Humean causal analysis depends on very simple models, which may 'dangerously oversimplify' complex events. Thirdly, in complex analysis cause and effect may be non-local, a view that is rejected by both Hume and Newton. And finally, cause and effect can be simultaneous, again an idea that is rejected by Hume (see also Forrester 1971; Sterman 2002: 511).

The central issue is that in complex systems there is a 'tangle of actions, interactions, and feedback' (Morin 2008: 84; see also Bertuglia and Vaio 2005: 282). This tangle is such that it is in practice not feasible to make sensible claims about causal processes. Complex systems are also subject to time's arrow, such that tracing causal processes, as many historians suggest, is an uncertain undertaking (Beaumont 2000: 178).

Complexity approaches therefore do not reject causality outright, but rather point to the phenomenal difficulties of ascertaining what those causes might be – given the characteristics of complex adaptive systems as non-linear, sensitive to initial conditions and subject to action at a distance and simultaneity. As a form of analysis, then, complexity theory suggests as an alternative the investigation of systems development, and in particular the forms of co-evolution between systems. While it may not be possible to isolate causes in a traditional sense, or perhaps even in the wider sense promoted by Kurki, understanding how systems have developed as they have remains a fruitful line of study.

The study of environmental issues It is a 'foundational myth' of international relations that the discipline was founded in the wake of the First World War to study the causes of war and promote ways of avoiding conflict (Smith 2000: 376). War has remained at the centre of the discipline, and for many scholars the prime form that such conflicts have taken is interstate war. While war, and the continued threat of the use of nuclear weapons, remains a threat to global welfare, the occurrence of interstate war has declined (Gleditsch et al. 2002) (the 2003 invasion of Iraq being a notable exception), and other dangers have appeared. Potentially the most significant of these are environmental issues, in particular climate change. In our view, international relations has a central role to play in the analysis of these issues – environmental questions are certainly trans-boundary and frequently global; and attempts to address environmental issues frequently involve international actors, whether states, international organizations or non-governmental organizations. Yet, as we saw in Chapter 5, international relations as currently configured has confronted considerable difficulties in addressing environmental matters. In Chapter 5 we argued for a 'complex ecologism' and in Chapter 6 we furthered this by proposing a posthuman international relations.

In short, a reorientation of the discipline is needed in order to tackle the global issues that we confront.

We would argue for a posthuman approach because it provides a way of analysing interactions between a range of systems, and examines the ways in which those systems have co-evolved. As we saw in Chapter 4, international systems are not independent of other systems but are better envisaged as embedded and interacting and co-evolving with a range of other systems. Furthermore, international systems are embedded in a range of non-human and inanimate systems, and considering these as complex adaptive systems opens a mean of analysing their interactions. By decentring the human, posthuman international relations stresses the contingent character of human existence and the embedded and overlapping character of human and non-human systems. Rather than seeing humans as the centre of analysis, posthuman international relations stresses that human activity depends on and affects the multi-variety of other systems that comprise the globe. Hence posthuman international relations provides a means of considering these interrelations, but also stresses an ethic of shared dependence on the biosphere.

The costs of a complexity approach

While we advocate the development of a posthuman international relations, we are very much aware that this comes with costs. These are costs that some within the discipline may be unwilling to bear. Though it is not our intention to dismiss all non-complexity theorizing, if complexity is a feature of the social world (a judgement that will ultimately be one made by the reader), then the logical conclusion is that theorizing that does not take that into account will ultimately be limited and unreliable. Policy built on such foundations will be potentially hazardous.

Limits to knowledge As we have seen, the core of Newtonian physics is the idea that we can look for regularities in phenomena and assume that these regularities are the basis for making causal statements about the world. The observation that democracies don't go to war with each other (a dubious claim in the first place) has been the basis of a democratic peace theory, and is perhaps a flawed element in the making of US foreign policy. For complexity theorists, such claims are dubious. While patterns may exist for a while, these can change suddenly and inexplicably. Ultimately, the derivation of laws of activity is not possible, and the future is unknowable and unpredictable.

Events cannot be controlled through knowledge, as the same actions may result in different consequences as complex adaptive systems change over time. Hence, to see the discipline as one that can make reliable predictions about the future is futile.

Policy relevance An important claim for a significant part of the discipline has been that it can provide policy-relevant information and predictions for state leaders. Even some critical approaches (for example, Marxism) have assumed that there are patterns of activity that can provide predictions for the basis of future events which can be used to develop a political programme. As we have seen, complexity approaches are sceptical about such claims. Uncertainty, as Robert Boardman (2010: 38) notes, is a 'certainty'.

A first reaction to this pervading uncertainty might be that there are no policy recommendations that can be made from a complexity perspective. An even more extreme position might be that policy is ultimately an irrelevance because policy-makers can never predict what the outcome of their policies will be, so there is no point in trying to alter the world – it will never work as was planned, and actions may be totally counterproductive with respect to intended and desired outcomes. Yet this is a deeply nihilistic and conservative position. And it is certainly not one that we advocate.

We will discuss some of the policy implications of complexity in the next section. The point that we are making here is that complexity theorizing implies a *different* form of policy advice. Policy cannot be based on claimed certainties – such as, for example, that states in a bipolar world will behave in a certain fashion. Instead, policy advice can be directed towards dealing with a complex world, and pursuing desired outcomes. In other words, the form of policy advice from a complexity perspective needs to be more grounded in uncertainty and ways of responding to that uncertainty.

Ideology What are the implications for ideological positions of a complexity perspective? Does it mean an end to ideology and political programmes? The starting point for the posthuman international relations that we are suggesting is an ontological claim – that complexity is an observable phenomenon. Ideas derived from complexity thinking have been used to develop analyses from a variety of perspectives, and in essence there is no specific ideological programme that develops from complexity thinking. Policy-makers confront complexity regardless of their political viewpoint. However, some theoretical positions in international relations may find complexity thinking more problematic than others. Realism, where there is a priority in retaining a focus on the state as an unchanging actor in an unchanging environment of anarchy, is likely to have problems with accepting insights from complexity, or will seek to abstract these so far from complexity that basic precepts are ignored. Realism and derivatives of classical realism have perceived themselves as based on Newtonian science from which a 'timeless wisdom' can be derived. Complexity thinking would therefore challenge such an approach epistemologically and ontologically.

Thinking in international relations that has focused on studying historical development would therefore find complexity approaches less threatening – Marxist thinking, Critical Theory (Frankfurt School) and historical sociology would all seem to exhibit characteristics which could be combined with complexity thinking – as well as anarchist contributions to international relations (see Cudworth and Hobden 2010). Mick Dillon (2000: 13) points to the overlaps between complexity thinking and poststructural approaches but argues that the former 'remains heavily strategic'.

Ultimately, then, complexity thinking can be seen as complementary to a number of theoretical perspectives. Does this mean that it lacks an ideological position or viewpoint about what might constitute an effective way to organize society? We would argue that it can be seen as 'critical' in Robert Cox's (1981: 129) sense of the term, in that it does not take the world as given, but instead seeks to analyse how the world has come into existence. It is also reflexive and aware of its own role in effecting social developments through entanglement and the effects of small variations in initial conditions. Likewise, Sylvia Walby (2009) has indicated the utility of complexity thinking in the analysis of complex inequalities.

Hence, while complexity approaches start from an observation about the characteristics of the animate and inanimate world, the conclusions that are drawn from this starting point will reflect the priorities and interests of the analyst. It may not be possible to wish complexity away, but the conclusions that are drawn regarding the implications of complexity are diverse. The complex ecologism discussed in Chapter 5 indicated the close interlinkages between human and non-human systems, whether animate or inanimate, and Chapter 6 argued for a rethinking that decentred the position of the human in international relations. These perspectives provide the starting point for considering complexity-related policy recommendations.

Policy implications – progress in a complex world

As we noted in the last section, if complexity is a feature, perhaps the defining feature, of existence, then it has great implications for policy-makers and the policy process. Perhaps it is the facility for analysis which might make complexity theory a valuable contribution to the policy-making process. As Euel Elliott and Douglas Kiel comment, most policy-making is based on 'assumptions of simplicity that fail to match the deep and multiple interactions that create complex phenomena' (Elliott and Kiel 1997: 77). While complexity theory may not be able to offer direct answers, it may be able to indicate some of the problems involved in the implementation of policy. A number of authors have considered the implications of complexity for policy-making. In this section we start by considering some of this work, before contributing some comments of our own.

Jay Forrester points to a number of counter-intuitive features of policy-making. First, 'social systems are inherently insensitive to most policy changes that people choose in an effort to alter the behavior of systems' (Forrester 1971: 11). This is because in complex systems there is often a large distance, spatially or temporally (or both), between cause and effect. In dealing with a particular symptom, policy-makers often make the mistake of seeing a local cause of a particular problem rather than considering a more remote cause. For example, in their discussion of terrorism, Robert Geyer and Samir Rihani (2010: 168) point to the tendency of governments to ascribe terrorist activities to 'creed and ethnic background or inbred hatred of democracy' rather than seeking more deep-rooted sources. A second counter-intuitive feature for Forrester (1971: 12) is that 'social systems seem to have a few sensitive influence points through which behavior can be changed'. The problem is that these high-influence points are very hard to identify. Furthermore, even when, whether by skill or plain luck, a high-influence point is chanced upon, there may well be a serious difference between the policy intention and the final outcome. Finally, Forrester (ibid.: 12) argues that there can be a considerable difference between policy outcomes in the short and long term. In particular, policies that show short-term improvements are likely to result in long-term degradation of the system. Forrester suggests that there are some serious problems for policy-makers operating in a complex world.

Gilberto Gallopín (2002), with reference to sustainable development, also points to problems confronting policy-makers in complex systems. First, there is the issue of willingness. Because of unequal power arrangements, vested interests and a perception of social systems as competitive rather than cooperative, some actors fail to see sustainable development policies as being in their interests. Secondly, policy-makers fail to understand the multifaceted linkages and inter-relationships in complex systems. This is compounded by 'compart-mentalized perceptions of reality and a scientific tradition and training that are still largely reductionist [which] impair the development of understanding' (ibid.: 362). Finally, there is a lack of capacity, when dealing with complex issues, in terms of institutions, financial and human resources and infrastructure. Difficulties with policy-making are compounded, Gallopín argues, by an increase in complexity. First, at an ontological level, humans are quite simply changing the world. At an environmental level this is to such an extent that some now claim we are in the anthropocene era (Dalby 2007, 2009: 100). Secondly, there are epistemological changes as complexity thinking becomes more widespread: 'this new understanding emphasizes that unpredict-ability and surprise may be woven into the fabric of reality' (Gallopín 2002: 364). Finally, there are changes in patterns of decision-making, becoming more participatory, involving a greater range of actors, and a larger range of concerns (such as the environment, human rights and animal rights). All of these factors contribute to the complexity of socio-ecological issues confronting policy-makers with a larger range of potential issues and side effects.

More positively, some of the contributors to the Gunderson and Holling (2002) *Panarchy* collection point to the resilience of human-ecological systems – in particular, human capabilities in applying and expanding adaptation possibilities. Marco Janssen (2002) argues that we can consider adaptation as a series of 'surprises' and 'insti-tutional phases'. A period of policy development will be followed by attempts at implementation. Should the policy be successful bureau-cratic procedures will develop that will formalize and institutionalize those procedures. At some point a surprise or a challenge will ap-pear which challenges those institutions and procedures. At which point alternatives will be considered. These alternatives might involve the continuation of existing institutions, but with novel policy pro-grammes, or a system change to a new type of institution. In either case, the cycle begins again with a new phase of policy development and implementation.

Climate change is perhaps an example which highlights the difficul-ties confronted by policy-makers (Mitchell 2009: 89–92). Policy-makers analysing the data produced by climate scientists are confronted by a very large number of variables, few of which are well understood, and at the same time they are aware that there are variables which will affect the outcome that haven't even been identified yet. These are all interconnected by positive and negative feedback loops. All of these variables may change in non-linear and even random ways. More detailed models of the climate system don't help as they simply add more variables, piling more complexity on top of complexity. A standard decision-making process, 'predict and act', makes little sense in such a scenario as prediction is in practical terms meaningless. Confronted by such uncertainty, it is perhaps unsurprising that there is a temptation to do little.

Sandra Mitchell suggests an approach to dealing with complexity, replacing both the 'predict' and the 'act' in conventional approaches with 'evaluate scenarios and adaptively manage'. She suggests that prediction should be replaced by models 'of multiple alternative futures' (ibid.: 90). The purpose is to use computing power to produce models that evaluate different variables and possible policy effects across as wide a range of scenarios as is possible. Scenario modelling should be complemented by adaptive management. Instead of invariant action plans, adaptive management aims to build uncertainty into the policy process. Carol Murray and David Marmorek (quoted in ibid.: 96) advocate 'a six-stage process: problem assessment, experimental design, implementation, monitoring, evaluation and management adjustment'. The aim is to build flexibility into the policy process, to learn from mistakes, and to adapt to changing situations – which may have been induced by the initial policy implementation. This requires, as they note, 'curiosity, innovation, courage to admit uncertainty, and a commitment to learning'.

Robert Axelrod and Michael Cohen suggest that it is possible to go farther, and harness complexity. What they mean by this is that it is possible to use the dynamics of complex systems in productive ways. There are three main interlinked ways (Axelrod and Cohen 1999: 155–8) in which advantage can be taken of complexity. First, by building variation into policy options. Variety is important because it increases the number of options that can be explored and allows more successful options to be pursued when certain possibilities fail. Too much variety can be problematic but, as in the 'predict and act' models discussed above, a lack of variety can be disastrous. Secondly, through developing internal and external interaction. Interaction is important in complex adaptive systems because it is through the interactions of units that emergent features develop. Hence, the effectiveness and robustness of a system can be increased by promoting interaction among its units. Interaction can also occur between systems. Interaction between systems can also be significant as a way of introducing variety, and through, for example, trade, promoting internal interactions. Variety and interaction therefore promote a more robust form of system: variety by increasing the options to deal with uncertain circumstances, and interaction by building links within and across systems. The third element, Axelrod and Cohen argue, is selection – the capacity to select the most appropriate options. This involves consideration of what the criteria are for success, and being prepared to identify short-term goals that can give an indication of whether a policy is having the desired effect or needs to be adapted.

From this very brief discussion of policy principles perhaps three general ideas could be derived. First, a precautionary principle. The study of complexity suggests that the possibilities for predicting the outcomes of certain policies are limited. This does not mean that all policies are doomed to failure, or that policy should not be made or implemented. However, 'we are not only failing to solve the persistent problems we face, but are in fact causing them' (Sterman 2002: 504). Policies may have expected outcomes, but in complex systems the unexpected should be anticipated, and hence the possible wider implications of policy options should be considered carefully before implementation. Morin (2008: 96) argues that policy-makers need a strategy, which he defines as 'the art of working with uncertainty'. While it should not be expected that the outcomes can be predicted, policy-makers and implementers should be aware of the possible wider impacts of specific strategies, and should allow both for unexpected results and for impacts distant from the point of implementation. The Chinese phrase 'crossing the river by feeling the stones', associated with Deng Xiaoping's economic reforms, could be a model here – the idea that advance should be slow, careful and always ready to make adjustments depending on the situation.

Secondly, a humility principle is required. Complexity approaches stress the character of overlapping and intersectionalized systems. Human systems are embedded in and coexist with uncountable animate and inanimate systems. Developments and processes within one system can ripple through systems, sparking different development trajectories. As Morin (ibid.: 96) points out, 'action escapes the will of the actor', and enters not only wider human society, but also potentially into non-human systems. Policy-makers need to avoid the 'arrogant dogmatism which rules non-complex forms of thinking' (ibid.: 97), and accept the human situation of being embedded within a potentially enormous range of other systems. Policy development in a complex world is clearly an area where there is room for much further research.

A third factor for effective policy-making would be to consider policy in terms of resilience. Issues of resilience – in other words, the capacity for natural and social systems to adapt successfully to changes in their environment – is at the forefront of the discussions of panarchy (Gunderson and Holling 2002). A central concern for policy-makers should be the extent to which policy proposals undermine or support the resilience of existing social systems. Clearly, those that reduce the resilience of human or non-human systems risk wider dislocations. These dislocations could occur as a direct result of the policy changes, or owing to the reduced capacity of a system to adapt to other (potentially totally unrelated) changes in the environment.

Future research

In addition to the problems of policy-making, confronting complexity presents many challenges for social research. The move from a Newtonian social science to a complexity-influenced one means: while the search for regularities remains a valid activity, there is no presumption that these regularities will persist; causal analysis will always be difficult because interlinked events may be separated spatially and temporally; systems are embedded and overlapping. There is clearly much work to be done! In terms of thinking about avenues for future research we can consider this in terms of ontology, epistemology and methodology. Here we offer no answers, but further questions.

Ontology A posthuman approach poses important questions regarding the focus of analysis in international relations. The state has often been perceived as the key actor. The differentiated complexity approach that we have outlined focuses on systems, suggesting perhaps that a major area for research could be the analysis of international systems as complex adaptive systems. A very preliminary sketch of such an emphasis was given in Chapter 4, but there is clearly more to be discussed in terms of the development of the system, the units, and ways in which system transformation has occurred in previous systems and the experience of periods of stability and instability.

The development of international systems as complex adaptive systems is closely interlinked with other systems, both in terms of units (states, international organizations, criminal groups) and other systems (the global economy, patriarchy, (post-)colonialism). We touched on some of these issues in Chapters 3 and 4 in relation to food and the environment, and central to the posthuman project is the awareness of human systems as embedded in and overlapping with non-human and inanimate systems. Hence the analysis of the development of international systems also requires a discussion of co-evolution with other systems.

Another area for research would be to expand the ways in which power can be analysed from a complex perspective in international relations. The notion of a fitness landscape provides a starting point, but the central question that needs elaboration is what constitutes 'fitness', and how has 'fitness' varied historically.

Epistemology Complexity raises major epistemological questions. There is considerable work to be done in exploring the implications for knowledge of making complexity the centre of study. Already considerable work has been done on this question in other fields (see, for example, Cilliers 2007; Sterman 2002), and there are possibilities for future research regarding the consequences for knowledge claims regarding international relations. There is also clearly room for complexity theory to engage with ongoing epistemological debates within international relations (Cudworth and Hobden 2011).

A starting point would be a discussion and examination of the limits to knowledge, and the implications of what those limits mean in terms of making statements about the character of international relations. To what extent do the conclusions drawn from complexity thinking support or undermine other positions in international relations?

Methodology As a result of the interconnections and overlapping character of systems, sensitivity to initial conditions, and potential spatial and temporal distance between causal effects and impacts, there are enormous methodological problems for the study of the social world. At the global level these problems are amplified to an exponential level. It is perhaps worth recalling James Rosenau's (1996: 309) statement that 'it is sheer craziness to dare to understand world affairs'. However, as he also noted, 'dare we must'. The complexity of the social world and the non-human world in which it is embedded makes the gaining of an understanding of the processes in which we are involved that much more difficult. However, to attempt to ignore or abstract from that complexity, tempting as that may be, potentially means we are overlooking a key feature of our being. As noted by Gerry Gingrich (quoted in Beaumont 2000: 4), complexity 'does not yield answers, at least not in the sense of those we have typically sought to describe our world and predict its events since the beginning of the Scientific Revolution. What it does yield is a new way of thinking about the world.'

The main methodological approach that has emerged with regard to thinking about complexity in international relations has been actor-based modelling, relying on computer power to develop simulations of complex situations (see the contributions to Harrison 2006a). Actor-based modelling has provided some significant case studies, yet we remain sceptical about its utility, as we noted in Chapter 2. Applying computer technology seems to imply a vision of complexity that is 'restricted' (Morin 2007), or 'thin'. For Roger Strand (2007: 201), a thin view of complexity is one that 'basically is compatible with the Simple View [Newtonian] if the latter revises some of its methodological prescriptions for science. Nature has seams, but they are finer, more intertwined and not in straight lines.' Our concern is that actor-based modelling fails to address 'general' or 'thick' complexity, and that modelling may just re-create humanist hubris that complexity can be measured and controlled (and indeed harnessed!)

Historical analysis provides an alternative to actor-based modelling. This involves the careful analysis and consideration of the development and co-evolution of systems. This would include an investigation of emergent properties by examining the interactions of units within a system, and looking at the ways in which systems progress in relation to each other. The intention is to attempt to understand how particular forms of social relations have come into existence, to identify power relations and inequalities, and highlight relations between human and non-human systems.

There have been many calls to rethink the discipline of international relations. Nonetheless, we make no apology for making yet another call. Ultimately, the study of international relations is just *too* important. As the study of global relations, it has to have global issues at its core, and we have to confront the circumstances in which we find ourselves. Together with the established questions of war, nuclear proliferation and human rights, there is a need to prioritize potentially disastrous global warming and the mass extinction of species (including possibly our own). At such a conjuncture the study of international relations in terms of narrow national interest seems plain perverse. An engagement with complexity theory indicates that to study the subject at a species level is equally misguided. Humans neither exist, nor have they developed, independently of other animate and inanimate systems, and to restrict international relations to the human abstracts, with potentially disastrous consequences, from these processes.

In calling for a posthuman international relations we thus call for a discipline that prioritizes the interests of earthlings rather than one particular species on 'Homeland Earth' (Morin 1999). While complexity theory offers no 'quick fix' for our predicament, and no immediate policy solutions, it does indicate why the challenges we face are so difficult, and why the outcome of our acts can be so different from our intentions. Acknowledging this complexity would be a first step towards more effective action. Awareness of our embedded and contingent existence should make us more thoughtful about what we seek to achieve. An international relations that can speak to such issues – indeed, a *posthuman international relations* – has much to contribute to understanding our situation.

Bibliography

Acampora, R. R. (2006) *Corporeal Compassion: Animal Ethics and Philosophy of Body*, Pittsburgh, PA: University of Pittsburgh Press.

Agamben, G. (2004) *The Open: Man and Animal*, trans. K. Attell, Stanford, CA: Stanford University Press.

Agar, M. (2004) 'We have met the other and we're all nonlinear: ethnography as a nonlinear dynamic system', *Complexity*, 10(2): 16–24.

Albert, M. and L. Cederman (2010) 'Introduction: systems theorizing in IR', in M. Albert et al. (eds), *New Systems Theories of World Politics*, Basingstoke: Palgrave, pp. 3–22.

Albert, M. and L. Hilkermeier (eds) (2004) *Observing International Relations*, London: Routledge.

Almond, G. A. and G. Bingham-Powell (1966) *Comparative Politics: A Developmental Approach*, Boston, MA: Little, Brown.

Anderson, K. (2001) 'The nature of "race"', in N. Castree and B. Braun (eds), *Social Nature: Theory, Practice, and Politics*, Oxford: Blackwell, pp. 64–83.

Annan, K. (2005) *In Larger Freedom: Development, Security and Human Rights: The Millennium Report*, New York: United Nations.

Archer, M. S. (2000) *Being Human: The Problem of Agency*, Cambridge: Cambridge University Press.

— (2003) *Structure, Agency and the Internal Conversation*, Cambridge: Cambridge University Press.

Arnold, D. (1996) *The Problem of Nature: Environment, Culture and European Expansion*, Oxford: Blackwell.

Arthur, W. B. (1994) 'Inductive reasoning and bounded rationality', *American Economic Review*, 84(2): 406–11.

Axelrod, R. M. (1997) *The Complexity of Cooperation: Agent-based Models of Competition and Cooperation*, Princeton, NJ: Princeton University Press.

Axelrod, R. M. and M. D. Cohen (1999) *Harnessing Complexity: Organizational Implications of a Scientific Frontier*, New York: Free Press.

Badmington, N. (2004) *Alien Chic: Posthumanism and the Other Within*, London: Routledge.

Baker, P. L. (1993) 'Chaos, order and sociological theory', *Sociological Inquiry*, 63(2): 123–49.

Barabási, A. (2002) *Linked: The New Science of Networks*, Cambridge, MA: Perseus Publishing.

Barnett, J. (2001) *The Meaning of Environmental Security: Ecological Politics and Politics and Policy in the New Security Era*, London: Zed Books.

Barry, A. (2001) *Political Machines: Governing a Technological Society*, London: Athlone Press.

— (2010) 'Materialist politics: metallurgy', in B. Braun and S. J. Whatmore (eds), *Political Matter: Technoscience, Democracy* and *Public Life*, Minneapolis, MN: University of Minnesota Press.

Batty, M. (2005) *Cities and Complexity: Understanding Cities with Cellular Automata, Agent-based Models, and Fractals*, London: MIT Press.

Bauman, Z. (1991) *Modernity and Ambivalence*, Cambridge: Polity.

Beaumont, R. (2000) *The Nazis' March to Chaos: The Hitler Era through the Lenses of Chaos-Complexity Theory*, Westport, CT: Praeger.

Beck, U. (1999) *World Risk Society*, Cambridge: Polity.

— (2000) 'Risk society revisited', in B. Adam et al. (eds), *The Risk Society and Beyond: Critical Issues for Social Theory*, London: Sage, pp. 211–29.

Behnke, A. (2006) 'Grand theory in the age of its impossibility: contemplations on Alexander Wendt', in S. Guzzini and A. Leander (eds), *Constructivism and International Relations: Alexander Wendt and His Critics*, London: Routledge, pp. 48–56.

Beinhocker, E. (2006) *The Origin of Wealth: Evolution, Complexity and the Radical Remaking of Economics*, London: Random House.

Bekoff, M. (2002) *Minding Animals: Awareness, Emotions and Heart*, Oxford: Oxford University Press.

Bennett, J. (2004) 'The force of things', *Political Theory*, 32(3): 347–72.

— (2005) 'In parliament with things', in L. Tønder and L. Thomassen (eds), *Radical Democracy: Politics between Abundance and Lack*, Manchester: Manchester University Press.

— (2010) *Vibrant Matter: A Political Ecology of Things*, Durham, NC: Duke University Press.

Benton, T. (1993) *Natural Relations: Ecology, Animal Rights and Social Justice*, London: Verso.

Bertram, E. et al. (1996) *Drug War Politics: The Price of Denial*, Berkeley: University of California Press.

Bertuglia, C. S. and F. Vaio (2005) *Nonlinearity, Chaos and Complexity: The Dynamics of Natural and Social Systems*, Oxford: Oxford University Press.

Bhavnani, R. (2006) 'Agent-based models in the study of ethnic norms and violence', in N. E. Harrison (ed.), *Complexity in World Politics: Concepts and Methods of a New Paradigm*, Albany, NY: SUNY, pp. 121–36.

Boardman, R. (2010) *Governance of Earth Systems: Science and Its Uses*, Basingstoke: Palgrave.

Bohman, J. (2007) *Democracy Across Borders: From Demos to Demoi*, Cambridge, MA: MIT Press.

— (2010) 'Democratising the global order: from communicative freedom to communicative power', *Review of International Studies*, 36(2): 431–47.

Bonanno, A. et al. (eds) (1994) *From Columbus to ConAgra: The Globalization of Agriculture and Food*, Lawrence: University Press of Kansas.

Bonanno, A. and D. H. Constance (2001) 'Globalization, Fordism and post-Fordism in agriculture and food: a critical review of the literature', *Culture and Agriculture*, 23(2): 1–18.

Bookchin, M. (1980) *Towards an Ecological Society*, Montreal: Black Rose Books.

— (1986) *The Modern Crisis*, Philadelphia, PA: New Society.

— (1990) *The Philosophy of Social Ecology*, Montreal: Black Rose Books.

— (2005) *The Ecology of Freedom: The Emergence and Dissolution of Hierarchy*, Edinburgh: AK Press.

Bordo, S. (1993) 'Feminism, Foucault and the politics of the body', in C. Ramazanoglu (ed.), *Up Against Foucault: Explorations of Some Tensions between Foucault and Feminism*, London: Routledge, pp. 179–202.

Bostrom, N. (2003) 'Human genetic enhancement: a transhuman perspective', *Journal of Value Inquiry*, 37(4): 493–506.

— (2008) 'Why I want to be posthuman when I grow up', in B. Gordjin and R. Chadwick (eds), *Medical Enhancement and Posthumanity*, London: Routledge, pp. 107–36.

Brah, A. and A. Phoenix (2004) 'Ain't I a woman? Revisiting intersectionality', *Journal of International Women's Studies*, 5(3): 75–86.

Brassett, J. and W. Smith (2010) 'Deliberation and global civil society: agency, arena, affect', *Review of International Studies*, 36(2): 413–30.

Braudel, F. (1995) *The Mediterranean and the Mediterranean World in the Age of Philip II*, vol. 1, Berkeley: University of California Press.

Braun, B. and S. Whatmore (2010) 'The stuff of politics: an introduction', in B. Braun and S. Whatmore (eds), *Political Matter: Technoscience, Democracy and Public Life*, Minneapolis and London: University of Minnesota Press, pp. ix–xl.

Bretherton, C. and J. Vogler (2006) *The EU as a Global Actor*, 2nd edn, London: Routledge.

Brock, L. (1997) 'The environment and security: conceptual and theoretical issues', in N. P. Gleditsch (ed.), *Conflict and the Environment*, Dordrecht: Kluwer Academic Press, pp. 17–34.

Buchanan, M. (2003) *Small World: Uncovering Nature's Hidden Networks*, London: Phoenix Books.

Bull, H. (1977) *The Anarchical Society: A Study in World Order*, London: Macmillan.

Burke, M. and D. Lobell (2010) 'Climate effects on food security', in D. Lobell and M. Burke (eds), *Climate Change and Food Security: Adapting Climate Change to a Warmer World*, Dordrecht: Springer, pp. 13–30.

Buzan, B. and R. Little (2000) *International Systems in World History: Remaking the Study of International Relations*, Oxford: Oxford University Press.

Byrne, D. (1998) *Complexity Theory and the Social Sciences*, London: Routledge.

— (2005) 'Complexity, configurations and cases', *Theory, Culture and Society*, 22(5): 95–111.

Calvocoressi, P. (1987) *A Time for Peace: Pacifism, Internationalism and Protest Forces in the Reduction of War*, London: Hutchinson.

Camilleri, J. A. and J. Falk (2009) *Worlds in Transition: Evolving Governance across a Stressed Planet*, Cheltenham: Edward Elgar.

Capra, F. (1975) *The Tao of Physics*, London: Flamingo.

— (1983) *The Turning Point*, London: Fontana.

— (1996) *The Web of Life: A New Synthesis of Mind and Matter*, New York: HarperCollins.

— (2002) *The Hidden Connections: A Science for Sustainable Living*, London: HarperCollins.

— (2007) 'Complexity and life', in F. Capra et al. (eds), *Reframing Complexity: Perspectives from*

North and South, Mansfield, MA: ISCE Publishing, pp. 1–25.

Carter, B. and N. Charles (2011) 'Human–animal connections: an introduction', in B. Carter and N. Charles (eds), *Human and Other Animals: Critical Perspectives*, Basingstoke: Palgrave, forthcoming.

Castellani, B. and F. Hafferty (2009) *Sociology and Complexity Science: A New Field of Inquiry*, Berlin: Springer.

Castells, M. (1996) *The Information Age: Economy, Society and Culture*, Oxford: Blackwell.

— (1997) *The Power of Identity. The Information Age: Economy, Society and Culture*, vol. 2, Oxford: Blackwell.

— (1998) *End of Millennium. The Information Age: Economy, Society and Culture*, vol. 3, Oxford: Blackwell.

Casti, J. L. (1994) *Complexification: Explaining a Paradoxical World through the Science of Surprise*, New York: HarperCollins.

Castree, N. (2001) 'Marxism, capitalism and the production of nature', in N. Castree and B. Braun (eds), *Social Nature: Theory, Practice and Politics*, Oxford: Blackwell, pp. 189–207.

Caulkins, J. et al. (2005) *How Goes the 'War on Drugs'?: An Assessment of U.S. Drug Programs and Policy*, Santa Monica, CA: Rand Corporation, www.rand.org/pubs/occasional_papers/2005/RAND_OP121.pdf.

Cavalieri, P. and P. Singer (eds) (1993) *The Great Ape Project: Equality Beyond Humanity*, London: Fourth Estate.

Caygill, H. (2000) 'Liturgies of fear: biotechnology and culture', in B. Adam et al. (eds), *The Risk Society and Beyond*, London: Sage, pp. 155–64.

Cederman, L. (1997) *Emergent Actors in World Politics: How States and Nations Develop and Dissolve*, Princeton, NJ: Princeton University Press.

Cilliers, P. (1998) *Complexity and Postmodernism: Understanding Complex Systems*, London: Routledge.

— (2000) 'Knowledge, complexity and understanding', *Emergence*, 2(4): 7–13.

— (ed.) (2007) *Thinking Complexity: Complexity and Philosophy*, vol. 1, Mansfield, MA: ISCE Publishing.

Clack, B. and R. York (2005) 'Carbon metabolism: global capitalism, climate change, and the biospheric rift', *Theory and Society*, 34(2): 391–428.

Claude, I. L. (1965 [1956]) *Swords into Plowshares: The Problems and Progress of International Organization*, London: University of London Press.

Clemens, W. C. (2001) *The Baltic Transformed: Complexity Theory and European Security*, Lanham, MD: Rowman and Littlefield.

CNA (2009) *National Security and the Threat of Climate Change*, CNA Corporation, securityandclimate.cna.org/report/.

Cockburn, A. (1995) 'A short, meat-orientated history of the world from Eden to the Mattole', in S. Coe (ed.), *Dead Meat*, New York: Four Walls Eight Windows, pp. 5–36.

Cooke, A. M. et al. (2009a) 'Introduction: agriculture, trade, and the global governance of food', in S. R. Curran et al. (eds), *The Global Governance of Food*, London: Routledge, pp. 2–7.

— (2009b) 'Conclusion: negotiating the dynamics of global complexity', in S. R. Curran et al. (eds), *The Global Governance of Food*, London: Routledge, pp. 209–17.

Coole, D. (2005) 'Rethinking agency: a phenomenological approach to embodiment and agentic capacities', *Political Studies*, 53(1): 124–42.

Cortes, F. et al. (1974) *Systems Analysis for Social Scientists*, London: John Wiley and Sons.

Cox, R. (1981) 'Social forces, states and world orders: beyond international relations theory', *Millennium*, 10(2): 126–55.

Crenshaw, K. W. (1991) 'Mapping the margins: intersectionality, identity politics and violence against women of color', *Stanford Law Review*, 43(6): 1241–99.

Cudworth, E. (2003) *Environment and Society*, London: Routledge.

— (2005) *Developing Ecofeminist Theory: The Complexity of Difference*, Basingstoke: Palgrave.

— (2007) 'Complexity theory and the sociology of natures', *International Journal of Interdisciplinary Social Sciences*, 2(3): 351–8.

— (2011) *Social Lives with Other Animals: Tales of Sex, Death and Love*, Basingstoke: Palgrave.

Cudworth, E. and S. Hobden (2010) 'Anarchy and anarchism: towards a theory of complex international systems', *Millennium*, 39(2): 399–416.

— (2011) 'The foundations of complexity, the complexity of foundations', *Philosophy of the Social Sciences*, forthcoming.

Dalby, S. (2002a) 'Security and ecology in the age of globalization', *Environmental Change and Security Report*, 8: 95–108.

— (2002b) *Environmental Security*, Minneapolis: University of Minnesota Press.

— (2002c) 'Environmental security: ecology or international relations', Paper presented at the annual convention of the International Studies Association, New Orleans, March.

— (2007) 'Ecology, security, and change in the anthropocene', *Brown Journal of World Affairs*, 13(2): 155–64.

— (2009) *Security and Environmental Change*, Cambridge: Polity.

Darwin, C. (1871) *The Descent of Man, and Selection in Relation to Sex*, London: John Murray.

Deleuze, G. and F. Guattari (1987) *A Thousand Plateaus: Capitalism and Schizophrenia*, trans. B. Massumi, Minneapolis: University of Minnesota Press.

Demeritt, D. (2001) 'Being constructive about nature', in N. Castree and B. Braun (eds), *Social Nature*, Oxford: Blackwell, pp. 22–40.

Derrida, J. (2002) 'The animal that therefore I am (more to follow)', trans. D. Wills, *Critical Inquiry*, 28(2): 369–418.

Detraz, N. (2009) 'Environmental security and gender: necessary shifts in an evolving debate', *Security Studies*, 18(2): 345–69.

Deudney, D. (1990) 'The case against linking environmental degradation and national security', *Millennium*, 19(3): 461–76.

Devereux, S. and J. Edwards (2004) 'Climate change and food security', *IDS Bulletin*, 35(3): 22–30.

Diamond, J. (2005) *Collapse: How Societies Choose to Fail or Survive*, London: Allen Lane.

Dickens, P. (1992) *Society and Nature: Towards a Green Social Theory*, Hemel Hempstead: Harvester Wheatsheaf.

— (1996) *Reconstructing Nature: Alienation, Emancipation and the Division of Labour*, London: Routledge.

Dillon, M. (2000) 'Poststructuralism, complexity and poetics', *Theory, Culture and Society*, 17(5): 1–26.

Dillon, M. and L. Lobo-Guerrero (2008) 'Biopolitics of security in the 21st century: an introduction', *Review of International Studies*, 34(2): 265–92.

Dobson, A. (2006) 'Do we need (to protect) nature?', in J. Huysmans et al. (eds), *The Politics of Protection: Sites of Insecurity and Political Agency*, London: Routledge, pp. 175–88.

Dobson, A. and D. Bell (2005) 'Introduction', in A. Dobson and D. Bell (eds), *Environmental Citizenship*, Cambridge, MA: MIT Press, pp. 1–20.

Dobson, A. and R. Eckersley (eds) (2006) *Political Theory and the Ecological Challenge*, Cambridge: Cambridge University Press.

Dryzek, J. S. (2006) *Deliberative Global Politics: Discourse and Democracy in a Divided World*, Cambridge: Polity.

Durkheim, E. (1952) *Suicide*, London: Routledge.

— (1966) *The Rules of Sociological Method*, New York: Free Press.

Dyer, H. (2001) 'Theoretical aspects of environmental security', in E. Petzold-Bradley et al. (eds), *Responding to Environmental Conflicts: Implications for Theory and Practice*, Dordrecht: Kluwer Academic, pp. 67–82.

Earnest, D. C. and J. N. Rosenau (2006) 'Signifying nothing? What complex systems theory can and cannot tell us about global politics', in N. E. Harrison (ed.), *Complexity in World Politics: Concepts and Methods of a New Paradigm*, Albany, NY: SUNY Press.

Easton, D. (1981) 'The political system besieged by the state', *Political Theory*, 9(3): 303–25.

Eckersley, R. (1992) *Environmentalism and Political Theory: Toward an Ecocentric Approach*, London: University College London Press.

— (1999) 'Discourse ethics and the problem of representing nature', *Environmental Politics*, 8(2): 24–49.

— (2004) *The Green State: Rethinking Democracy and Sovereignty*, Cambridge, MA: MIT Press.

— (2009) 'Environmental security, climate change, and globalizing terrorism', in D. Grenfell and P. James (eds), *Rethinking Insecurity, War and Violence: Beyond Savage Globalization?*, London: Routledge, pp. 85–97.

EEA (2008) *Energy and Environment Report 2008*, Copenhagen: European Environment Agency.

Elliott, E. and L. D. Kiel (1997) 'Nonlinear dynamics, complexity and public policy: use, misuse, and applicability', in R. A. Eve et al. (eds), *Chaos, Complexity, and Sociology: Myths, Models, and Theories*, London: Sage, pp. 64–78.

Enloe, C. (1988) *Does Khaki Become You? The Militarisation of Women's Lives*, London: Pandora.

— (1990) *Bananas, Beaches and Bases: Making Feminist Sense of International Politics*, Berkeley: University of California Press.

— (2000) *Maneuvres: The International Politics of Militarizing Women's Lives*, Berkeley: University of California Press.

European Commission (2001) *Environment 2010: Our Future, Our Choice – the Sixth Environment Action Programme*, Brussels: Commission of the European Communities.

— (2009) *Adapting to Climate Change:*

Towards a European Framework for Action, Brussels: Commission of the European Communities.

Evans, A. (2009) *The Feeding of the Nine Billion: Global Food Security for the 21st Century*, London: Chatham House.

Evans, L. T. (1998) *Feeding the Ten Billion: Plants and Population Growth*, Cambridge: Cambridge University Press.

FAO (2009) *The State of Food Insecurity in the World, 2009*, Rome: Food and Agriculture Organization.

Fenn, D., O. Suleman, J. Efstathiou and N. F. Johnson (2008) 'How does Europe make its mind up? Connections, cliques and compatibility between countries in the Eurovision Song Contest', arxiv.org/PS_cache/physics/pdf/0505/0505071v1.pdf.

Fleming, L. and O. Sorenson (2001) 'Technology as a complex adaptive system: evidence from patent data', *Research Policy*, 30(7): 1019–39.

Forrester, J. W. (1971) 'Counterintuitive behavior of social systems', *Technology Review*, 73(3): 52–68.

Fortmann, M. et al. (2004) 'Conclusions: balance of power at the turn of the new century', in T. V. Paul et al. (eds), *Balance of Power: Theory and Practice in the 21st Century*, Stanford, CA: Stanford University Press, pp. 360–74.

Foucault, M. (1971) *The Order of Things: Archaeology of the Human Sciences*, New York: Pantheon.

— (1973) *The Birth of the Clinic: An Archaeology of Medical Perception*, trans. A. Sheridan, London: Routledge.

— (1976) 'Two lectures', in M. Kelly (ed.), *Critique and Power*, Cambridge, MA: MIT Press, pp. 17–46.

— (1978) *The History of Sexuality*, vol. 1: *The Will to Knowledge*, trans. R. Hurley, London: Penguin.

— (1979) *Discipline and Punish: The Birth of the Prison*, trans. A. Sheridan, Harmondsworth: Penguin.

— (1980) 'Body/power', in C. Gordon (ed.), *Michel Foucault: Power/Knowledge*, Brighton: Harvester, pp. 55–62.

— (1984) 'Right of death and power over life', in P. Rabinow (ed.), *The Foucault Reader*, New York: Pantheon, pp. 258–72.

— (2003) *Society Must Be Defended: Lectures at the Collège de France 1975–76*, trans. D. Macey, New York: Picador.

— (2007) *Security, Territory, Population: Lectures at the Collège de France*, Basingstoke: Palgrave.

Fox, W. (1986) *Approaching Deep Ecology: A Response to Richard Sylvan's Critique of Deep Ecology*, University of Tasmania.

Franco Parellada, R. (2007) 'Modeling of social organizations: necessity and possibility', in F. Capra et al. (eds), *Reframing Complexity: Perspectives from North and South*, Mansfield, MA: ISCE Publishing, pp. 151–68.

Franklin, A. (1999) *Animals and Modern Cultures: A Sociology of Human–Animal Relations in Modernity*, London: Sage.

Friedmann, H. (1993) 'The political economy of food', *New Left Review*, 197: 29–57.

Friedmann, H. and P. McMichael (1989) 'Agriculture and the state system: the rise and decline of national agricultures, 1870 to the present', *Sociologia Ruralis*, 29(2): 93–117.

Fudge, E. (2006) 'Two ethics: killing animals in the past and in the present', in Animal Studies Group (eds), *Killing Animals*, Urbana:

University of Illinois Press, pp. 99–119.

Fukuyama, F. (2002) *Our Posthuman Future: Consequences of the Biotechnology Revolution*, London: Profile Books.

Gallopín, G. C. (2002) 'Planning for resilience: scenarios, surprises, and branch points', in L. H. Gunderson and C. S. Holling (eds), *Panarchy: Understanding Transformations in Human and Natural Systems*, Washington, DC: Island Press, pp. 361–94.

Gane, N. and D. Haraway (2006) 'When we have never been human, what is to be done? An interview with Donna Haraway', *Theory, Culture and Society*, 23(7/8): 135–58.

Gatrell, A. (2005) 'Complexity theory and geographies of health: a critical assessment', *Social Science and Medicine*, 60(12): 2661–71.

Gell-Mann, M. (1994) *The Quark and the Jaguar: Adventures in the Simple and the Complex*, London: Little, Brown.

Gershenson, C. et al. (eds) (2007) *Worldviews, Science and Us: Philosophy and Complexity*, London: World Scientific Publishing.

Geyer, R. and S. Rihani (2010) *Complexity and Public Policy: A New Approach to Twenty-first Century Politics, Policy and Society*, London: Routledge.

Ghosh, J. (2010) 'The unnatural coupling: food and global finance', *Journal of Agrarian Change*, 10(1): 72–86.

Gilbert, S. F. (2002) 'The genome in its ecological context: philosophical perspectives on interspecies epigenesis', *Annals of the New York Academy of Science*, 981: 202–18.

Gill, G. (2008) 'Reflections on researching the rugged fitness landscape', *Informing Science*, 11: 165–96.

Gleditsch, N. P. et al. (2002) 'Armed conflict 1946–2001: a new dataset', *Journal of Peace Research*, 39(5): 615–37.

Gleick, J. (1988) *Chaos: Making a New Science*, London: Heinemann.

Goldblatt, D. (1996) *Social Theory and the Environment*, Cambridge: Polity.

Gregory, D. (2001) '(Post)colonialism and the production of nature', in N. Castree and B. Braun (eds), *Social Nature*, Oxford: Blackwell, pp. 84–111.

Guha, R. (1989) 'Radical American environmentalism and wilderness protection: a critique', *Environmental Ethics*, 11(1): 71–83.

— (1997a) 'The environmentalism of the poor', in R. Guha and J. Martinez-Alier (eds), *Varieties of Environmentalism: Essays North and South*, London: Earthscan, pp. 3–21.

— (1997b) 'Mahatma Gandhi and the environmental movement', in R. Guha and J. Martinez-Alier (eds), *Varieties of Environmentalism: Essays North and South*, London: Earthscan, 153–68.

Gulbenkian Commission (1996) *Open the Social Sciences: Report of the Gulbenkian Commission on the Restructuring of the Social Sciences*, Stanford, CA: Stanford University Press.

Gunaratne, S. (2003) 'Thank you Newton, welcome Prigogine: unthinking old paradigms and embracing new directions', *Communications*, 28(4): 435–55.

Gunderson, L. H. and C. S. Holling (eds) (2002) *Panarchy: Understanding Transformations in Human and Natural Systems*, Washington, DC: Island Press.

Guzzini, S. and A. Leander (eds) (2006) *Constructivism and International Relations: Alexander Wendt and His Critics*, London: Routledge.

Haas, E. (1953) 'The balance of power: prescription, concept, or propaganda?', *World Politics*, 5(4): 442–77.

Habermas, J. (1996) 'Three normative models of democracy', in S. Behabib (ed.), *Democracy and Difference: Contesting the Boundaries of the Political*, New York: Columbia University Press, pp. 21–30.

Hables Gray, C. (2001) *Cyborg Citizen: Politics in the Posthuman Age*, London: Routledge.

Hajer, M. (1995) *The Politics of Environmental Discourse: Ecological Modernization and the Policy Process*, Oxford: Clarendon.

Halberstam, J. and I. Livingston (1995) *Posthuman Bodies*, Bloomington: Indiana University Press.

Haraway, D. (1991) *Simians, Cyborgs and Women: The Reinvention of Nature*, London: Free Association Press.

— (1996) *Modest_Witness@Second_Millennium.FemaleMan©_Meets_Oncomouse™: Technoscience and Feminism*, London: Routledge.

— (2003) *The Companion Species Manifesto: Dogs, People and Significant Otherness*, Chicago, IL: Prickly Paradigm Press.

— (2008) *When Species Meet*, Minneapolis: University of Minnesota Press.

Harris, M. (1987) *The Sacred Cow and the Abominable Pig: Riddles of Food and Culture*, New York: Touchstone Books.

Harrison, N. E. (ed.) (2006a) *Complexity in World Politics: Concepts and Methods of a New Paradigm*, Albany, NY: SUNY Press.

— (2006b) 'Thinking about the world we make', in N. E. Harrison (ed.), *Complexity in World Politics: Concepts and Methods of a New Paradigm*, Albany, NY: SUNY Press, pp. 1–23.

— (2006c) 'Complex systems and the practice of world politics', in N. E. Harrison (ed.), *Complexity in World Politics: Concepts and Methods of a New Paradigm*, Albany, NY: SUNY Press, pp. 183–96.

— (2006d) 'From economics to ecology: towards new theory for international environmental politics', in E. Laferrière and P. Stoett (eds), *International Ecopolitical Theory*, Vancouver: UBC Press, pp. 52–69.

Harvey, D. (1996) *Justice, Nature, and the Geography of Difference*, Oxford: Blackwell.

— (2009) 'Complexity and case', in D. Byrne and C. Ragin (eds), *The Sage Handbook of Case-based Methods*, London: Sage.

Hathaway, D. E. and M. D. Ingco (1996) 'Agricultural liberalization and the Uruguay Round', in W. Martin and L. A. Winters (eds), *The Uruguay Round and the Developing Countries*, Cambridge: Cambridge University Press.

Hawkins, G. (2010) 'Plastic materialities', in B. Braun and S. J. Whatmore (eds), *Political Matter: Technoscience, Democracy and Public Life*, Minneapolis: University of Minnesota Press, pp. 119–38.

Hayles, K. (1990) *Chaos Bound: Orderly Disorder in Contemporary Literature and Science*, Ithaca, NY: Cornell University Press.

— (1991) *Chaos and Order: Complex Dynamics in Literature and Science*, Chicago, IL: University of Chicago Press.

— (1999) *How We Became Posthuman: Virtual Bodies in Cybernetics, Literature and Informatics*, Chicago, IL: University of Chicago Press.

Heimann, M. and M. Reichstein (2008) 'Terrestrial ecosystem carbon dynamics and climate feedbacks', *Nature*, 451(7176): 289–92.

Helm, D. (2008) 'Climate change policy: why has so little been achieved?', *Oxford Review of Economic Policy*, 24(2): 211–38.

Hine, R. V. and J. M. Faragher (2000) *The American West: A New Interpretive History*, New Haven, CT: Yale University Press.

Hobden, S. (1998) *International Relations and Historical Sociology: Breaking Down Boundaries*, London: Routledge.

Hoffman, A. J. (2006) *Getting Ahead of the Curve: Corporate Strategies that Address Climate Change*, Arlington, VA: Pew Centre on Global Climate Change.

Hoffmann, S. (1977) 'An American social science: international relations', *Daedalus*, 106(3): 41–60.

Holling, C. S. et al. (2002a) 'In quest of a theory of adaptive change', in L. H. Gunderson and C. S. Holling (eds), *Panarchy: Understanding Transformations in Human and Natural Systems*, Washington, DC: Island Press, pp. 3–22.

— (2002b) 'Sustainability and panarchies', in L. H. Gunderson and C. S. Holling (eds), *Panarchy: Understanding Transformations in Human and Natural Systems*, Washington, DC: Island Press, pp. 63–102.

— (2002c) 'Discoveries for sustainable futures', in L. H. Gunderson and C. S. Holling (eds), *Panarchy: Understanding Transformations in Human and Natural Systems*,

Washington, DC: Island Press, pp. 395–418.

Holsti, K. (1985) *The Dividing Discipline: Hegemony and Diversity in International Theory*, London: Allen and Unwin.

Homer-Dixon, T. (2009) 'The newest science: replacing physics, ecology will be the master science of the 21st century', *Alternatives Journal*, 35(4): 8–38.

Hipel, K. W. et al. (2010) 'Systems of systems approach to policy development for global food security', *Journal of Systems Science and Systems Engineering*, 19(1): 1–21.

Hulme, M. and H. Neufeldt (2010) *Making Climate Change Work for Us: European Perspectives on Adaptation and Mitigation Strategies*, Cambridge: Cambridge University Press.

Hutchinson, F. et al. (2002) *The Politics of Money: Towards Sustainability and Economic Democracy*, London: Pluto Press.

Intergovernmental Panel on Climate Change (2007) *Climate Change 2007: Impacts, Adaptation and Vulnerability: Contribution of Working Group II to the Fourth Assessment Report*, Cambridge: Cambridge University Press.

Irvine, L. (2004) *If You Tame Me: Understanding Our Connections with Animals*, Philadelphia, PA: Temple University Press.

Janssen, M. A. (2002) 'A future of surprises', in L. H. Gunderson and C. S. Holling (eds), *Panarchy: Understanding Transformations in Human and Natural Systems*, Washington, DC: Island Press, pp. 241–60.

Jervis, R. (1997) *System Effects: Complexity in Social and Political Life*, Princeton, NJ: Princeton University Press.

Jhaveri, N.J. (2004) 'Petroimperialism: US oil interests and the Iraq War', *Antipode*, 36(1): 2–11.

Johnson, A. (1991) *Factory Farming*, Oxford: Blackwell.

Johnson, C. (2002) *Blowback: The Costs and Consequences of American Empire*, London: Time Warner.

Johnson, N. F. (2009) *Simply Complexity: A Clear Guide to Complexity Theory*, Oxford: One World.

Johnson, N. F., P. Jeffries and P. M. Hui (2003) *Financial Market Complexity*, Oxford: Oxford University Press.

Johnson, N. F., M. Spagat, J. Restrepo, J. Bohorquez, N. Suarez, E. Restrepo and R. Zarama (n.d.) 'From old wars to new wars and global terrorism', personal.rhul. ac.uk/uhte/014/PaperLANL6.pdf.

Jordan, A. et al. (2010) 'Climate change policy in the EU: an introduction', in A. Jordan et al. (eds), *Climate Change Policy in the European Union: Confronting the Dilemmas of Mitigation and Adaptation*, Cambridge: Cambridge University Press, pp. 3–26.

Kaldor, M. et al. (eds) (2007) *Oil Wars*, London: Pluto Press.

Kaplan, M. (1957) *System and Process in International Politics*, New York: John Wiley and Sons.

Kauffman, S. (1993) *The Origins of Order: Self Organization and Selection in Evolution*, Oxford: Oxford University Press.

— (1995) *At Home in the Universe: The Search for Laws of Self Organization and Complexity*, Oxford: Oxford University Press.

— (2000) *Investigations*, Oxford: Oxford University Press.

— (2008) *Reinventing the Sacred: A New View of Science, Reason and Religion*, New York: Basic Books.

Kavalski, E. (2007) 'The fifth debate and the emergence of complex international relations theory: notes on the application of complexity theory to the study of international life', *Cambridge Review of International Affairs*, 20(3): 435–54.

Klare, M. T. (2001) *Resource Wars: The New Landscape of Global Conflict*, New York: Metropolitan Books.

Kratochwil, F. (1993) 'The embarrassment of changes: neo-realism as the science of realpolitik without politics', *Review of International Studies*, 19(1): 63–80.

Krauthammer, C. (1991) 'The unipolar moment', *Foreign Affairs*, 70(1): 23–33.

Kropotkin, P. (1987a [1902]) *Mutual Aid: A Factor of Evolution*, London: Freedom Press.

— (1987b [1911]) *The State: Its Historic Role*, London: Freedom Press.

Kuehls, T. (1996) *Beyond Sovereign Territory: The Space of Ecopolitics*, Minneapolis: University of Minnesota Press.

Kurki, M. (2008) *Causation in International Relations: Reclaiming Causal Analysis*, Cambridge: Cambridge University Press.

Lake, A. (2009) *Hierarchy in International Relations*, Ithaca, NY: Cornell University Press.

Lang, T. (2010) 'Crisis? What crisis? The normality of the current food crisis', *Journal of Agrarian Change*, 10(1): 87–97.

Lansing, J. S. (2003) 'Complex adaptive systems', *Annual Review of Anthropology*, 32: 183–204.

— (2006) *Perfect Order: Recognizing Complexity in Bali*, Princeton, NJ: Princeton University Press.

Laplace, P. S. (1902 [1840]) *A Philosophical Essay on Possibilities*, trans. from the French, 6th edn, New York: John Wiley.

Latouche, S. (1993) *In the Wake of the Affluent Society: An Exploration of Post-Development*, London: Zed Books.

Latour, B. (1993) *We Have Never Been Modern*, Hemel Hempstead: Harvester Wheatsheaf.

— (1999) *Pandora's Hope: Essays on the Reality of Science Studies*, Cambridge, MA: Harvard University Press.

— (2004) *The Politics of Nature: How to Bring the Sciences into Democracy*, trans. C. Porter, Cambridge, MA: Harvard University Press.

— (2005a) *Reassembling the Social: An Introduction to Actor-Network Theory*, Oxford: Oxford University Press.

— (2005b) 'From real politik to dingpolitik: or how to make things public', in B. Latour and P. Weibel (eds), *Making Things Public*, Cambridge, MA: MIT Press, pp. 14–41.

— (2009) 'A plea for earthly sciences', in J. Burnett et al. (eds), *New Social Connections: Sociology's Subjects and Objects*, Basingstoke: Palgrave, pp. 72–84.

Law, J. and J. Urry (2004) 'Enacting the social', *Economy and Society*, 33(3): 390–410.

Leakey, R. and R. Lewin (1996) *The Sixth Extinction: Biodiversity and Its Survival*, London: Weidenfeld & Nicolson.

Le Billon, P. (2005) 'The geopolitical economy of "resource wars"', in P. Le Billon (ed.), *The Geopolitics of Resource Wars*, London: Frank Cass, pp. 1–28.

Lee, M. E. (1997) 'From enlightenment to chaos: toward nonmodern social science', in R. A. Eve

et al. (eds), *Chaos, Complexity and Sociology: Myths, Models, and Theories*, London: Sage, pp. 15–29.

Levy, J. (1988) 'Domestic politics and war', *Journal of Interdisciplinary History*, 18(4): 653–73.

Levy, M. (1995) 'Is the environment a national security issue?', *International Security*, 20(2): 35–62.

Lewin, A. Y. and H. W. Volberda (1999) 'Prolegomena on coevolution: a framework for research on strategy and new organizational forms', *Organization Science*, 10(5): 519–34.

Light, A. (1998) 'Bookchin and/as social ecology', in A. Light (ed.), *Social Ecology after Bookchin*, New York: Guilford Press, pp. 1–23.

Lin, M. (2006) 'Substance, attribute and mode in Spinoza', *Philosophy Compass*, 1(2): 144–53.

Little, R. (2007) *The Balance of Power in International Relations: Metaphors, Myths and Models*, Cambridge: Cambridge University Press.

Lobell, D. and M. Burke (2010) 'Global and regional assessments', in D. Lobell and M. Burke (eds), *Climate Change and Food Security: Adapting Climate Change to a Warmer World*, Dordrecht: Springer, pp. 177–92.

López, J. and J. Scott (2000) *Social Structure*, Buckingham: Open University Press.

Lorenz, E. (1993 [1972]) 'Predictability: does the flap of a butterfly's wings in Brazil set off a tornado in Texas', Presented to the 139th meeting of the American Association for the Advancement of Science, reprinted in E. Lorenz, *The Essence of Chaos*, Seattle: University of Washington Press, pp. 181–4.

Lövbrand, E. and J. Stripple (2006)

'The climate as a political space', *Review of International Studies*, 32(2): 217–35.

Lovelock, J. (2000) *Ages of Gaia: A Biography of our Living Earth*, 2nd edn, Oxford: Oxford University Press.

— (2009) *The Vanishing Face of Gaia: A Final Warning*, London: Allen Lane.

Luhmann, N. (1993) *Risk: A Social Theory*, Stanford, CA: Stanford University Press.

— (1995) *Social Systems*, Stanford, CA: Stanford University Press.

Lujala, P. et al. (2005) 'A diamond curse? Civil war and a lootable resource', *Journal of Conflict Research*, 49(4): 538–62.

Luke, T. W. (1999) *Capitalism, Democracy and Ecology: Departing from Marx*, Champaign, IL: University of Illinois Press.

Macnaghten, P. (2003) 'Embodying the environment in everyday life practices', *Sociological Review*, 51(1): 62–84.

Mainzer, K. (2007) *Thinking in Complexity: The Computational Dynamics of Matter, Mind, and Mankind*, Berlin: Springer.

Mandelbrot, B. and R. L. Hudson (2004) *The (Mis)Behaviour of Markets: A Fractal View of Risk, Ruin, and Reward*, London: Profile Books.

Mann, M. (1986) *The Sources of Social Power*, vol. 1: *A History of Power from the Beginning to A.D. 1760*, Cambridge: Cambridge University Press.

Margulis, L. (1981) *Symbiosis in Cell Evolution*, San Francisco, CA: W. H. Freeman and Co.

Margulis, L. and D. Sagan (1986) *Microcosmos: Four Billion Years of Evolution from Our Microbial Ancestors*, New York: Summit.

— (1995) *What Is Life?*, New York: Simon and Schuster.

— (2002) *Acquiring Genomes: A Theory of the Origins of Species*, New York: Basic Books.

Marres, N. (2010) 'Front-staging non-humans: publicity as a constraint on the political activity of things', in B. Braun and S. J. Whatmore (eds), *Political Matter: Technoscience, Democracy and Public Life*, Minneapolis: University of Minnesota Press, pp. 177–210.

Martinez-Alier, J. (1997) 'From political economy to political ecology', in R. Guha and J. Martinez-Alier (eds), *Varieties of Environmentalism: Essays North and South*, London: Earthscan, pp. 22–45.

Marx, K. (1954) *Capital*, vol. 1, London: Lawrence and Wishart.

Mason, J. and M. Finelli (2006) 'Brave new farm?', in P. Singer (ed.), *In Defence of Animals: The Second Wave*, Oxford: Blackwell, pp. 104–22.

Masson, J. M. (2004) *The Pig Who Sang to the Moon: The Emotional World of Farm Animals*, London: Jonathan Cape.

Matthew, R. A. (2002) 'In defense of environment and security research', *Environmental Change and Security Project Report*, 8: 109–24.

Maturana, H. and F. J. Varela (1980) *Autopoiesis and Cognition: The Realization of the Living*, Dordrecht: Kluwer Academic.

— (1987) *The Tree of Knowledge: The Biological Roots of Human Understanding*, Boston, MA: Shambhala.

McCall, L. (2005) 'The complexity of intersectionality', *Signs*, 30(3): 171–80.

McClintock, A. (1995) *Imperial Leather: Race, Gender and*

Sexuality in the Colonial Contest, London: Routledge.

McGlade, J. and E. Garnsey (2006) 'The nature of complexity', in E. Garnsey and J. McGlade (eds), *Complexity and Co-evolution: Continuity and Change in Socio-Economic Systems*, Cheltenham: Edward Elgar, pp. 1–21.

McMichael, P. (1997) 'Rethinking globalization: the agrarian question revisited', *Review of International Political Economy*, 4(4): 630–62.

— (1998) 'Global food politics', *Monthly Review*, 50(3): 97–111.

McNeill, J. R. (2000) *Something New under the Sun: An Environmental History of the Twentieth Century*, New York: Norton.

Mearsheimer, J. (2001) *The Tragedy of Great Power Politics*, New York: Norton.

Mellor, M. (1992) *Breaking the Boundaries: Towards a Feminist Green Socialism*, London: Virago.

Merchant, C. (1980) *The Death of Nature: Women, Ecology and the Scientific Revolution*, San Francisco, CA: Harper and Row.

Miah, A. (2007) 'A critical history of posthumanism', in B. Gordijn and R. Chadwick (eds), *Medical Enhancement and Posthumanity*, London: Routledge, pp. 71–94.

Midgely, M. (1996) *Utopias, Dolphins and Computers: Problems of Philosophical Plumbing*, London: Routledge.

Mies, M. (1986) *Patriarchy and Accumulation on a World Scale*, London: Zed Books.

— (1993) 'The need for a new vision: the subsistence perspective', in M. Mies and V. Shiva (eds), *Ecofeminism*, London: Zed Books, pp. 297–324.

Mihata, K. (1997) 'The persistence of "emergence"', in R. A. Eve et al. (eds), *Chaos, Complexity, and Sociology: Myths, Models, and Theories*, London: Sage, pp. 30–8.

Miller, D. (1984) *Anarchism*, London: J. M. Dent.

Miller, J. H. and S. E. Page (2007) *Complex Adaptive Systems: An Introduction to the Computational Models of Social Life*, Princeton, NJ: Princeton University Press.

Milner, H. (1991) 'The assumption of anarchy in international relations', *Review of International Studies*, 17(1): 67–85.

Mitchell, S. D. (2009) *Unsimple Truths: Science, Complexity and Policy*, Chicago, IL: University of Chicago Press.

Moore, J. W. (2009) 'Ecology and the accumulation of capital: a brief environmental history of neoliberalism', Paper prepared for the workshop Food, Energy, Environment: Crisis of the Modern World-System, Fernand Braudel Center, Binghampton University, jasonwmoore.com/uploads/Moore__Ecology_and_Accumulation__Neoliberalism__5_October_2009_.pdf.

— (2010) 'The end of the road? Agricultural revolutions in the capitalist world-ecology, 1450–2010', *Journal of Agrarian Change*, 10(3): 389–413.

Moravec, H. (1988) *Mind Children: The Future of Robot and Human Intelligence*, Cambridge, MA: Harvard University Press.

Morgan, K. et al. (2006) *Worlds of Food: Place, Power and Provenance in the Food Chain*, Oxford: Oxford University Press.

Morgenthau, H. J. (1960) *Politics among Nations: The Struggle for Power and Peace*, 3rd edn, New York: Knopf.

Morin, E. (1999) *Homeland Earth: A*

Manifesto for the New Millennium, Cresskill, NJ: Hampton Press.

— (2007) 'Restricted complexity, general complexity', in C. Gershenson et al. (eds), *Worldviews, Science and Us: Philosophy and Complexity*, Singapore: World Scientific Publishing, pp. 5–29.

— (2008) *On Complexity*, Cresskill, NJ: Hampton Press.

Naess, A. (1973) 'The shallow and the deep, long-range ecology movement: a summary', *Inquiry*, 16(1–4): 95–100.

— (1989) *Ecology, Community and Lifestyle: Outline of an Ecosophy*, Cambridge: Cambridge University Press.

Neocleous, M. (2008) *Critique of Security*, Edinburgh: Edinburgh University Press.

Nibert, D. (2002) *Animal Rights/Human Rights: Entanglements of Oppression and Liberation*, Lanham, MD: Rowman and Littlefield.

Nowotny, H. (2005) 'The increase of complexity and its reduction', *Theory, Culture and Society*, 22(5): 15–31.

Oberthür, S. and C. Kelly (2008) 'EU leadership in international climate policy: achievements and challenges', *International Spectator*, 43(3): 35–50.

O'Brien, R. and M. Williams (2010) *Global Political Economy: Evolution and Dynamics*, Basingstoke: Palgrave.

Oswald Spring, U. (2007) 'International security, peace, development, environment', in U. Oswald Spring (ed.), *Encyclopaedia on Life Support Systems*, vol. 39, Oxford-EOLSS, online.

— (2008a) *Gender and Disasters. Human, Gender and Environmental Security: A HUGE Challenge*, Bonn: UNU-EHS, Intersection.

— (2008b) 'A HUGE gender security approach: towards human, gender and environmental security', in H. G. Brauch et al. (eds), *Facing Global Environmental Change: Environmental, Human, Energy, Food, Health and Water Security Concepts*, Berlin: Springer-Verlag, pp. 1157–82.

Parsons, T. (1951) *The Social System*, London: Routledge and Kegan Paul.

— (1960) *Structure and Process in Modern Societies*, Glencoe, IL: Free Press of Glencoe.

Pechlaner, G. and G. Otero (2008) 'The third food regime: neoliberal globalism and agricultural biotechnology in North America', *Sociologia Ruralis*, 48(4): 351–71.

Peet, R. and M. Watts (eds) (1996) *Liberation Ecologies: Environment, Development, Social Movements*, London: Routledge.

Pepper, D. (1993) *Eco-Socialism: From Deep Ecology to Social Justice*, London: Routledge.

Perona, E. (2007) 'The confused state of complexity economics', in M. Salzano and D. Colander (eds), *Complexity Hints for Economic Policy*, Milan: Springer, pp. 33–53.

Phoenix, A. and P. Pattynama (2006) 'Editorial: Intersectionality', *European Journal of Women's Studies*, 13(3): 187–92.

Pierson, P. (2000) 'Increasing returns, path dependency and the study of politics', *American Political Science Review*, 94(2): 251–68.

Pinstrup-Andersen, P. (2002) 'Food and agricultural policy for a globalizing world: preparing for the future', *American Journal of Agricultural Economics*, 84(5): 1201–14.

Ploeg, J. D. van der (2010) 'The food

crisis, industrialized farming and the imperial regime', *Journal of Agrarian Change*, 10(1): 98–106.

Plumwood, V. (1993) *Feminism and the Mastery of Nature*, London: Routledge.

— (2002) *Environmental Culture: The Ecological Crisis of Reason*, London: Routledge.

Pollan, M. (2003) 'Power steer', *New York Times Magazine*, 31 March.

Prigogine, I. (1980) *From Being to Becoming: Time and Complexity in the Physical Sciences*, San Francisco, CA: Freeman.

— (2003) *Is Future Given?*, New Jersey: World Scientific.

Prigogine, I. and I. Stengers (1984) *Order out of Chaos*, New York: Bantam.

Pritchard, B. (2009) 'The long hangover from the second food regime: a world-historical interpretation of the collapse of the WTO Doha Round', *Agriculture and Human Values*, 26(4): 297–307.

Przeworski, A. (1985) *Capitalism and Social Democracy*, Cambridge: Cambridge University Press.

— (2000) *Democracy and Development*, Cambridge: Cambridge University Press.

Reinalda, B. (2009) *Routledge History of International Organizations: From 1815 to the Present Day*, London: Routledge.

Renner, M. (2002) *The Anatomy of Resource Wars*, Washington, DC: World Watch Institute.

Rescher, N. (1998) *Complexity: A Philosophical Overview*, New Brunswick, NJ: Transaction Publishers.

Richards, D. (ed.) (2000) *Political Complexity: Non-linear Models of Politics*, Ann Arbor: University of Michigan Press.

Rifkin, J. (1994) *Beyond Beef: The Rise and Fall of Cattle Culture*, London: Thorsons.

Rihani, S. (2002) *Complex Systems Theory and Development Practice: Understanding Non-linear Realities*, London: Zed Books.

Rose, N. (1999) *Powers of Freedom: Reframing Political Theory*, Cambridge: Cambridge University Press.

Rosecrance, R. and J. Taw (1990) 'Japan and the theory of international leadership', *World Politics*, 42(2): 184–209.

Rosenau, J. (1990) *Turbulence in World Politics: A Theory of Change and Continuity*, London: Harvester Wheatsheaf.

— (1996) 'Probing problems persistently: a desirable but improbable future for international relations', in S. Smith et al. (eds), *International Theory: Positivism and Beyond*, Cambridge: Cambridge University Press, pp. 309–17.

Rostow, W. W. (1959) 'The stages of economic growth', *Economic History Review*, 12(1): 1–16.

Russell, B. and N. Morris (2006) 'Armed forces are put on standby to tackle threat of wars over water', *Independent*, 28 February, p. 1.

Sachs, W. et al. (1998) *Greening the North: A Post-Industrial Blueprint for Ecology and Equity*, London: Zed Books.

Salleh, A. (2009) 'Ecological debt: embodied debt', in A. Salleh (ed.), *Eco-Sufficiency and Global Justice: Women Write Political Ecology*, London: Pluto Press, pp. 291–312.

Scheffer, M. et al. (2002) 'Dynamic interaction of societies and ecosystems – linking theories from ecology, economy and sociology', in L. H. Gunderson and C. S. Holling (eds), *Panarchy: Understand-*

ing *Transformations in Human and Natural Systems*, Washington, DC: Island Press, pp. 195–240.

Schmidt, B. (1998) *The Political Discourse of Anarchy: A Disciplinary History of International Relations*, Albany, NY: SUNY Press.

Shiva, V. (1988) *Staying Alive: Women, Ecology and Development*, London: Zed Books.

Singer, J. D. (1961) 'The level-of-analysis problem in international relations', *World Politics*, 14(1): 77–92.

Smith, S. (1996) 'Positivism and beyond', in S. Smith et al. (eds), *International Theory: Positivism and Beyond*, Cambridge: Cambridge University Press, pp. 11–44.

— (2000) 'The discipline of international relations: still an American social science', *British Journal of Politics and International Relations*, 2(3): 374–402.

Solé, R. and J. Montoya (2002) 'Small world patterns in food webs', *Journal of Theoretical Biology*, 214(3): 405–12.

Soper, K. (1995) *What Is Nature?*, Oxford: Blackwell.

Spier, F. (2010) *Big History and the Future of Humanity*, Oxford: Wiley-Blackwell.

Spitzner, M. (2009) 'How global warming is gendered', in A. Salleh (ed.), *Eco-Sufficiency and Global Justice: Women Write Political Ecology*, London: Pluto Press, pp. 218–24.

Stacey, R. (1996) *Complexity and Creativity in Organizations*, San Francisco, CA: Berrett Koehler.

Steinfeld, H. et al. (2006) *Livestock's Long Shadow*, Rome: UN FAO.

Stengers, I. (2000) *The Invention of Modern Science*, trans. D. W. Smith, Minneapolis: University of Minnesota Press.

— (2010a) *Cosmopolitics I*, trans. R. Bononno, Minneapolis: Minnesota University Press

— (2010b) 'Including nonhumans in political theory: opening Pandora's box?', in B. Braun and S. J. Whatmore (eds), *Political Matter: Technoscience, Democracy and Public Life*, Minneapolis: University of Minnesota Press, pp. 3–34.

Sterman, J. D. (2002) 'All models are wrong: reflections on becoming a systems scientist', *System Dynamics Review*, 18(4): 501–31.

Strand, R. (2007) 'Complexity, ideology, and governance', in F. Capra et al. (eds), *Reframing Complexity: Perspectives from North and South*, Mansfield, MA: ISCE Publishing, pp. 195–217.

Sylvester, C. (1994) 'Empathetic cooperation: a feminist method for IR', *Millennium*, 23(2): 315–34.

— (2004) 'Woe or whoa! International relations where it's not supposed to be', *Brown Journal of World Affairs*, 10(2): 57–68.

Tainter, J. (1988) *The Collapse of Complex Societies*, Cambridge: Cambridge University Press.

Talbott, S. (2008) *The Great Experiment: The Story of Ancient Empires, Modern States, and the Quest for a Global Nation*, New York: Simon & Schuster.

Thomas, H. (1993) *The Conquest of Mexico*, London: Hutchinson.

Thomas, K. (1983) *Man and the Natural World: Changing Attitudes in England 1500–1800*, London: Allen Lane.

Thrift, N. (1999) 'The place of complexity', *Theory, Culture and Society*, 16(3): 31–69.

— (2005) *Knowing Capitalism*, London: Sage.

— (2010) 'Halos: making more

room in the world for new political orders', in B. Braun and S. J. Whatmore (eds), *Political Matter: Technoscience, Democracy and Public Life*, Minneapolis: University of Minnesota Press, pp. 139–76.

Tickner, J. A. (2001) *Gendering World Politics: Issues and Approaches in the Post-Cold War Era*, New York: Columbia University Press.

Tilly, C. (1990) *Coercion, Capital and European States, A.D. 990–1990*, Oxford: Blackwell.

Trombetta, M. J. (2008) 'Environmental security and climate change: analysing the discourse', *Cambridge Review of International Affairs*, 21(4): 585–602.

Turner, B. S. (1996) *The Body and Society: Explorations in Social Theory*, London: Sage.

Turner, F. (1997) 'Foreword: Chaos and social science', in R. A. Eve et al. (eds), *Chaos, Complexity and Sociology: Myths, Models and Theories*, London: Sage, pp. xi–xxv.

Ulanowicz, R. E. (2007) 'Ecology: a dialogue between the quick and the dead', in F. Capra et al. (eds), *Reframing Complexity: Perspectives from North and South*, Mansfield, MA: ISCE Publishing, pp. 27–46.

UNDP (1994) *Human Development Report 1994: New Dimensions of Human Security*, New York: United Nations Development Programme.

UNEP (2007) *Sudan: Post-Conflict Environmental Assessment*, Nairobi: United Nations Environment Programme.

Urry, J. (2000) *Sociology beyond Societies: Mobilities for the Twenty-First Century*, London: Routledge.

— (2003) *Global Complexity*, Cambridge: Polity.

— (2004) 'The global complexities of

September 11th', *Theory, Culture and Society*, 19(4): 57–69.

Van Duyn, R. (1969) *Message of a Wise Kabouter*, London: Duckworth.

Velten, H. (2007) *Cow*, London: Reaktion.

Wæver, O. (1996) 'The rise and fall of the inter-paradigm debate', in S. Smith et al. (eds), *International Theory: Positivism and Beyond*, Cambridge: Cambridge University Press, pp. 149–85.

— (1998) 'The sociology of a not so international discipline: American and European developments in international relations', *International Organization*, 52(4): 687–727.

Walby, S. (2003) 'Complexity theory, globalization and diversity', Paper presented to the British Sociological Association Annual Conference, University of York, April.

— (2007) 'Complexity theory, systems theory, and multiple intersecting social inequalities', *Philosophy of the Social Sciences*, 37(4): 449–70.

— (2009) *Globalization and Inequalities: Complexity and Contested Modernities*, London: Sage.

Waldrop, M. M. (1994) *Complexity: The Emerging Science at the Edge of Order and Chaos*, London: Penguin Books.

Walker, R. B. J. (2006) 'On the protection of nature and the nature of protection', in J. Huysmans et al. (eds), *The Politics of Protection: Sites of Insecurity and Political Agency*, London: Routledge, pp. 189–202.

Wallace, M. M. and O. Martin-Ortega (2009) *International Law*, 6th edn, London: Thomson Reuters.

Wallerstein, I. (1974) *The Modern World-System*, vol. 1: *Capitalist*

Agriculture and the Origins of the European World-Economy in the Sixteenth Century, San Diego, CA: Academic Press.

— (1979) *The Capitalist World-Economy*, Cambridge: Cambridge University Press.

— (1984) *The Politics of the World-Economy*, Cambridge: Cambridge University Press.

— (1991) *Unthinking Social Science: The Limits of Nineteenth-Century Paradigms*, Cambridge: Polity.

— (2000) 'From sociology to historical social science', *British Journal of Sociology*, 51(1): 25–35.

— (2003) *The Decline of American Power: The US in a Chaotic World*, New York: New Press.

— (2004) *The Uncertainties of Knowledge*, Philadelphia, PA: Temple University Press.

Waltz, K. N. (1959) *Man, the State, and War: A Theoretical Analysis*, New York: Columbia University Press.

— (1979) *Theory of International Politics*, New York: Random House.

— (1986) 'Reflections on theory of international politics: a response to my critics', in R. O. Keohane (ed.), *Neorealism and Its Critics*, New York: Columbia University Press, pp. 322–45.

— (2000) 'Structural realism after the Cold War', *International Security*, 25(1): 5–41.

Warren, K. (1994) *Ecological Feminism*, London: Routledge.

— (1997) 'Taking empirical data seriously: an ecofeminist philosophical perspective', in K. Warren (ed.), *Ecofeminism: Women, Nature, Culture*, Bloomington: Indiana University Press, pp. 3–20.

Watson, A. (1992) *The Evolution of International Society: A Comparative Historical Analysis*, London: Routledge.

Watts, D. J. (2004) *Small Worlds: The Dynamics of Networks between Order and Randomness*, Princeton, NJ: Princeton University Press.

Weber, M. (1968) *Economy and Society*, vols 1, 2 and 3, New York: Bedminster.

Wendt, A. (1987) 'The agent-structure problem in international relations theory', *International Organization*, 41(3): 335–70.

— (1992) 'Anarchy is what states make of it: the social construction of power politics', *International Organization*, 46(2): 391–425.

— (1999) *Social Theory of International Politics*, Cambridge: Cambridge University Press.

— (2003) 'Why a world state is inevitable', *European Journal of International Relations*, 9(4): 491–542.

— (2006) 'Social theory as Cartesian science: an auto-critique from a quantum perspective', in S. Guzzini and A. Leander (eds), *Constructivism and International Relations: Alexander Wendt and His Critics*, London: Routledge, pp. 181–219.

— (2010) 'Flatland: quantum mind and the international hologram', in M. Albert et al. (eds), *New Systems Theories of World Politics*, Basingstoke: Palgrave, pp. 279–310.

Westley, F. S. et al. (2002) 'Why systems of people and nature are not just social and ecological systems', in L. H. Gunderson and C. S. Holling (eds), *Panarchy: Understanding Transformations in Human and Natural Systems*, Washington, DC: Island Press, pp. 103–20.

Whatmore, S. (2006) 'Materialist

returns: practicing cultural geographies in and for a more-than-human world', *Cultural Geographies*, 13(4): 600–10.

Wilson, E. O. (1999) *Consilience: The Unity of Knowledge*, London: Abacus.

Wohlforth, W. C. (1995) 'Realism and the end of the Cold War', *International Security*, 19(3): 91–129.

Wohlforth, W. C. et al. (2007) 'Introduction: Balance and hierarchy in international systems', in S. J. Kaufman et al. (eds), *The Balance of Power in World History*, Basingstoke: Palgrave, pp. 1–21.

Wolfe, C. (2003) *Animal Rites: American Culture, the Discourse of Species and Posthumanist Theory*, Chicago, IL: Chicago University Press.

— (2008) 'Flesh and finitude: thinking animals in (post) humanist philosophy', *SubStance*, 37(3): 8–36.

— (2010) *What is Posthumanism?*, Minneapolis: University of Minnesota Press.

Worldwatch Institute (2004) *State of the World 2004*, Washington, DC: Worldwatch Institute.

Wright, S. (1932) 'The roles of mutation, inbreeding, crossbreeding and selection in evolution', *Proceedings of the Sixth International Congress of Genetics*, 1: 356–66.

WTO (2010) *International Trade Statistics 2010*, Geneva: World Trade Organization.

Yearley, S. (1996) *Sociology, Environmentalism, Globalization: Reinventing the Globe*, London: Sage.

Index

Entries for material presented in tables are indicated by (tab.) after the page number, e.g. Dalby, Simon, 112 (tab.).

Acampora, Ralph, 146–7
actor-based modelling, 11, 13, 21, 170, 187 *see also* computer modelling
actor network theory, 98–9
adaptation policies, 121–3
Afghanistan, 78
Agamben, Giorgio, 142
agency, 150–9
Albert, Mathias, 13–14
anarchism, 127–33, 180
anarchy, 55–8, 73, 83, 85–6, 89, 172
animals *see* non-human animals
anthropocene, 114, 146, 182
anthropocentrism, 17, 126–7, 140–6, 150–4 *see also* 'human', as category
Archer, Margaret, 152–4
Arthur, Brian, 28–9
assemblages, 149, 152–3, 156
autopoiesis *see* self-organization
Axelrod, Robert, 183–4

Baker, Patrick, 170–1
Baku–Tbilisi–Ceyhan pipeline, 156
balance of power, 53–4, 77–8, 84–7 *see also* equilibrium
Barabási, Albert-László, 46
Barnett, Jon, 113
Barry, Andrew, 156
Batty, Michael, 34
Beaumont, Roger, 32–3, 65
Bell, Derek, 156
Bennett, Jane, 97, 148–9, 151–5, 157–8
Bertuglia, Cristoforo, 171, 173
bicycle gearing, 69

biodiversity, 106–7, 115
biophysical posthumanism, 144–6
biopower, 3, 24, 160–5 *see also* embodiment
biotechnology, 106, 133–4, 149
Boardman, Robert, 179
bodies *see* biopower; embodiment
Bookchin, Murray, 126–8, 130–3
Bostrom, Nick, 144, 150
Brah, Avtar, 70
Brassett, James, 159–60
Brock, Lothar, 117
Brown, Gordon, 157
buffalo, 103
Bull, Hedley, 71, 89
Burke, Marshall, 108
butterfly effect, 66, 171–2 *see also* non-linearity
Buzan, Barry, 15, 53, 60–2, 71–3
Byrne, David, 34

Camilleri, Joseph, 92–3
capitalism *see also* economics; environmental consumerism; globalization: Capra on, 146; in ecofeminist thought, 135–6; financial markets, 27–9; Foucault on, 164; Kropotkin on, 129–30; as system, 7–8, 58–60, 64, 72, 95–7, 102, 133
Capra, Fritjof, 18, 42–5, 79, 131, 145–6
Carter, Bob, 152–4
Castellani, Brian, 33
Castells, Manuel, 34, 146
causality, 170, 176–8, 181, 185 *see also* non-linearity; predictability
Cederman, Lars-Erik, 80–1
chaos, 4, 13, 41, 83 *see also* turbulence
Charles, Nickie, 152–4

quantum theory, 5, 44, 65, 172

About Zed Books

Zed Books is a critical and dynamic publisher, committed to increasing awareness of important international issues and to promoting diversity, alternative voices and progressive social change. We publish on politics, development, gender, the environment and economics for a global audience of students, academics, activists and general readers. Run as a co-operative, Zed Books aims to operate in an ethical and environmentally sustainable way.

Find out more at:

www.zedbooks.co.uk

For up-to-date news, articles, reviews and events information visit:

http://zed-books.blogspot.com

To subscribe to the monthly Zed Books e-newsletter, send an email headed 'subscribe' to:

marketing@zedbooks.net

We can also be found on **Facebook, ZNet, Twitter** and **Library Thing**.